1007/=

Zionism and its l

Zionism and its Discontents

A Century of Radical Dissent in Israel/Palestine

Ran Greenstein

PlutoPress
www.plutobooks.com

First published 2014 by Pluto Press
345 Archway Road, London N6 5AA

www.plutobooks.com

Copyright © Ran Greenstein 2014

The right of Ran Greenstein to be identified as the author of this work
has been asserted by him in accordance with the Copyright, Designs and
Patents Act 1988.

British Library Cataloguing in Publication Data
A catalogue record for this book is available from the British Library

ISBN   978 0 7453 3468 4   Hardback
ISBN   978 0 7453 3467 7   Paperback
ISBN   978 1 7837 1203 8   PDF eBook
ISBN   978 1 7837 1205 2   Kindle eBook
ISBN   978 1 7837 1204 5   EPUB eBook

Library of Congress Cataloging in Publication Data applied for

This book is printed on paper suitable for recycling and made from fully
managed and sustained forest sources. Logging, pulping and manufacturing
processes are expected to conform to the environmental standards of the
country of origin.

10   9   8   7   6   5   4   3   2   1

Typeset by Stanford DTP Services, Northampton, England
Text design by Melanie Patrick
Simultaneously printed digitally by CPI Antony Rowe, Chippenham, UK
and Edwards Bros in the United States of America

Contents

Preface

This book examines Zionism through the lenses used by critical political movements, who have sought to challenge its conceptual bases as well as confront its practices on the ground. These include the bi-nationalist movement of the British Mandate period; the Palestinian Communist Party of the same period; the Palestinian national movement in its various permutations, beginning with the Mandate period and continuing to the present; and the Matzpen group of the 1960s to 1980s. Zionist activists and scholars may find it strange to see their movement reflected through the eyes of its critics and opponents. This is an essential operation, however, to avoid the usual writing of history from the perspective of victors, and to provide a counter-view that examines political alternatives as they unfolded in their own time.

Inevitably, we tend to look at historical developments in retrospect, knowing their outcomes. I tried to avoid this approach by looking forward, from the temporal perspective of the actors discussed in the book, and not from the vantage point of the present. None of these actors managed to achieve their primary political goals, but they all made valuable contributions – by way of analysis and practice – which should serve us today in charting a new course of action. Hence, the importance of their stories. In their different ways they provide essential starting points for a critique of the present. I hope this will be of interest not only to scholars but also to activists who seek to learn the lessons of the past in order to shape their struggles in the present and achieve greater success in the future.

These stories focus on the evolution of intellectual positions and political perspectives. I have paid less attention to organizational issues. The goal here is to allow the reader to appreciate the broad alternative points of view developed by different forces, rather than trace the development of a party apparatus or the mechanism of a movement's resource mobilization. Above all, it is a history of ideas which shaped reality, albeit not always in an obvious or predictable manner.

As far as possible original sources were used and secondary analyses were relied on to a lesser extent. The aim here has been to reflect on radical ideas and political alternatives from the perspectives of actors directly involved in their formulation, instead of evaluating them from a remote scholarly vantage point. I make no secret of my own views, especially in the concluding chapter, and cannot claim political neutrality, but have strived to present an account that is accurate, accessible and, above all, engaging with historical and contemporary concerns.

Why study these movements specifically? The choice was made with a view to identifying comprehensive responses to the rise of the Zionist settlement project, which remains the crucial actor shaping the history of Israel/Palestine for the last century. With the exception of the bi-nationalist movement, all the others offered alternatives that attacked Zionism from the outside and sought to replace its policies and principles with a completely different orientation, rather than suggest internal correctives. Even bi-nationalism involved a radical rejection of the notion of a Jewish state, which increasingly became the goal unifying all other Zionist movements, and still is the crucial common denominator of Zionism today. Examples set by these radical currents serve as a form of 'subjugated knowledges' that have experienced a degree of 'insurrection' in the last two decades. This book aims to assist this process further.

In this respect, I wish to join the wave of studies that challenge the central assumptions of mainstream Zionism from within Israeli society as well as from outside its boundaries. Academics such as Baruch Kimmerling, Ariella Azoulay, As'ad Ghanem, Nur Masalha, Oren Yiftachel, Shlomo Swirski, Ilan Pappe, Honaida Ghanim, Dimitry Shumsky, Yehouda Shenhav, Shlomo Sand, Adi Ophir and others have contributed to this work. Many of them identify their perspective as post-Zionist rather than anti-Zionist, but to some extent at least they follow in the footsteps of the pioneering Matzpen approach (discussed in chapter 4), without necessarily being aware of their debt to it. Critical questions about the structures of domination of Israeli state and society, the relations between Zionism and colonialism, and the role of Israeli policies in entrenching imperial control in the Middle East, which were considered radical heresy when raised in the 1960s, are being raised openly in respectable public and academic forums. The answers may differ but the willingness to raise difficult questions is a testimony to the spread of dissent beyond the margins.

Although I do not discuss this directly, my geographical/intellectual location in South Africa had an impact on some of the book's contents. This is not meant to be a comparative book, but here and there some reflections of a more comparative nature entered the discussion. This is particularly the case in chapter 3, where I set up the South African liberation movement as a benchmark (or 'ideal type') against which to examine Palestinian nationalism, and to a limited extent in chapters 4 and 5 as well. The task of a full-fledged study of the issue is best left for another project, though. The South African dimensions mentioned here are meant simply to illustrate historical possibilities in Israel/Palestine, not to offer extended discussion in their own right.

Finally, what can the activist/scholar expect from this book? Two things in particular: (1) a concise but thorough review of the ideas and historical records of the movements in question, written from a sympathetic perspective that identifies the 'best case' that can be made for each of them. I do not always agree with the positions developed by these movements but always strive to present them in a way that would make sense to a reader located remotely in space and time. And, (2) an analysis that places these movements in their historical and theoretical contexts, while examining their relevance for their times and ours. The answers they offered are not always suitable for us today (and some answers may not have been suitable for them either), but the questions they raised are still relevant as ever. Above all, my goal is to enable readers to look at contemporary political and cultural issues with the benefit of historical depth. I hope this task has been achieved.

1

The Bi-nationalist Perspective During the British Mandate, 1917–48

From its early days in the late nineteenth century, the modern Jewish settlement of Palestine faced criticism from within its own ranks as well as from outsiders. Alongside the resistance of indigenous Arabs (initially 'mute' but becoming increasingly vocal over time),[1] it experienced dissent from various Jewish constituencies. Three critical trends were particularly important: religious rejection of secular nationalism; left-wing opposition which elevated universal socialist principles above nationalist aims; and, liberal-humanist critique of the quest for a Jewish state in Palestine, and its associated exclusionary practices, as the ultimate goal of the settlement project.

Even before the formal establishment of the Zionist movement in 1897, these trends had become evident. While the religious rejection of Zionism could be seen as an internal critique, concerned with the implications of nationalism for the traditional definition and practice of Judaism,[2] the other two trends directed attention to relations between Jews and Arabs in Palestine. Although many things have changed since the early days of settlement, the main themes of the critique which were raised initially more than 120 years ago have remained valid to this day.

The liberal-humanist critique – on which this chapter focuses – is associated with the Russian Jewish thinker Asher Ginsberg, better known by his pen name Ahad Ha'am ('one of the people'). In a landmark article, written after his first visit to the new settlements in 1891, titled *Truth from the Land of Israel [Eretz Israel]*, he sharply criticised the nascent settlement project for the unhealthy relations it established between Jewish farmers and Arab workers. He went on to debunk some of the myths involving notions such as 'land without a people for a people without land', which implicitly informed the settlement project:

From abroad, we are accustomed to believe that Eretz Israel is presently almost totally desolate, an uncultivated desert, and that anyone wishing to buy land there can come and buy all he wants. But in truth it is not so. In the entire land, it is hard to find tillable land that is not already tilled . . . From abroad we are accustomed to believing that the Arabs are all desert savages, like donkeys, who neither see nor understand what goes on around them. But this is a big mistake . . . The Arabs, and especially those in the cities, understand our deeds and our desires in Eretz Israel, but they keep quiet and pretend not to understand, since they do not see our present activities as a threat to their future . . . However, if the time comes when the life of our people in Eretz Israel develops to the point of encroaching upon the native population, they will not easily yield their place. . .

Instead of treating the local population with 'love and respect . . . justice and righteousness', the settlers, who had been oppressed in their countries of origin, suddenly became masters and began behaving accordingly:

This sudden change has engendered in them an impulse to despotism . . . and behold, they walk with the Arabs in hostility and cruelty, unjustly encroaching on them, shamefully beating them for no good reason, and even bragging about what they do, and there is no one to stand in the breach and call a halt to this dangerous and despicable impulse. To be sure, our people are correct in saying that the Arab respects only those who demonstrate strength and courage, but this is relevant only when he feels that his rival is acting justly; it is not the case if there is reason to think his rival's actions are oppressive and unjust. Then, even if he restrains himself and remains silent forever, the rage will remain in his heart and he is unrivalled in 'taking vengeance and bearing a grudge'.[3]

Ahad Ha'am did not know then that his prophetic warnings coincided with the first documented expression of Arab protest against organized Jewish immigration, in June 1891. Local Muslim and Christian leaders sent a telegram from Jerusalem to Istanbul, the Ottoman imperial capital, demanding a stop to the immigration of Russian Jews into the country and to the purchase of land by them.[4] These two themes, immigration and land, remained at the core of the conflict between Jewish settlers and Palestinian-Arab residents for much of its history.

A few years later, following in the footsteps of Ahad Ha'am, another veteran thinker and activist, Yitzhak Epstein, voiced similar criticism of

Jewish settlement, though with a more political focus. In a 1905 speech, published as an article in 1907 and titled *A Hidden Question*, he addressed the 'one question that outweighs all the others: the question of our attitude toward the Arabs'. It was an important question, he argued, because Zionists tended to 'forget one small detail: that there is in our beloved land an entire people that has been attached to it for hundreds of years and has never considered leaving it'. Epstein's concern was with land acquisition. Given that most land was already cultivated, 'what will the fellahin do after we buy their fields?' he asked. Although Zionist associations bought land legally, the owners usually were large landlords who had acquired their title to it 'by deceit and exploitation and lease it to the fellahin'. It was customary for the tenants to remain on the land when it changed hands, 'but when we buy such a property, we evict the former tillers from it . . . [and] we must admit that we have driven impoverished people from their humble abode and taken bread out of their mouths'.

This practice created local and broader problems and had moral and practical implications. Practically, 'will those evicted really hold their peace and calmly accept what was done to them? Will they not in the end rise up to take back with their fists what was taken from them by the power of gold? Will they not press their case against the foreigners who drove them from their land?'

Even though an 'Arab movement in the national and political sense of that term' did not exist (yet), local resistance would have serious consequences for the settlers. To avoid such consequences, 'when we come to buy lands in Eretz Israel, we must thoroughly check whose land it is, who works it, and what the rights of the latter are, and we must not complete the purchase until we are certain that no one will be worse off'.

Epstein was convinced that by targeting land carefully to avoid dispossession, and showing Arab farmers that their lives would be improved by Jewish settlement, the land would 'support Jewish settlers as well as the fellahin'. The residents will benefit from new scientific farming methods, better health care and education, and will recognize 'us as their benefactors and comforters'. This approach should be based on respect for 'the national rights of every people and tribe'. It will be reciprocal: 'while we try to establish our nation, we will also support the revival of the inhabitants and will reinforce their national feeling in the best sense of the term'. Therefore, Jews must open all their public institutions to residents of the country: hospitals, pharmacies, libraries, banks, schools, kindergartens and cultural activities. The spirit of this exchange, learning each other's language and culture, is opposed to

Short-sighted and small-minded nationalism that regards only itself . . . [since] our intention is not to Judaize the Arabs, but to prepare them for a fuller life, to refine them, to develop them, to free them from their narrow vision, so that, in the course of time, they will become loyal allies, friends, and brothers.[5]

From today's perspective, these early texts sound patronizing in an Orientalist fashion, yet their prescient analysis is striking, especially when seen against the wilful blindness to the issue displayed by other Zionist observers and activists. Neither thinker discussed political nationalism outright – it did not exist at the time – but rather focused on Arab local patriotism and fears of dispossession. To a remarkable extent their views are in line with recent scholarship which indicates that a full-fledged Palestinian-Arab national identity had begun developing only in the last decade of the Ottoman period, and became dominant with British rule starting in 1917–18.

They operated alongside another group of activists and commentators of Mizrahi and Sephardi origins, whose legacy is less well-known. People like Shimon Moyal and Nissim Malul, writing in Hebrew and Arabic, advocated a more tolerant and linguistically assimilationist approach towards the Arab residents of the country, based on identification with the shared homeland of Palestine within the framework of the Ottoman Empire. Their approach could be referred to as inclusive Zionism, which was attuned to local conditions in Palestine, the co-existence of two peoples in the country, and the need for all of them to live together in the same physical space. In this sense it was a more peaceful and realistic approach than the dominant trend of exclusive Zionism.[6]

Without advocating explicit political programmes these critical voices, although a small minority within their respective constituencies, laid the foundations for the bi-national perspective in the British Mandate period (which lasted until 1948), to which I now turn.[7]

THE BALFOUR DECLARATION AND THE PALESTINE MANDATE

Before the First World War Palestine was not a clearly demarcated political unit. It had been divided into different districts, which were ruled from the regional centres of Beirut and Damascus, as well as directly from Istanbul. The British occupation of the country, towards the end of the war, established the country for the first time in centuries as a distinct political entity. This was reinforced by the Balfour Declaration of November 1917, in which the British Foreign Secretary conveyed his Government's commitment to 'the establishment in Palestine of a national home for the Jewish people'. This was based on the understanding that 'nothing shall be done which may prejudice the civil and religious rights of existing non-Jewish communities in Palestine, or the rights and political status enjoyed by Jews in any other country'.

The Declaration was incorporated into the Palestine Mandate, adopted by the Council of the League of Nations in July 1922, which went further to recognize 'the historical connection of the Jewish people with Palestine'. It asserted the need to place 'the country under such political, administrative and economic conditions as will secure the establishment of the Jewish national home . . . the development of self-governing institutions, and . . . safeguarding the civil and religious rights of all the inhabitants of Palestine, irrespective of race and religion'. The main issues of contention identified in Ottoman times as of crucial importance – land and immigration – were noted as well, mandating the new administration to 'facilitate Jewish immigration', to encourage 'close settlement by Jews on the land', and to 'facilitate the acquisition of Palestinian citizenship by Jews who take up their permanent residence in Palestine'. In all matters affecting the establishment of the Jewish national home, 'an appropriate Jewish agency' would operate alongside the Government, a role allocated to the Zionist Organization.

In these respects, the creation of Palestine as a political unit went hand in hand with granting Jews and their settlement project a privileged position. Much has been written about the lack of symmetry between the two groups in the country: Jews were mentioned explicitly while Arabs were not. They were not even recognized as a group but rather as a collection of 'non-Jewish communities', and their political rights were ignored – only their civil and religious rights were noted. And yet, the call for developing country-wide self-governing institutions for all residents could have been seen as a counter-balance to the obligation to build the Jewish national home. That neither the meaning of 'national home', nor the powers of and limitations on self-governance, were specified in the documents, was not an accident. There was a deliberate ambiguity there that potentially allowed for creative policies and negotiated spaces beyond the quest of both national movements for exclusive control. It is precisely into this space that the bi-nationalist movement fitted, though it had to confront other interpretations of the Declaration.

Initially, the organized Palestine Jewish community (known as the new *Yishuv*) saw the Declaration as an opportunity to make a political claim on behalf of the entire Jewish people. A late-1918 conference of local representatives demanded that Palestine become a Jewish state[8] and that it be governed by an Executive Committee chosen by the Zionist Organization, working under a British Governor General. It would adopt the name *Eretz Israel*, the Zionist flag and the Jewish days of rest. Hebrew and Arabic would be official languages. These demands were seen as too radical by the World Zionist Organization, which put forward a more modest proposal, calling on world powers to 'recognise the historic title of the Jewish people to Palestine and the right of the Jews to reconstitute in Palestine their National Home'.[9] Having to work in an international arena, contending with contradictory forces and expectations, the broader Zionist movement – unlike the over-enthusiastic local Jewish community – realized that it had to present its case in a way that would minimize opposition and allow it to appear accommodating.

The need to temper Jewish expectations was brought home sharply by the report of the King-Crane commission, appointed by US President Wilson in 1919 to explore the implications of self-determination in the Middle East. The commission recommended 'serious modification of the extreme Zionist program for Palestine of unlimited immigration of Jews, looking finally to making Palestine distinctly a Jewish State', because it was resolutely opposed by Arabs, who were 90 per cent of the country's population: 'To subject a people so minded to unlimited Jewish immigration, and to steady financial and social pressure to surrender the land, would be a gross violation of the principle [of national self-determination]. . . and of the people's rights.' Faced with such local and regional opposition, the Zionist project 'could [not] be carried out except by force of arms'. Only 'a greatly reduced Zionist program' can be attempted, 'and even that, only very gradually initiated'.[10]

The usual Zionist response to such arguments consisted of three core components:

- Palestine was a small part of the overall Arab homeland. Therefore, the rights of Arabs in general were not violated by Jewish settlement and political control in Palestine. They could still exercise their political rights freely in Egypt, Syria, Iraq, and so on.
- While Jews were a minority of the population in the country, this was a temporary situation. Impending massive immigration would shift the demographic balance in their favour. When that happens,

'normal' democratic rule would ensue, but until then only national-communal autonomy could be a proper form of governance.

- Local opposition to Zionism reflected jealousy and the narrow interests of reactionary feudal and commercial Arab elites, who used their position to incite the ignorant masses. The latter would benefit, however, from social and technological progress brought about by Jewish settlement.[11]

Without questioning these principles, some Jewish activists saw a need to put forward alternative visions to alleviate fears of Zionist plans. This was especially important in view of the clear rejection of the Balfour Declaration by Arabs, and the threat of violent resistance to its imposition. Among these activists was Haim Kalvarisky, who had already acquired a reputation as a leading settlement official, involved in land purchases and in facilitating a Jewish–Arab dialogue. In 1919 he came up with a formula intended to serve as a basis for negotiation with Arab nationalists: 'Palestine constitutes the homeland of all its residents: Jews, Muslims and Christians are citizens on equal footing.' Its government would not discriminate against anyone, its administration will be open to all, its schools will promote bilingual education, and social services will be provided by the state with no distinction between people on the basis of religious origins. At the same time, the country will be considered a Jewish national home and thus open to Jewish immigration and transfer of capital without restrictions.[12]

Like other Zionist negotiators, Kalvarisky positioned his formula within the context of broader Arab unity, which made the relations between Jews and Arabs asymmetrical: Jews regarded the country as their entire homeland, while for Arabs it was a small part of their overall territory. It was impossible to get the consent of Palestinian Arabs to the Zionist project, as their clash over the country was seen in mutually exclusive terms. But, from this perspective, Arab nationalists outside of Palestine were expected to give up exclusive claims to some land in exchange for other benefits. However, even when they were willing to do so, they were overruled by local Palestinian nationalists. The agreements Zionists were able to reach with other Arabs – members of the Hashemite family in particular – did not carry any weight inside the country, and did not change the nature of the political conflict between the two competing nationalist projects.[13]

Tempering the initial Balfour Declaration euphoria, with a focus on the need to accommodate opponents within the country itself, Ahad Ha'am discussed in 1920 the difference between two national home formulas. The first consisted of making Palestine the national home of the Jewish people and it meant that Jews could do whatever they wished in the country, regardless of opposition by local Arabs. The second, that of building the national home *in* Palestine, had a different meaning: it implied that the historical rights of Jews to the country could be realized there, but not be used to deny the rights of other residents of the country. These Arab residents had lived there for many generations and they too claimed the country as their national home. The co-existence of two national homes in the same country was possible, he argued, if they had the freedom to run their internal affairs on their own, and run jointly the common affairs of the country as a whole (possibly with an external authority in charge if they did not get along, which would ensure equality).[14]

These positions were not merely abstract statements. They aimed to make local Jews aware that their expectations of becoming politically dominant in the country, despite comprising only 10 per cent of the population, were premature (a fact that the less insular Zionist leadership in Europe understood clearly). The Jerusalem riots of March 1920, repeated on larger scale with a series of armed attacks against Jews in Jaffa and neighbouring settlements in May 1921, brought home the realization that the Arabs would not 'easily yield their place', as Ahad Ha'am had predicted 30 years earlier. This notion encouraged the Yishuv's *Va'ad Leumi* (National Committee) to invite Yitzhak Epstein, as an old expert on 'Arab affairs', to address it on the topic. Epstein called for 'involving the natives in all our activities. In actual practice we must take it upon ourselves – from the points of view of justice and necessity – to involve them in everything'. However, his call for local initiative was met with 'cold silence'.[15] Launching armed attacks against Jewish communities was a powerful way of expressing political grievances, and of making Jews acutely aware of the need to address Arab concerns, but it also made the prospect of getting Arabs involved in 'everything' very unappealing to Jewish residents of the country.

The 1921 riots created an environment that was not conducive for inter-communal collaboration. As the Haycraft Commission of Inquiry, set up by the British to investigate the riots, saw it,

> It has been impossible to avoid the conclusion that practically the whole of the non-Jewish population was united in hostility to the Jews. During the riots all discrimination on the part of the Arabs between different categories of Jews was obliterated. Old-established colonists and newly

arrived immigrants, Chalukah Jews and Bolshevik Jews, Algerian Jews and Russian Jews, became merged in a single identity, and former friendships gave way before the enmity now felt towards all.[16]

This outcome has been reinforced by every round of violence ever since: expressions of external hostility inevitably led to the consolidation of internal solidarity and to weakening of prospects for crossing boundaries between the two communities. Instead of exposing rifts within the camps, fighting resulted in strengthening the need to stand together to confront the enemy, especially when it made no distinctions between different components of the opposing camp, and offered no attractive alternatives.

THE ROOTS OF BI-NATIONALISM

In a sense, the bi-nationalist associations of the Mandate period charted a course in between Epstein's enthusiasm for total involvement and the organized Yishuv's cold silence. They adhered to a version of Zionism which supported the formation of a Jewish national home, frequently understood as a 'spiritual centre' rather than a political entity. They rarely deviated from the quest for Jewish immigration to the country and settlement on the land, but they distanced themselves from the mainstream Zionist position, which viewed the national home as a prelude to a state (sometimes referred to vaguely as a 'commonwealth') in which Jews would dominate demographically and politically. Their aim was to create a solid basis for the Jewish community in the country, without making it the dominant group. Other Zionists saw that modest goal as jeopardising the entire settlement project: if Jews were doomed to remain a non-dominant minority, in what way would Palestine be different from all other places in which Jews lived at the time?

While the distinction between spiritual and political Zionism was potentially important, it could be seen as largely rhetorical in nature. Advocates of the spiritual approach, such as Martin Buber, proposed to the 12th Zionist Congress of 1921 a resolution that urged Jews to reject 'with abhorrence the methods of nationalistic domination, under which they themselves have long suffered', and renounce any desire 'to suppress another people or to dominate them', since in the country 'there is room both for us and its present inhabitants'. The way forward was to establish 'a just alliance with the Arab peoples', in order 'to turn our common dwelling-place into a community that will flourish economically and culturally, and whose progress would bring each of these peoples unhampered independent development.' In that way, members of both nations will develop 'feelings of mutual respect and goodwill, which will operate in the life of both the community and its individual members'.[17]

The official Zionist position, as adopted by that Congress, noted 'the enmity of a part of the Arab inhabitants, incited by unscrupulous elements to commit deeds of violence', but also asserted 'our will to live at peace and in mutual respect with the Arab people, and together with them, to make our common home in a flourishing commonwealth whose reconstruction will assure undisturbed national development for each of its peoples'. It mandated its leadership body, the Zionist Executive, 'to secure an honourable entente with the Arab people on the basis of this declaration and in strict accordance with the Balfour Declaration . . . [without infringing] upon the rights and needs of the working Arab nation.'[18]

In retrospect, the differences between Buber's approach and the official resolution seem minor, but Buber did not condition agreement with Arabs on acceptance of the Balfour Declaration. The official Zionist position was a non-starter. No Arab leader in Palestine could possibly have accepted the Declaration as a basis for negotiating the future of the country, since it gave the Jewish minority (and non-resident Jews) a privileged position vis-à-vis the Arab majority. The British attempts to create representative institutions (a legislative or advisory council, an Arab Agency to parallel the work of the Jewish Agency) failed because they were premised on acceptance of the Mandate framework, which itself was premised on the Balfour Declaration. Willingness to compromise on – but not necessarily abandon – basic Zionist principle served to distinguish what became known as the bi-nationalist approach from other political perspectives.

BRIT SHALOM

While moderate voices had a long history, it was only with the formation of the Brit Shalom association in 1925 that they became consolidated into a more coherent perspective. In its statutes, the association defined its objective as follows: 'to arrive at an understanding between Jews and Arabs as to the form of their mutual social relations in Palestine on the basis of absolute political equality of two culturally autonomous peoples, and to determine the lines of their co-operation for the development of the country'. Its proposed mode of operation included conducting studies, disseminating information, encouraging friendly relations between Jews and Arabs, and shaping public opinion favourable to mutual understanding between communities.

Its founders came from different political and personal backgrounds. Some of them were well established Yishuv leaders, who saw reconciliation with Arabs as a practical necessity (Arthur Ruppin, the senior Zionist settlement official, was prominent among them). Others were officials and activists who developed relationships with local rural leaders, and had a strategic vision of co-existence beyond its practical benefits (Yitzhak Epstein and Haim Kalvarisky stood out among them). Still others were inspired by moral convictions, and saw the need to incorporate the needs and concerns of local people – not only of Jews – into the Zionist mission. Martin Buber was senior among them – though he only settled in Palestine in the late 1930s – together with academics affiliated with the newly-established Hebrew University in Jerusalem. From among this group, members such as Hugo Bergmann, Gershom Scholem, Ernst Simon, Robert Weltsch and Hans Kohn, became known as the radical circle, and have received the most scholarly attention.[19]

Because of this diversity of personalities and perspectives, and the nature of the association as a study group and lobby for Jewish–Arab understanding rather than a political party with a distinct programme of its own, its story tends to become fragmented. Most studies deal more with the individual members on which we have information, than with the movement as a whole, and it is difficult to reconstruct a coherent narrative of the evolution of its thought. Bearing this in mind, the association's journal, *She'ifoteinu* ('Our Aspirations'), is a useful source for shifting positions and emphases during the period of its publication, 1927 to 1933.

From its inception the movement and in particular its academic members encountered opposition by Yishuv activists. Ruppin, as a senior settlement official, found himself in-between his Labour allies who regarded Brit Shalom as 'delusional', and his radical colleagues who were calling for supporting the Arab demand for a constitution, against the opposition of the Zionist leadership:

> These demands put me in an embarrassing position. My tendency is apolitical, I would prefer that Brit Shalom not address current political issues as long as we have not clarified for ourselves the principles for future cooperation with the Arabs. In my view Brit Shalom should

be a study, research and debating club, and only later develop a concrete programme.

Ruppin's motivation reflected anxiety that Zionism could not be realized in accordance with 'general ethical demands', and therefore that it would 'deteriorate into pointless chauvinism' and that it would become impossible 'to allocate a sphere of action to a growing number of Jews in Palestine without oppressing the Arabs'. Land was a particular concern, since 'soon, when land is no longer available, the settlement of a Jew will inevitably result in the dispossession of a [Arab] peasant . . . and then what?'[20]

This concern stemmed from the unprecedented goal of Zionism, 'to bring the Jews, as a second nation, to a country already settled by another nation – and to do that peacefully'. The Zionist movement made the situation worse, as 'it ignored completely the existence of Arabs', and then 'encouraged delusions that obscured the difficulties involved in dealing with the Arab problem'. In reality there were 'very serious contradictions of interest between the Jews and the Arabs': it was impossible to reconcile 'free immigration and free economic and cultural development' for Jews – 'essential conditions for Zionism' – without 'damaging the interests of the Arabs'.

The clash of interests was related to issues of land, labour, immigration: 'any place where we buy land and settle people on it of necessity requires that the current cultivators be removed from it, be they owners or tenants'. Further, 'since our immigration is predominantly that of people with few or no resources, it is possible that these immigrants would deprive the Arabs of their sustenance'. Although the principle of employing only Jews in Jewish-owned enterprises 'is in accordance with our national interests', it 'deprives the Arabs of the wages they used to earn'. Therefore, 'we are far from able to convince the Arabs rationally that our interests are compatible' and, if given a chance, 'the Arabs, as a majority, would take advantage of the rights guaranteed to them by the constitution in order to prevent any economic advancement of the Jewish minority', thereby 'putting an end to the Zionist movement'.[21]

Ruppin's dilemma was typical of many liberal Zionists who wanted to reconcile adherence to universal principles of justice and equality with loyalty to particular group interests. This proved especially difficult at times of intense political conflict, as was the case following the riots of 1929. The relatively quiet period of the early-mid 1920s, during which Brit Shalom was formed, had been transformed into a more sharply focused and violent confrontation between mutually exclusive political visions for the country by the end of the decade.

For Ruppin this meant loss of hope for reaching an agreement with the Arab leadership, leading him increasingly to distance himself from Brit Shalom. His conclusion is worthy of particular consideration:

> We must recognise that in our entire history of relations with the Arabs we have not made an effort to find a formula that will satisfy not only the essential interests of the Jews but also the essential interests of the Arabs . . . Paradoxically I would say: *What we can get* (from the Arabs) – *we do not need, and what we need – we cannot get.* At most, what the Arabs are willing to give us is rights of a Jewish national minority in an Arab state, similar to the rights of [minority] nationalities in Eastern Europe. But we have learnt from the state of affairs in Eastern Europe, how difficult it is to force a majority nation holding power to grant the minority true national equality. The fate of the Jewish minority in Palestine will forever depend on the good will of the Arab majority holding power. Such an arrangement definitely will not satisfy Eastern European Jews who are the majority of Zionists; on the contrary, this would diminish their enthusiasm for Zionism and Palestine. A Zionism willing to reach such a compromise with the Arabs [and thus entrench Jews as a minority in the country] will lose the support of Jews in Eastern Europe and will quickly become *Zionism without Zionists.*[22]

What could be done then? In Ruppin's view at the time, using language that echoes all the way to the present:

> [N]o negotiations with the Arabs *at present* will allow progress, since the Arabs still hope to be able to get rid of us . . . it is not negotiations but the development of Palestine to increase our share in the population and to strengthen our economic power that might lead to reduction of tensions. When time comes and the Arabs realize that they are not called upon to grant us something we do not have already, but to recognize reality as it is – the *weight of facts* on the ground will lead to reduced tensions. The existence or demise of the Zionist movement depends on our ability – with the help of the Mandatory government – to increase in the next five to ten years our numbers and power here, until we reach balance with the Arabs, more or less. It may be a bitter truth, but it is The Truth in my view.[23]

The basic problem was that Arabs 'reached national consciousness quicker than we estimated, and they reject our presence in Palestine. They will fight us with all means possible'. Zionists could rely ultimately only on themselves, therefore it was

> important to postpone the decisive battle until we are numerically stronger than we are at present. To achieve this goal we have to compromise. Peace will not be possible through 'agreement' with the Arabs, but will eventually come, when we have become so strong that the Arabs would not be certain of the outcome of the fight and would be forced to recognise us as a *fait accompli*.[24]

The Ruppin quotes are important not only because of his official position and for showing how liberals were transformed under the impact of intensifying conflict. They also illustrate how the logic of creating 'facts on the ground' and building an 'iron wall' to deter Arab opposition became dominant in the Jewish community. Of course, not all activists moved in the same direction, as shown by Hans Kohn who broke off with the Zionist movement and eventually left Brit Shalom following the 1929 uprising. Already before then he had expressed dissatisfaction with the reluctance of the association to express its views in more radical terms for fear of breaking decisively with the Zionist consensus.[25] The 1929 events were a crucial catalyst in pushing him further away from the mainstream.

Kohn identified with Zionism not in political terms but as a 'moral-cum-spiritual movement' that was compatible with his pacifist, radical, and anti-imperialist positions. But, it became increasingly difficult for him to sustain this approach alongside the official Zionist line:

> I cannot concur with this policy when the Arab national movement is being portrayed as the wanton agitation of a few big landowners. I know all too well that frequently the most reactionary imperialist press in England and France portrays the national movements in India, Egypt, and China in a similar fashion – in short, wherever the national movements of oppressed peoples threaten the interest of the colonial power.

When the Zionist movement adopted such a false and hypocritical attitude, it was a sign of something deeply problematic in its approach.

The uprising of 1929 was carried out by Arabs, who 'perpetrated all the barbaric acts that are characteristic of a colonial revolt'. They were motivated by a deep cause:

We have been in Palestine for twelve years [since 1917] without having even once made a serious attempt at seeking through negotiations the consent of the indigenous people. We have been relying exclusively upon Great Britain's military might. We have set ourselves goals which by their very nature had to lead to conflict with Arabs. We ought to have recognized that these goals would be the cause, the just cause, of a national uprising against us . . . But for twelve years we pretended that the Arabs did not exist and were glad when we were not reminded of their existence.

Without the consent of local Arabs, Jewish existence in Palestine will only be possible 'first with British aid and then later with the help of our own bayonets . . . But by that time we will not be able to do without the bayonets. The means will have determined the goal. Jewish Palestine will no longer have anything of that Zion for which I once put myself on the line.'[26]

Kohn's main problem was the development of Zionism into 'the militant-reactionary wing of Judaism', which had to be confronted by a resolute and determined opposition from a united movement. But, instead of forming such a movement many Brit Shalom activists became tied up with Zionist institutions and loyalties, and unwilling to take a decisive step away from them. The best example of that was the eviction of tenants from land bought by Zionist settlement agencies. This 'immeasurable barbarity' was led by Brit Shalom member Ruppin (not named explicitly), despite his repeated assurances of opposition to the removal of Arab tenants from their land. Instead of fighting these practices Brit Shalom formulated lofty peace proposals and bypassed the real issues. It 'enveloped itself in a cloud of naivety' with no public impact. Under these circumstances Kohn saw no point in continuing his membership in the movement.[27]

Ruppin and Kohn offered opposite solutions to the same dilemma: the difficulty of reconciling universal humanism with Zionist nationalism. When crisis erupted, Ruppin chose nationalism and Kohn chose universalism, but other members continued to believe there was no inherent contradiction between the two. This had to do largely with their understanding of Zionism, seen more in its spiritual and internal implications for Jewish constituencies than in relation to Arabs in the country. It seems strange from our perspective today, but at the time the Jewish Question was much more prominent than the Arab Question in the thinking of many progressive activists. Academic and public intellectuals such as Hugo Bergmann, Gershom Scholem and Ernst Simon, illustrate this point.

In their contributions to Brit Shalom's journal, frequently without using their names, activists put forward a fairly consistent set of positions revolving around their understanding of Zionism and the policies of the Zionist movement, the Arab question, the meanings of bi-nationalism, and the way forward for resolving the intensifying conflict in the country. Beyond the diversity of views, key points were reiterated regularly. They saw Zionism as a movement to create a spiritual centre that would revitalise Jewish religious and intellectual life in an environment free of fear and stagnation. The creation of the centre in Palestine would help Jews elsewhere to pursue their spiritual needs in an invigorated manner. Political domination and demographic majority in the country were not necessary for that. In fact, diverting energies away from the spiritual and cultural tasks towards accumulating state power and – in the process – collaborating with imperial forces against the local population, would harm the project and make it unviable.

Zionism from this perspective was not an attempt to 'solve' the Jewish problem by concentrating all Jews in Palestine in their own state, but rather a way of reviving Jewish global existence by creating a new anchor for it in the country. To facilitate this endeavour, accommodation with the local Arab population was essential. This was the case for practical reasons – working against the wishes of the Arabs made the task difficult if not impossible – as well as substantive reasons. Judaism had to renew its links to the Orient – its historical and spiritual home – to revitalise itself. This realignment had political implications: when the Zionist leadership linked its fate to British imperialism it turned its back on potential allies in the region and undermined its own prospects.

A political alliance with the new forces of the awakening Orient should not come at the expense of the fundamental principles of Zionism, however. These principles included the commitment to the Jewish national home and ongoing Jewish immigration into the country. Common criticism by mainstream Zionist forces, which portrayed Brit Shalom as so intent on reconciliation with the Arab movement that it gave up the basic Zionist positions, was wrong. The notion that Jewish immigration and land settlement must not be disrupted was central, but Brit Shalom insisted that these activities must not be carried out at the expense of

Arabs or lead to their dispossession. For example, when land is bought by Jewish agencies some of it must be allocated to the tenants, or they could be employed on part of it and so on. Opposition to the principles of sole ownership and 100 per cent 'Hebrew Labour' in Jewish-owned enterprises set Brit Shalom apart.

The key concept that framed the entire approach of Brit Shalom was that of political parity: the idea that Jews and Arabs should share state power equally, regardless of their proportion in the population, which at the time saw a small Jewish minority alongside a large Arab majority. In matters involving culture, religion and education, each national community would be autonomous and free to pursue its own course. Common matters with no specific communal aspect, involving issues such as trade, industry, public services, roads, health, and so on, would be handled by the authorities as in 'normal' countries. In these matters lines of division between citizens cut across communal affiliation and are based rather on a socio-economic or class basis. Thus they would be unlikely to pit one community against another.[28]

Issues of land, immigration and jobs – which of necessity affect the size and spread of the communities and thus the relations between them – would be handled in a way that reconciles conflicting interests. The precise mechanism for this operation had to be worked out, but in principle it would be based on recognising the legitimacy of both national movements, trying to ensure that the vital interests of each would be guarded: ongoing immigration for Jews and protection from dispossession for Arabs. Neither a Jewish state nor simple majority rule could guarantee that, only a bi-national state entrenching equality between groups and individuals.

Thus, Hugo Bergmann addressed Ben-Gurion's proposals for an interim regime that would see autonomy in communal matters, overseen by the British bureaucracy to ensure that Jewish immigration and settlement would not be disrupted. This scheme allowed no representation for citizens in central institutions, and the reliance on colonial power was particularly strange as a plan devised by self-proclaimed Labour socialists such as Ben-Gurion and his colleagues. Bergmann insisted that a democratically elected parliament was essential, but one that would not have power over the essential national interests of the two communities. These would be sorted out either by a neutral party (the British) or by a committee including local Jews and Arabs nominated by the country-wide parliament as well as international experts from the League of Nations.[29]

Ernst Simon provided a more detailed response following the 17th Zionist Congress in February 1931, the first to be convened after the 1929 uprising. He celebrated the fact that the Congress finally recognised the need to deal with 'the Arab question' and rejected the Zionist-Revisionist notion that Jewish majority in Palestine was the ultimate goal of Zionism. But, the Congress did define the solution of the Jewish problem in Palestine as the movement's goal. Simon rejected that. Instead he proposed an explicit renunciation of the demand for a majority, and a statement that Zionism – the quest to create a secure basis for the Jewish people in Palestine according to international law – could be realized in a bi-national country, with no need for a Jewish majority. This would alleviate the Arab fear that Zionism was merely a scheme to take over the country and marginalize non-Jews.

This approach was linked to a broader concern; that Zionism had to be cleansed of its false messianic expectations in order to preserve the kernel of Judaism, which was never dependent on political domination. Although Palestine was the only place where Jews could become a nation-state, they had to operate together and in equality with the Arabs, possibly as part of an overall regional alliance.[30] Simon, like his colleagues, did not adhere to the idea that the Jewish Diaspora was a 'problem', for which massive immigration into Palestine was the 'solution'. Jews were destined to live in many countries, and the goal of Zionism was to allow all the dispersed Jewish communities to benefit from the creation of a centre in Palestine that would facilitate the rejuvenation of spiritual, religious and intellectual life of all Jews. It was a matter of the quality of Jewish life established in the country rather than of the number of Jews who settle there.

Perhaps more adamant in pursuing these points was Gershom Scholem, a young academic still at the beginning of his career, who later became one of the greatest scholars in Jewish Studies of the twentieth century. His starting point was the need for a Jewish 'national organism' in Palestine as a cornerstone for efforts to revive Jewish life around the world, infusing it with renewed spiritual energy to ensure its survival for generations to come. That energy was mobilized through Zionist efforts, not in Palestine itself but elsewhere. The quest for a spiritual and cultural Jewish centre in Palestine encouraged many European Jews to become concerned with, involved in and enthusiastic about Jewish organized life. This was not a prelude for building a Jewish state but a positive outcome in its own right. Zionism, Scholem argued, thus fulfilled its historical role – reviving Judaism – despite its failure to build a substantial basis in Palestine itself.

In addition to this intra-Jewish dimension, the Zionist movement was facing an external problem of having sided with reactionary historical forces – its alliance with the British tied its fate to that of the declining imperial powers. Despite its progressive pretensions, Zionism turned its back on the forces of tomorrow, the oppressed people of the region. A choice must be made: it is impossible to combine the two, imperialism and socialism, water and fire. However, by now (1931) it may have become too late to switch sides: 'Either Zionism will be swept away together with the water of imperialism or it will burn in the revolutionary fire of the awakening Orient.' There is danger either way, but it is better to find yourself on the right side of the barricades and risk the fire of revolution than to die together with the forces of reaction.[31]

This kind of radical rhetoric was not typical to Brit Shalom (reflecting Scholem's personal style above all), but behind it was the common attitude among its members that an alliance with the Arabs of Palestine and the broader region was essential, on moral and practical grounds. An anti-imperialist alliance with the Arabs against the British was going a bit too far for most of them, though they did frequently express reluctance with the need to base the Zionist project on British bayonets. That the labour movement shared with the rest of the Zionist movement this reliance on military power to stem the rise of the natives was disappointing for Brit Shalom, due to its affinity with the Left.[32] Clearly, though, it did not regard itself as part of the Zionist Left due to its secularism and lack of regard for tradition. Without an ongoing link to religion – in a spiritual rather than ritualistic sense – Zionism would be reduced to crude political nationalism and lose its claim to be a continuation of Judaism.[33] Even a large Jewish majority in Palestine would not help if the achievements of the movement were devoid of traditional Jewish content.[34]

The intense political and theoretical debates on the pages of *She'ifoteinu* in 1931–32, giving a sense of engagement and dynamism, turned out to have been the swansong of Brit Shalom. The last issue of the publication appeared in early 1933, coinciding with the rise to power of the Nazis in Germany. The general shift in focus of attention from the Arab question to the plight of Jews in Germany and further afield, and the sense of impending doom, made the Yishuv even less tolerant of dissidents and uninterested in reaching a compromise with Palestinians involving restrictions on immigration and land settlement. Indeed, the 1930s saw 200,000 Jews moving to Palestine, more than doubling the Jewish population and its relative proportion in the country. Rapid increase in its financial resources, technical and scientific skill, industrial activities and military power accompanied this growth.

Brit Shalom's critique of mainstream Zionism's inability to offer a spiritual alternative to Jews, and its refusal to turn its face towards 'the awakening East' seemed out of touch with reality. Its willingness to consider curbs on immigration and give up Jewish claims to a majority and a state were a source of constant criticism from intellectuals and activists towing the official line. Its operation outside the official channels was seen as opening up dangerous dissension at times that required national unity. Its members found it difficult to stand against the nationalist tide, some were demoralised and withdrew altogether and the organization ceased its activities. The absence of willingness by Arabs to compromise on their central demands concerning immigration and land transfer isolated Brit Shalom further.

Palestinians were engulfed by their own sense of impending doom. The transformation of the Jewish community from a small vulnerable minority into a solid segment of society, comprising 30 per cent of the population, with dense institutional network and organizational capacity, meant that the trend was going against Palestinian hopes for quick independence and majority rule. The mid-late 1930s saw them mobilizing on an unprecedented scale to put a stop to immigration and land transfer to Jewish institutions, and to demand a national government. This culminated with the General Strike of April–October 1936 and a subsequent armed revolt that lasted until 1939. The Jewish community took advantage of these events to increase military cooperation with the British and actively assist them in repressing the Arab Revolt, and also to increase its economic autonomy and reduce dependence on Arab labour and produce. By the eve of the Second World War, it had become a more consolidated and stronger entity, while Palestinians had suffered not only a military defeat from the outside, but intense factional fights that split them from the inside and created a bitter legacy of divisions and paralysed institutions.

THE INTERIM PERIOD

With Brit Shalom no longer on the scene, others sought to fill the gap and motivate for renewed efforts to reach reconciliation between Jews and Arabs in the country, usually without an explicit political programme. They had to tread carefully not to alienate the organized community in the same way that Brit Shalom had. Thus, the newly-established Kedma Mizraha ('Forward to the East') defined itself in 1936 as 'a non-partisan organization with the goal of getting to know the East, forging cultural, social and economic relations with the peoples of the East, and providing a correct understanding [*hasbara*] of the work of the Jewish people in the country'. It brought together people with different opinions but united in the realization that it was essential for the Jewish community to find ways to speak directly to Palestinian Arab representatives.

In this sense Kedma Mizraha was an apolitical version of the early Brit Shalom as envisaged by Ruppin – an association for studying Jewish–Arab relations and promoting social and cultural interaction, with no explicit programme of its own. Distinguishing itself from Brit Shalom was an important aspect of the way it was presented. It saw itself operating within the framework of the Yishuv and under the guidance of 'national institutions'. This meant clearing its activities with the leadership and renouncing claims to be negotiating from an independent position.[35]

Brit Shalom moved from initial concern with a Jewish–Arab dialogue to the promotion of its own proposals about constitutional arrangements. It was willing to consider compromises on issues of immigration and settlement in order to reach an agreement with Arabs. And, it was opposed to core ideas of mainstream Zionism: regarding Palestine as the site for the solution of the Jewish problem, working for a Jewish majority in the country, and calling for a Jewish state as the ultimate goal of the movement. In all these respects it was considered to be too radical, with positions verging on treason to the 'national cause'.

In contrast, Kedma Mizraha was not interested in adopting a specific political stance. It saw its task as encouraging the authorities – especially the Jewish Agency headed by Ben-Gurion – to take the issue of dialogue with Arabs seriously. In addition, it made repeated calls for using the press and other means to disseminate information about Zionism and the Yishuv and launch propaganda and 'hasbara' efforts with a focus on the benefits that Palestinians and Arabs in general may derive from the Zionist project. In this sense it positioned itself clearly on the side of the authorities in relation to their opponents.

The only publication by the association, titled simply *A Collection of Articles on the Arab Question*, came out in 1936 during the general strike. Almost every article laments the failure to be more active in informing and educating the Arab masses about the actual and potential gains that Jewish settlement brought in its wake. The failure of the Zionist movement to target Arabs as an important constituency, they argued, resulted in leaving the field open to the operation of hostile Arab nationalist forces who disseminated false notions about the impact of settlement. The Arab masses were thus constantly exposed to propaganda about the evil nature of Zionism, its designs on the land, its intentions to dispossess the indigenous population and take over the country for the exclusive use of Jews. An Arab-language newspaper, dedicated to refuting these notions and informing the masses about the true purpose of the Zionist movement, was desperately needed as a result, they insisted. This focus was similar to that of Sephardi activists in the late Ottoman period, with their emphasis on the need for bilingualism, not surprising in that Kedma Mizraha was the only association of the period that included Sephardi and Mizrahi voices that were virtually absent from all other Zionist movements of the period.

Very few of the contributors saw a need to examine critically Zionist intentions and policies and evaluate whether Arab concerns and fears had any basis. The main issue for most of them was the absence of effective communication rather than Zionist practices. Perhaps the sole exception in this regard was a short piece by Moshe Smilansky, a veteran activist from the agricultural sector, who was critical of official policies in general and in particular the campaign for evicting Arab workers from Jewish-owned farms and enterprises. Smilansky highlighted the need for coexistence of two nationalities in the same country, who must cooperate economically in order to survive, in the fields of labour, trade and industry. Such pragmatic cooperation eventually would lead to closer social and political relations as well.[36]

Others focused on the need for Jews to learn Arabic at their schools and to allow Arab children to be educated in Hebrew-medium schools. Lack of familiarity with each other's language and culture was a recipe for misunderstanding and allowed people to fall prey to simplistic slogans. This called for formulating systematic activities overseen by dedicated officials and departments. In particular, contributors lamented the frame of mind that regarded such matters as unimportant, given that the source of the conflict was political in nature rather than cultural. In a meeting with representatives of the association, Ben-Gurion responded that knowledge of German language and culture did not help Jews facing the Nazi regime, nor did ability to speak Arabic alleviate the conditions of Jews in Yemen. His generally dismissive attitude was summarized by his decision to endorse whatever cultural activities Kedma Mizraha wished to pursue, but without making any commitment on his part to undertake action in a similar vein. And, he explicitly rejected the right of anyone other than official representatives to negotiate or explore possibilities on behalf of the Yishuv and the Zionist movement.[37]

Kedma Mizraha sought to distance itself from Brit Shalom but not all members were happy with such an approach that diluted the critique of the Zionist leadership and depoliticized the quest for Jewish–Arab reconciliation. Although initially reluctant due to 'obsessive Zionist loyalty that borders on civil sin' and caution not to become a 'scapegoat' for the failure of others,[38] some activists revived an explicit political stance in a March 1939 publication, *Al Parashat Darkeinu* ('The Parting of Our Ways'), with reference to a classical collection by Ahad Ha'am, *Parting of the Ways*. It included not only former members of both movements and veterans such as Kalvarisky, but also a new generation of socialist activists to the left of the Ben-Gurion leadership of the labour movement.

A guiding principle in these efforts was the wish for 'the Arabs to recognise a Jewish national home within a Jewish–Arab Palestine that would be willing to enter – under British sponsorship and with proper guarantees – a future grand Arab confederation'.[39] This seemed to provide a way of going beyond the specific problem of Palestine which proved so difficult to resolve and pose the question in a broader context. The scale of territory and population in the region (Palestine, Lebanon, Syria, Jordan and Iraq) would have made Palestine-specific issues easier to address, especially given the 'racial' affinity between Jews and Arabs.[40] The constant stumbling block was the gap between the fears of Palestinians, who were directly affected and intensely opposed the idea, and other Arabs who had less to fear from the scheme, but also less interest in it, and their potential support was at best too lukewarm to offset Palestinian opposition.

An interesting addition to the debate on the Arab Question in the 1930s were voices positioned to the left of the mainstream labour party – Mapai – which controlled the Histadrut, and had been led since its launch by David Ben-Gurion, the chairman of the Jewish Agency. Moshe Erem of Left Poalei Zion and Yaakov Hazan of Hashomer Hatza'ir argued that a necessary step towards defusing tensions in the country was organizing workers on the basis of class interests instead of separating them on an ethnic basis as the Histadrut had done. By rejecting the notion of a joint labour organization, the Histadrut was making conflict inevitable and undermining any basis for cooperation across national boundaries. By insisting on evicting all Arab workers from Jewish-owned enterprises, it was poisoning the atmosphere and leaving workers open to the nationalist incitement of their reactionary leadership.[41] As usual, the leadership simply ignored these concerns.

Various other initiatives were undertaken in the same period, seeking to come up with proposals acceptable to all sides, loosely based on the notion of political parity between Jews and Arabs in the country and the principle of non-domination of one by the other. In a quest to form a broader political structure, the League for Jewish–Arab Rapprochement and Cooperation was launched in 1939, shortly after the *Parting of Our Ways* publication, with many contributors to it playing a leading role. Initially the League was a loose coalition of groups and individuals who generally adhered to notions of cooperation between the two national groups, and acted as a lobby without having an agreed political platform of its own. It expressed its goals in vague terms similar to those of Kedma Mizraha: 'The League unites all those who recognise the need for Jewish–Arab rapprochement and strives for cooperation between the two nations – The Jewish and Arab – and also all of those who consider it necessary that the Palestine question be solved on the basis of economic advancement and freedom of national culture and social development of both nations together.'[42]

With left-wing Zionist movements joining it a few years later it acquired a bigger mass basis, but at the cost of diluting some of the distinctive features of the Brit Shalom legacy. Thus, in 1942, it issued a statement of principles premised on 'the construction of Palestine as a common homeland for the Jewish people returning to it and the Arab people residing therein', based on 'lasting mutual understanding and agreement between the two peoples'. It asserted that 'the principle of the return of the Jews to their historical homeland to build their independent national life in it is unequivocal, as are the rights of the Palestine Arabs to their independent national life, and their ties with other parts of the Arab people'. It thus reiterated the notions of cooperation and sharing that had been the mainstay of the bi-nationalist approach, but with a few crucial differences. Its vision was that of two national communities that live independently alongside each other with little to hold them together. This was a move away from the Brit Shalom approach, which distinguished between general issues handled through common institutions (municipal services, health, transport, trade and so on), and specific national questions that would be handled through negotiations and attempts to reach consensus between the communities.

Regarding the crucial national questions of immigration and land, the League recognized 'the right of the Jews to immigrate and settle in Palestine in accordance with its maximum absorptive capacity and to an extent that shall ensure the growth of the Jewish community in Palestine toward a full and independent economic, social, cultural, and political life, in cooperation with Arab people'. It agreed to immigration quotas 'for a number of years', but was opposed to 'any aim to perpetuate the position of the Jewish community as a minority in Palestine'. In these respects too, the League set itself apart from Brit Shalom, whose focus was on building a Jewish spiritual-cultural centre in Palestine, for which massive immigration was not a requirement. Although it supported immigration, many of its leading members were willing to consider quotas (not just for a few years), and set the target for Jewish demographic growth as reaching no more than half of the population, and realistically even less (a common figure used was 40 per cent). As for land, Brit Shalom's insistence on ensuring no dispossession of Arab peasants and its willingness to consider restrictions on land transfer and settlement did not feature in the League's statements.

We can contrast these ideas with the initiative undertaken a few years earlier by the Group of Five, prominent individuals who got together in the midst of the Arab general strike of 1936, in order to facilitate negotiations between the Jewish and Arab leaderships in the country. A key issue was that of immigration, since 'All Arab circles believe that at the present rate of immigration, the Jews will soon be a majority in Palestine and the Arabs a subjugated minority'.[43] The basis for negotiation proposed by the Five was to restrict immigration for a period of ten years, during each of which 30,000 Jews would be allowed to enter the country, bringing their numbers to 800,000 – 40 per cent of the total population – by 1946. Other ideas proposed by the group included restrictions on the amount of land that small Arab farmers were allowed to sell (no more than 75 per cent of their land), and a mandatory allocation of part of the land to tenant cultivators, in the event the land was sold by the nominal landowner. Politically, they proposed a legislative council on the basis of parity, and representation of both Jews and Arabs in government's senior administrative and executive bodies.

The response of the Jewish Agency executive was to demand that the basis for the immigration quotas would be double that of the proposal (62,000 as was the case for 1935, the highest figure for the entire period). This would have allowed the Jewish community to double its size in six to seven years, and reach demographic parity with the Arab population by the end of the period. From an Arab perspective there was no point in reaching an agreement that would have reinforced their fears of Jewish immigration rather than alleviate them. The Agency was aware of that, of course, and had no intention of going along with any proposal that would restrict Jewish land acquisition and immigration. Nothing came out of the initiative as a result.

The same official attitude undermined other initiatives, such as the commission to investigate Jewish–Arab relations that was convened by the Jewish Agency in 1940, in response to an earlier call by the World Zionist

Congress. Chaired by Shlomo Kaplansky, a veteran activist in the labour movement, it included people of different positions including advocates of bi-nationalism (Judah Magnes and Haim Kalvarisky), alongside more mainstream persons. Its work overlapped with that of another commission created by the League for Jewish–Arab Rapprochement, in order to inform the Kaplansky commission. It became known as the Bentov commission after its chair, Mordekhai Bentov of Hashomer Hatza'ir.[44]

Kaplansky set out by highlighting the realistic goals of the two groups, which potentially could be reconciled without sacrificing long-term goals: 'For the Arabs – self government, an Arab federation, prevention of economic eviction, particularly of the fellahin'. For the Jews, 'self government, immigration and settlement with no political limits to their growth'. He called for a government in 'partnership of the two nations' on the basis of parity and equality, and for agreement on immigration 'until numerical parity was achieved between the Jews and Arabs, with guarantees for the continuation of immigration at the end of this experimental period', in line with the country's absorptive capacity. Other elements included combination of personal-communal and territorial autonomy (recognizing an overlap between the two principles due to demographic concentration of people in fairly homogeneous regions) and possible entry of Palestine into a Middle Eastern federation in a treaty with Britain.[45] The Bentov report was based on similar principles, with greater emphasis on territorial rather than personal autonomy within the proposed Jewish–Arab federal state, and with a call for international – rather than British – supervision during the transitional period. It also offered more detailed discussion of possible constitutional and administrative arrangements in anticipation of potential problems.

Neither of the reports was published at the time, adopted by any official body, or served as a basis for negotiation with Palestinian forces, so they remained mere thought experiments. Even the League did not adopt the Bentov report which it had commissioned. Overall, it is clear that the League was more of a mainstream Zionist organization than other bi-nationalist movements, as demonstrated by its activities jointly with and within the most important Zionist social-economic agency, the Histadrut.[46] This was due both to the presence of the settlement-oriented Hashomer Hatza'ir and other labour parties, and to the changing global and local context.

Locally, in the decade between the demise of Brit Shalom and the rise of the League, the Jewish community had grown from 200,000 people to almost half a million (from 18 per cent of the population to 30 per cent). This growth was not only demographic in nature; it reflected large industrial expansion and consolidation of organizational and military strength. This last aspect was particularly important given the decline in the capacity of the Palestinian-Arab community to organize itself and challenge British rule and Zionist settlement. The defeat of the Arab Revolt and the bitter legacy of factionalism in its aftermath reduced the ability of Palestinians to face their opponents from a position of strength.

Globally, the gamble of parts of the Arab leadership – headed by Hajj Amin al-Husseini – on victory for the Axis forces seemed to have paid off in the first years of the war, but by the end of 1942 the tide had turned. The Allies were beginning to reverse their early defeats with the battles of el-Alamein and Stalingrad, reinforced by the growing involvement of the USA in the war. At the same time, the crisis of European Jewry was intensifying and news of the holocaust was beginning to spread, though its dimensions were yet unknown. Under these circumstances the willingness of the Jewish leadership in Palestine to compromise on the practical core of Zionism – immigration and land settlement – was naturally much reduced.

The quest for a Jewish state, no longer hidden by euphemisms about a national home, became the official goal of the movement with the Biltmore programme of 1942, and even those who were not happy about such explicit statement of the goal found it difficult to oppose it in public. And yet, amidst these conditions, a new bi-nationalist movement emerged, in many respects a true successor to Brit Shalom. That was the Ihud (Union) Association, led by Judah Magnes and Martin Buber, veteran critics of mainstream politics.

THE IHUD ASSOCIATION

Clearly adhering to Zionism, Ihud declared its support for a 'Union between the Jewish and Arab peoples as essential for the upbuilding of Palestine and for cooperation between the Jewish world and the Arab world in all branches of life'. To realize that, the association called for: 'Government in Palestine based upon equal political rights for the two peoples', a federal union between Palestine and neighbouring countries, 'to guarantee the national rights of all the people within it', and a covenant between that Union and 'an Anglo-American Union which is to be part of the future Union of the free peoples'.[47]

This was followed by an important programmatic article written by Magnes. Acknowledging the Jewish link to the country, he added the need to distinguish between 'messianic expectations and hard reality', and recognize that 'Palestine is small and is not empty. Another people have been in possession for centuries, and the concept of Palestine as a Jewish state is regarded by many Arabs as equivalent to a declaration of war against them.' To prevent the danger of war due to uncompromising positions on both sides, the options of Palestine as a Jewish state or an Arab state must be rejected. The masses will rejoice over the prospect of a settlement that 'might enable them to live together and to develop their common country in peace.'

The principle of bi-nationalism was central for Magnes (although not specifically mentioned in the Ihud programme): 'Palestine as a bi-national state must provide constitutionally for equal political rights and duties for both the Jewish and Arab nations, regardless of which is the majority and which the minority. In this way neither people will dominate the other'. This would be guaranteed by the regional and global federations of which Palestine will be a part.

The most difficult issue the state would have to address is immigration, since 'no Jew can agree to a fiat which would arbitrarily stop immigration into Palestine', and 'Arabs will not agree to unrestricted Jewish immigration. It would build up a Jewish majority and might mean Jewish dominance in Palestine'. This was a 'genuine impasse', but in the context of a regional federation the numbers would be of lesser importance as the Arabs 'would be relieved of their present fear of being swamped and dominated by a majority of Jews'. If a federation would not come into existence, other proposals could be resurrected and modified, such as that of the Group of Five in 1936, which had envisaged Jews increasing their proportion up to 40 per cent. Magnes, a few years later, modified that proposal to ensure that 'the Jewish population would never be permitted to become more than one half of the total population'. An Anglo-American victory would facilitate the task, he argued, by providing guarantees of economic development to the benefit of Jews and Arabs in Palestine and the broader region.[48]

Magnes left unexplained how he could see Palestinians agreeing to an increase of the Jewish population to 50 per cent of the total, when they had failed to reach an agreement on a more modest proposal of 40 per cent in the past. This was a consistent stumbling block, as the only expression of willingness to deviate from the standard nationalist position rejecting any additional Jewish immigration was in the framework of a regional Arab federation. Such a federation could not be guaranteed (and indeed never materialized), with the result that the entire quest for Jewish–Arab reconciliation in Palestine hinged on a factor that was beyond the control of all local parties. The attempt to dilute the nature of the Palestine conflict by positioning it within the broader Arab and Middle Eastern, and even global, contexts was not new nor was it restricted to that period, and in one way or another it survives – and continues to fail – to this day.

Despite moving on the question of immigration toward the position of the League for Jewish–Arab Rapprochement, Magnes did not become a mainstream Zionist. In a 1942 letter to an American Reform rabbi, he defined Jewish nationalism as 'unhappily chauvinistic and narrow and terroristic in the best style of Eastern European nationalism'.[49] When this statement became public and he was subjected to harsh criticism, he defended his views: 'What I had in mind was not the few extremists . . . but rather, definite acts which some important leaders and groups have not repudiated and which take on the aspect of being, to say the least, not contrary to their national policy. Definite tendencies have thus been fostered among our youth which are causing many persons the gravest concern'. This was a clear reference to the growing reliance on the use of force and the nurturing of militarism within the ranks of the organized Jewish community. Forced to distance himself from that position, he reasserted his Zionism, but only 'if this term does not have to mean maximalist aims which in the opinion of many people cannot be achieved within our lifetime'.[50] This reluctance to embrace the Zionist consensus despite intense pressure marked Magnes and Ihud to the end of their political careers.

These principles did not change even with the revelations of the scale of destruction of European Jewry by the Nazis. Towards the end of the Second World War Magnes published a long letter in the *New York Times*, in which he asserted the need for a bi-national arrangement for the country (not just politically but administratively as well) and argued against partition of Palestine, which will 'create two irredentas, irreconcilable and activist, on either side of the borders. That is the way to never-ceasing warfare, the kind that made the Balkans a byword'. It was a 'surgical operation' that would kill the patient. How will the immigration issue be resolved? Allowing it up to parity, but its 'tempo' will depend on 'the economic capacity of Palestine to absorb new immigrants', which itself will be determined by an international body consisting of Jewish, Arab and UN representatives. If the arrangements result in improving relations between the two groups in the country, future issues related to immigration would be resolved in a spirit of cooperation between them. But the key is lifting discussion 'out of the narrow parochialism of Palestine politics and put[ting it] on the higher and wider plane of international interests'.[51]

Alongside Magnes, Martin Buber was an important intellectual inspiration for Ihud, a role he had played for Brit Shalom as well, although not a member officially. In a dialogue between a 'patriot' and a 'traitor', where he played the latter role, he put forward his position regarding the implications of a Jewish state: 'Of course, you don't intend to deny them [Arabs] anything but collective political equality. But if two nations live in the same state and one of them rules the other, and if the ruling nation's productivity is manifestly greater, the other nation will naturally be reduced to the status of second-class citizens in the state's economy, one way or another'. While this kind of politics may make sense to Jews as a solution to their immediate problems, 'short-term politics does not go well with morality, while long-term politics merges with morality at certain crucial junctures'.[52]

Zionism from his perspective meant that 'as many Jews as possible come to Palestine', while for Ben-Gurion it meant for Jews 'to become the majority in the country'. Posing the issue in such terms implies relations of power, 'and this is not what we aspire to. Just as we do not want our neighbours to determine our fate, we do not want to be in the position determining theirs'. Ben-Gurion promised justice and equality, 'but can we expect the Arabs to accept that promise as a commitment limiting our future actions regarding them, a commitment that the generations of our descendants will fulfil in its entirety?' The contradiction here is that 'Ben-Gurion goes so far as to say that no written promises can really guarantee any of the Jewish people's vital interests. Doesn't that necessarily apply to both sides?' Only by giving up the quest to become the majority in the country, can relationships between the two national groups be built on a basis of equality, free of conflict.[53]

By the mid-1940s, even before the end of the war, the global scene had changed irrevocably, and with it internal Jewish debate. The rise of the USA and the Soviet Union as world powers made British policy concerns, with their wish to avoid alienating Arab public opinion, less central to shaping the future of the country. The creation of groups of internally displaced populations – hundreds of thousands of Jews who survived the war but whose communities had been destroyed and they had no home to return to – gave the question of immigration into Palestine a new sense of urgency. The notion of a Jewish state gained ground, among its constituency in Palestine and as a proposed solution to the problem of European Jewish refugees. Local Arab opposition did not change, but its capacity to block the growing trend towards political power for Jews in the country weakened as a result. Ihud, as the only Jewish political force opposing both statehood and unrestricted immigration, found itself isolated from the mainstream Jewish community.

There was another force calling for a bi-national solution – Hashomer Hatza'ir – but it did that from a different conceptual and political starting point. Standing firmly on ground shared by all Zionist parties, Hashomer Hatza'ir adhered to an expansive interpretation of Jewish rights: the historical right to the country, the moral right to immigrate into it without political restrictions, the notion that transfer of land from Arab to Jewish hands and consequent settlement on it do not hurt the Arab population due to the almost unlimited absorptive capacity of the country. In fact, Arabs derived great social and material benefits from the labour of and investment by Jews. That they did not wish to be overwhelmed demographically in their own country by people who were foreigners to them was understandable, but not reason enough to restrict immigration. In the grand scheme of things, the real needs of Jews fleeing persecution and death took precedence over the imaginary needs of Arabs fearing future persecution by Jews.[54]

Ideally, the goals of Zionism – especially immigration and land settlement – would be realized with the agreement of Arabs, but going forward with the settlement tasks did not require their prior consent. This hard-line position was tempered however with dissent regarding the ultimate goal of the movement. The quest for a massive Jewish immigration into the country, which would turn the existing Palestinian-Arab population into a minority, did not equate to a call for a Jewish state. Even if ongoing immigration would result in Jews becoming a majority, there was no need for the state to become 'Jewish' in the sense of granting Jews privileges and relegating Arabs to second-class status. Instead, the goal was a Jewish–Arab state or simply a territorial Palestinian state in which people would enjoy equal individual and collective rights regardless of their numerical proportion of the total population.

The question of demography provides an interesting contrast with Brit Shalom and Ihud. For the bi-nationalist associations there was no question that the increase in the size of Palestine's Jewish population (both in relative and absolute terms) would disadvantage the local Arabs. Before the British Mandate period began Arabs had been the vast majority of the population, facing hardly a challenge to their dominance of the public sphere in most places (Tel Aviv and the agricultural Jewish settlements were the only exceptions). Their language, culture, religious practices, and sheer physical presence were the norm in the country as a whole and they felt no threat to their collective national existence or their fate as individuals spread over hundreds of communities in the countryside, towns and big cities. They had no reason to expect that their immediate future would set them apart from other Arabs in the region, or that their ability to control their own lives and determine their future would be hampered as a result of political forces coming from outside the country and operating with complete disregard for their concerns.

The sense of loss of control, that Palestine was slipping away from them and being taken over by strangers and their society was undergoing severe dislocation – expressed above all in communal land being privatized and frequently sold away, villagers falling into debt and forced off the land with tenants moving to urban slums, becoming dependent on wage labour – all these fed Arab nationalist agitation throughout the period, especially from the early 1930s onwards. Data about growing overall wealth in the country, the rise in industrial and agricultural productivity, and rapid modernization, did little to change the prevalent feeling of impending national doom. It is not surprising that the humanist intellectuals of Brit Shalom and Ihud were more sensitive to the power of such feelings – and thus the need to address them – than the Marxist-inspired activists of Left Zionist movements.

The latter, including Hashomer Hatza'ir, sought to prove that Palestinians benefited from Jewish settlement and therefore their fears were not grounded in material reality. They dismissed Arab concerns about rapid social dislocation as psychological in nature, reflecting jealousy or narrow-minded conservatism rather than an experience of being undermined politically and suffering the consequences of growing social and economic instability. However, not only were the fruits of material prosperity not spread equally, but its foundations were shaky. They were based on land sales that generated revenue but led to permanent loss of physical and social ground, the war economy of the 1940s did create jobs but these were temporary in nature, wages were higher but offered no security of tenure or prospects of long-term development for the poor peasants and unskilled workers. Above all, the gradual but consistent expansion of a Jewish-only exclusion zone, from which all Arabs were barred – as residents, employees, and service providers – cast a deep shadow over all instances of material improvement.

Given that the two major Zionist slogans were Redemption of Land and Conquest of Labour, both of which led to the removal of Arabs to be replaced by Jewish immigrants, it is hardly surprising that repeated assertions by mainstream Jewish leaders that they did not intend to dispossess Arabs because there was enough room in the country for both groups were not taken at face value. That the most prominent leader of the Zionist movement and the Jewish community since the mid-1930s – David Ben-Gurion – had built his political career around the campaign for Hebrew Labour, did not make it easier for Arabs to accept the assurances that they would not be dispossessed when Palestine became a Jewish state.

Realising that Jewish immigration and settlement had consequences that were not only symbolic and political but also material in nature prompted bi-nationalist activists to offer compromises (from a Zionist point of view) regarding the size and pace of immigration. Although convinced that Jews have the moral right to immigrate to Palestine, especially at periods in which they faced mortal danger in Europe, they realized that the fears and concerns of local Arabs were genuine and had to be accommodated in order to reach a peaceful resolution of the conflict.

Hashomer Hatza'ir took a different line: it refused to offer any concessions on immigration and land settlement, but was ready for a political compromise on the goal of a Jewish state. It offered three principles that would establish a bi-national state and shape relations in the country: shared sovereignty over the country, which would be neither Jewish nor Arab but both; giving each community power to manage its internal affairs without domination of one over the other; and, parity in power and representation as the basis for the inter-group relationship, regardless of the overall size of the groups or their proportion in the population. For this to work, reducing the inequality in living standards while encouraging economic cooperation and interdependence between communities was essential. Political equality could not remain stable if it continued to coexist with sharp social inequalities. The socialist orientation of the movement was clearly visible here as it was in its general focus on socio-economic issues.

On a practical note, the proposed bi-national solution of Hashomer Hatza'ir was based on the notion of ethnic federalism: two autonomous ethnic units within the overall national framework, which determine their own policies in communal affairs – education, culture – and share power on issues with no specific ethnic component, such as health, industry, transport and so on. All this would be framed by the need to gain the support of both communities on matters of crucial importance to the nature of the country, such as immigration and land settlement. Jewish and Arab representatives may transcend their national affiliation when dealing with neutral issues – taxation, roads, trade – but take their own side on key national questions. To avoid conflict, the principle of uninterrupted Jewish immigration would be entrenched and would not be subject to change through an occasional majority. It could be expected that within 20 years the Jewish population would reach three million people through immigration, and Arabs would reach two million through natural increase. This state of affairs would lead to normalization of relations and the removal of ethnic majority–minority issues from the national agenda, provided that questions of economic resources and social policies are handled through a political mechanism that treats all citizens as equal without giving preference to one segment over another.

The additional concern with social and economic issues was an important dimension that had been neglected by other bi-nationalist movements. But, the insistence on uninterrupted Jewish immigration (theoretically restricted by the absorptive capacity of the country, a notion without effective limits) made the proposal of Hashomer Hatza'ir a non-starter from the perspective of Arab nationalists. Guarantees of material development in some undefined future were a poor substitute for the immediate prospect of national independence and political control that was their most pressing goal, nor was bi-nationalism an adequate alternative. This became clear in testimonies to the 1946 Anglo-American Committee of Inquiry, presented by the Ihud delegation on the one hand and the Arab Office on the other.[55]

Magnes and Buber represented Ihud at the inquiry, putting forward the association's position 'for the union of Jews and Arabs in a bi-national Palestine based on the parity of the two peoples; and for the union of the bi-national Palestine with neighbouring countries'. This latter principle was important because 'Palestine must be lifted out of the parochialism to which its tiny size might condemn it. Palestine represents an inter-national, inter-religious idea of deep concern to millions of Jews, Christians and Moslems throughout the world'.

While recognizing that both Jews and Arabs had rights in the country, Ihud made a distinction between the 'historical rights' of the former and 'natural rights' of the latter. The two overlapped to a degree but essentially balanced each other out: historical rights were ideological in nature, reflecting the position of Palestine (Eretz Israel) in Jewish history and consciousness, while natural rights had a greater practical component, reflecting the long presence of Arabs in the country and their role in shaping its society and culture. Ultimately both were of 'equal validity' and the task of negotiations and commissions of inquiries was to reconcile them in a way that would satisfy the basic needs of both, particularly addressing issues of immigration, land and self-government. Immigration was, of course, the biggest stumbling block. Ihud recognized that from the Arab point of view every additional Jewish immigrant represents a demographic threat. It called for an immediate admission of 100,000 European Jewish refugees as a humanitarian gesture dealing with those displaced by the war. Such a number would not offset the demographic balance, and would not exceed what some Arab representatives had agreed to before the war. In addition, a period of a decade or more would allow Jews to reach parity with the Arab population, subject to the absorptive capacity of the country (a concept that had to allow for 'imponderables' that could creatively expand the economic potential of the country). Beyond that, any further immigration would be subject to agreement, with the expectation that the growing trend towards regional unity would ease the fears of local Arabs and make them consent to Jewish immigrants who would not threaten them with being numerically 'swamped' any longer. A solution to that issue would facilitate a solution for the land issue as well.

MOVING TOWARDS PARTITION

The political structure of the country would provide both communities with equal representation, on the assumption that in areas where the communal interest does not dictate a unified position – economy, trade, labour, social security and so on – Jews and Arabs would be able to overcome boundaries and operate jointly as members of the entire population. Cultural issues would be decided by each community separately, and matters of shared but also possibly opposed national interests would be resolved by consensus. This approach was premised on the involvement of international organizations – the Jewish Agency, the Arab League, the newly-created United Nations (UN) – which would help manage the relations between the local communities. On their own, these local forces were much more likely to reach a dead end and prove unable to resolve any issue without resort to the use of force, as their record up to 1946 had shown. As Magnes put it: 'Full cultural autonomy is combined with full allegiance to the multi-national State. National identity is safeguarded, yet there is coalescence in a larger political framework.'[56] Examples of such arrangements were found in Switzerland, the UK, the

Soviet Union, South Africa and Yugoslavia, all different but combining centralization and autonomy, on a communal or regional basis.

Magnes addressed the opposition by the Palestinian leadership to a dilution of the principles of independence and majority rule in two ways: first, a call to create broader frameworks (international, regional) that would remove the matter from the parochial concerns of local Jews and Arabs. As he put it: 'It is our conviction – at least, our hope – that the Arab League is going to be much more moderate than any local Arab body in any country.'[57] And, second, by invoking the big 'inarticulate' section of the Arab population – meaning ordinary people – who would be willing to accept such solutions as he was proposing, but do not have a voice and therefore cannot challenge their official leadership. In the absence of any contemporary studies it is impossible to say whether that was indeed the case, but clearly Magnes could not provide evidence that mattered politically for his point.

A direct response to Magnes's testimony was given by Arab-British academic, Albert Hourani, speaking for the Arab Office. Hourani opposed any change on immigration that would mean conceding to Zionists 'more than they can legitimately claim to weakening the Arab character of Palestine, and to admitting the principle of the National Home'. He opposed a bi-national state, which could work only 'if a certain spirit of cooperation and trust exists and if there is an underlying sense of unity to neutralize communal differences'. This spirit did not exist in Palestine and 'If it existed, the whole problem would have not arisen in this form', Hourani argued. Even if it were possible, a bi-national state would lead to one of two things: 'Either to a complete deadlock involving perhaps the intervention of foreign powers, or else to the domination of the whole life of the state by communal considerations.'

Above all, Hourani said, the integrity and sincerity of Magnes were not in doubt but he spoke for 'a very small section of the Jewish community in Palestine.' His scheme would satisfy his group of supporters 'but it would not satisfy the vast majority of Zionists.' If a bi-national state were established, he and his group 'would be swept aside and the majority of Zionists would use what Doctor Magnes had obtained for them in order to press their next demands'. Thus, he might become 'the first victim of political Zionism'.[58]

There was a point here that summed up Zionist practices and proved prophetic regarding future developments. The mainstream leadership under Ben-Gurion was pragmatic. It agreed to be part of any agreement that would grant it more than it already had acquired. Having started with very little, any political or territorial concession that brought it closer to its goals was seen as a victory and was embraced as a stepping stone for further progress. As conditions changed and more favourable offers were made, it took advantage of these in the same way, and thus was able to move constantly forward. Palestinians adopted an opposite approach. Having started out from a position of overwhelming demographic and territorial dominance, they regarded all concessions as setbacks. They tended to measure all potential agreements against that fixed starting point and an absolute notion of rights. Unlike Zionists, they rarely weighed new options at any given point in time based on what they could gain or lose in relation to the existing – but ever shifting – situation. They thus made themselves appear constantly as rejectionists, while their Zionist counterparts projected an image of willingness to compromise.

Magnes was well aware that his views of reconciliation and cooperation were shared only by a small minority among the Jewish community in the country, and had no open Arab support. In fact, that was one of his main arguments against partition: 'The only way to get people to work together is to get them to live together, to get them to know one another, and you can't do that by putting them into separate compartments.' If you do that, the feelings of fear and distrust, among the youth in particular 'will be accentuated to a very large degree. Unfortunately, at the present time you have a large amount of the bitterest nationalism, which you might call chauvinism, being given expression to both here and there'. If partition – an artificial division of the country – were to be enacted, the experience of living separately would increase hate and desire for revenge and result in more rather than less conflict.[59] Given that a Jewish state could be achieved only against the resistance of Arabs, the result would be more violence and growing resentment: 'The day we lick the Arabs, that is the day, I think, when we shall be sowing the seed of an eternal hatred of such dimensions that Jews will not be able to live in that part of the world for centuries to come.'[60]

The marginal position of Ihud was presented by Buber as a badge of honour, being 'the Cassandra of our time', referring to those 'who, equally free from the megalomania of the leaders and from the giddiness of the masses, discern the approaching catastrophe. They do not merely utter their warnings, but they try to point to the path which has to be followed if catastrophe is to be averted'.[61] This could be done only if the basic error of Zionism is reversed, and instead of siding with colonial forces and seeking international agreements that would override local concerns, agreement would be attempted between the local contenders who would then seek international sanction for it.

Ironically, despite its marginalized political position, Ihud's statement and testimony were taken up by the Anglo-American Committee in its April 1946 report. It did not use the notion of bi-nationalism explicitly but said:

> In order to dispose, once and for all, of the exclusive claims of Jews and Arabs to Palestine, we regard it as essential that a clear statement of the following principles should be made: I. That Jew shall not dominate Arab and Arab shall not dominate Jew in Palestine. II. That Palestine shall be neither a Jewish state nor an Arab state. III. That the form of government ultimately to be established, shall, under international guarantees, fully protect and preserve the interests in the Holy Land of Christendom and of the Moslem and Jewish faiths. Thus Palestine must ultimately become a state which guards the rights and interests of Moslems, Jews and Christians alike; and accords to the inhabitants, as a whole, the fullest measure of self-government, consistent with the three paramount principles set forth above.

It went on to warn: 'the hostility between Jews and Arabs and, in particular, the determination of each to achieve domination, if necessary by violence, make it almost certain that, now and for some time to come, any attempt to establish either an independent Palestinian State or independent Palestinian States would result in civil strife such as might threaten the peace of the world.'[62]

The Committee's recommendations were to continue with the Mandate until the United Nations assumed trusteeship as a step towards self-government and eventual independence and, in the meantime, to facilitate the immediate immigration of 100,000 Jewish displaced persons from Europe and remove restrictions on land settlement in Palestine (rescinding the Land Transfers Regulations of 1940). Since neither side was happy with these ideas – the Jewish leadership regarded them as offering too little and the Arab leadership as conceding too much – the conflict remained unchanged. Ihud was the only political force that welcomed the Committee's report, and indeed felt vindicated in its decision to attend the hearings despite opposition from official Zionist institutions – but not without reservations. These had to do mostly with the question of self-government and role of local residents in the administration of the country.[63]

In a letter published in the *New York Times* in June 1946, Magnes outlined the elements missing from the report, focusing critical attention on the principle that self-governing institutions could come into being only once the two communities expressed willingness to work together. On the contrary, he argued, 'this will to work together can be furthered best by setting up self-governing institutions . . . Good will can come through life, through the creation of common interests vital to both peoples. Active, responsible participation in Government is perhaps the most important of these common vital interests'. This applied to the constitution as well, which must not be imposed from the outside: 'Charge representatives of the two peoples with the task of helping to frame a constitution and the will to work together will thus appear'. It is the concrete experience of cooperation in day-to-day life that will give rise to common political consciousness and not the other way around.[64]

Much of the essence of the testimony given by Magnes on behalf of Ihud in 1946 was repeated in his appearance in front of another commission: the UN Special Committee on Palestine (UNSCOP), which collected evidence in July 1947. Identifying Arab-Jewish cooperation as the chief objective of policy, he lamented the absence of interest in it by any of the major parties to the conflict, including the Mandatory government.

Recognizing the validity of the principle of majority rule where conditions are appropriate, he invoked the more relevant examples of Belgium, Canada, Czechoslovakia, the Soviet Union, Switzerland and Yugoslavia as cases in which 'the equality of basic national rights of the different nationalities making up the state is protected against majority rule'. Bi-nationalism 'gives full protection to the various regions of the country, to the national languages, cultures, institutions', and yet maintains 'full allegiance to the political state'. This combination of unity at the state level with cultural and regional diversity overcomes the problem of dominant and dominated peoples, which 'leads to constant friction, breaks out in revolution, results in war'.[65]

To avoid all that, there was need for both sides to make concessions. Arabs 'would have to yield their ambition to set up in Palestine a uni-national, independent sovereign state', in exchange for enjoying 'the maximum of national freedom in a bi-national Palestine equally with their Jewish fellow-citizens'. Jews would give up 'their dream of a uni-national independent sovereign Jewish state', in exchange for being made 'a constituent nation' in Palestine, where they would not be classified as a minority, nor a majority, but with 'full national rights equally with their Arab fellow citizens'.[66] Integration within regional and global frameworks would supplement the picture and serve as mechanisms to resolve disputes between the two constituent nations, which they would not be able to agree among themselves on how to handle.

In this sense the bi-national arrangement – before independence for the country – would be different from the British Mandate, because it would have bridge-building between the two nations as an explicit goal, whereas the British saw their role as that of a referee standing in judgement over the two combatants who were doing all the work. Partition would make the task of bridge-building impossible.

Magnes acknowledged that from the Arab point of view immigration was a problem, bordering on foreign invasion, as 'people are coming from the outside who were not born here'. The Arab fear of Jewish domination was understandable but Jews were not really invaders as they did not come into the country to explore or seek wealth. The Arabs have material links to the country, and 'we contend that our claim is at least as strong – to be sure, not so material. This happens to be an instance where the Jewish people, which is accused of being a materialist people, is trying to emphasize spiritual bonds and trying to make these spiritual, historic bonds of equal validity at least with these material *kushans*, or deeds, which certain landlords have over the soil.'[67]

While Magnes was strong on principles, he had – or at least presented – an inflated view of the degree of support for the bi-national idea, referring to 'a very large proportion of the population definitely committed to the bi-national state', and even larger proportion who would accept it if it came into being. In this figure he included Ihud (admittedly a small association), Hashomer Hatza'ir, and the Communists, as well as 'a large section of the inarticulate population' who are 'very much in favour of some accommodation with the Arabs', even though there was no doubt that majority of Jews supported a Jewish state.[68]

In any event, the problem of Palestine had no finite solution, and the bi-national idea was meant to give 'the framework for the development of common interests between the Jews and the Arabs, who are both going to remain here unless the Arabs drive the Jews into the sea, as they say they once drove the Crusaders into the sea, or the Jews drive the Arabs into the desert, as some think perhaps they should be driven'.[69] Partition did not give any finality either, and rather was 'but the beginning of real warfare – warfare perhaps between Jew and Jew, and warfare between Jew and Arab'. The advantage of a bi-national Palestine was that it had already existed in practice as a demographic and social reality, and all that was needed was to combine this reality with the idea that Jews and Arabs were 'equal nationalities', whose relations were not governed by the majority-minority question.[70]

Ihud's presentation was reinforced in a subsequent testimony by Ernst Simon on behalf of the League for Jewish–Arab Rapprochement and Co-operation. The League united its members in the belief in a bi-national solution, based on individual and collective equality. It called for guaranteeing what each group needs most. For Jews it was immigration and settlement, for Arabs economic and social development, and for both peace and joint independence. Although Simon was an Ihud activist, and before that one of the radical members of Brit Shalom, when representing the League he was careful to stick to more mainstream Zionist positions, asserting the benefits Jewish settlement brought to Arabs (albeit marred by the insistence on political domination), and the unrestricted right for further Jewish immigration.[71]

Also speaking for the League, Aharon Cohen spent much of his presentation criticising the British authorities for failing to facilitate and actively hampering any improvement in Jewish–Arab relations:

There is a very large measure of freedom in this country for national incitement and sowing of hatred of one nation against the other. Newspapers or organizations which aim to widen the gulf between the two nations were hardly ever forbidden. In a land of two nations the Government and the censorship reveal unrestrained leniency towards insulting and inciting articles written in the papers of one nation against the other. On the other hand, the censorship is very severe not only with criticism aimed at the Government, but also at times makes it even impossible to refute the chauvinistic incitement and reveal the true nature of reactionary intrigues.[72]

This was lamentable especially since, in his view, the hostile attitude of the Arab leadership was not replicated in the feelings of grassroots constituencies who recognize the benefits brought by Jewish settlement. He gave examples of daily cooperation between ordinary people, for example in the Negev: 'The average Arab, even if he is under the influence of the current anti-Jewish slogan, "Defend the South against Jewish Invasion", welcomes Jewish settlement in his vicinity because he hopes that it will bring him water, bus transport, medical aid, and modern methods in many other fields.'

Due to the claimed discrepancy between official and popular attitudes, he said, there was room for optimism, since 'there exists a gap between the feelings of the wide masses of both peoples and the official proclamation made by their respective leaders. The policy of extremism which was nurtured during the recent years became popular under the misleading assumption that extremism pays'. But, if people realized that 'extremism leads to destruction', and that 'co-operation holds greater promise, that the attempt to bridge temporary conflicting interests presents greater hopes, then the mood of the two nations would definitely change'.

Such change would be based on the absence of conflict 'between the real interests and just aspirations of the two peoples. The Jews want freedom to develop unhindered their national home through immigration, settlement, and political independence. The Arabs seek progress, political independence, a rise in their standard of life, freedom from want and ignorance, freedom from economic backwardness and feudal domination'. Both sets of goals could be realized 'if Palestine is constituted as quickly as possible as the bi-national state in which they will live as two nations enjoying equal national status in Government regardless of their relative numbers'. A bi-national state based on these premises and 'taking into consideration the special needs of the country and the needs of the two nations involved', will stimulate 'the progressive and compromising forces in the two nations, and make them co-operate for the benefit of all the inhabitants'. This regime 'can open the gates of Palestine to the Jews waiting to enter; it can raise the standard of living of the Arabs to that of the Jews through joint development schemes, so that both of them may progress shoulder to shoulder. Such a regime can advance both nations quickly to independence in their common homeland'.

The contrast between immigration and settlement for Jews, with explicit political content, and raising living standards for Arabs, a more apolitical outcome, was noticed by the Committee. Cohen denied that this reflected a different approach to the national aspirations of the two groups. He clarified: 'Our League has never tried to organize Jews and Arabs within its framework. We are working primarily within the Jewish community and we are trying to encourage the rise of similar groups within the Arab community, so that we both can be cooperating together.' Earlier in his testimony he referred to the group *Falsatin al-Jadida* ('New Palestine'), with which the League had signed a memorandum a few months earlier, only to see its leader Fawzi al-Husseini assassinated shortly thereafter, as a result.

The memorandum was the only instance of a joint Jewish–Arab political platform during the entire period. It asserted the signatories' commitment to maintain the integrity of Palestine and seek a solution for its political problem through an Arab-Jewish accord based on the following principles: complete cooperation between the two peoples in all fields; political equality between them in Palestine toward the independence of the country; Jewish immigration according to the country's economic absorptive capacity, and the future alliance of independent Palestine with the neighbouring countries.[73]

With al-Husseini's demise less than two weeks after the document was signed, the opportunity to use it as a stepping-stone towards joint organization beyond national boundaries came to an abrupt end.

Cohen made much of the failure of the British authorities to solve the murder and take steps against the almost-certain culprits – the leadership of the Arab national movement, led by the al-Husseini family. He attributed that to the supposed British hostility for the prospect of Jewish–Arab reconciliation, though it is not clear what they would have gained from such an attitude if indeed they had held it. In any event, the really important question was different: if Cohen was right and the initiative was more than a negligible affair of passing interest, why did it prove so easy for nationalists on both sides to marginalize the activists in question? Was there ever a serious prospect of joint action to overcome national divisions? Why did testimonies such as those by Magnes and Simon, which impressed their audiences by offering rational discussion and a well-argued case based on liberal humanist principles, receive so little practical support from the public – Jews and Arabs alike? Did the support among the 'inarticulate population' dissipate or did it never exist in the first place?

We know that bi-nationalist activists were a small minority among Jews in the country but we do not know the extent of tacit support for their ideas, and know even less about support among Arabs. The crucial point though, is that even if many were sympathetic to these ideas or at least willing to go along with them if they proved viable, such support never stood on its own. Rather, it depended on the prevailing attitudes of the other side. In other words, the willingness of Jews to support bi-nationalism increased when they thought there was an Arab partner to the proposed arrangements and declined when no such partner was seen to exist. Arabs were more willing to consider compromises when they felt the other side was seriously considering curbing its goals, and less willing when they thought Zionist officials were merely playing for time by agreeing to compromises as temporary concessions until they were strong enough to demand more. All this resulted in a vicious cycle – political or physical aggression by one side led to the consolidation of public opinion behind aggressive policies by the other, which in turn served to 'vindicate' the initial aggression, and so on.

In this environment, the prospects for a virtuous cycle – mutually reinforcing expressions of willingness to cross the nationalist 'red lines' in order to address the other side's concerns – declined steadily. The expansion of the Zionist settlement project was seen as an act of aggression by the Arab leadership, diplomatic efforts failed to block it and led to frustration and use of force, as in 1921 and 1929. This exposed Jewish bi-nationalists such as Brit Shalom to accusations of being soft on the Arabs and – in their naivety and weakness – encouraging them to oppose Jewish settlement. Their inability to identify a clear partner for bi-nationalism on the Arab side undermined Brit Shalom and similar movements further. They were seen as making concessions which were not reciprocated but only led to Arab intransigence. The Arabs for their part saw no reason to make concessions in response to informal proposals that did not come from official Zionist sources, and were worried that reciprocating would not bring them any real benefits and just undermine their negotiating position. Mutual suspicions, fears of being taken advantage of, and the need to save face in order not to appear 'weak', prevented a breakthrough that could have opened the way to serious negotiations.

When the UNSCOP majority report called for partition of the country, Magnes warned that it would 'arouse the resentment of large numbers of Jews, of almost all the Arabs of Palestine, and of the Arab world', and require the use of force on an extensive scale, 'thus precipitating the irrepressible conflict, which today does not yet exist'.[74] Anticipating events, he argued that 'the war of the irredentas [to acquire more territory and get rid of members of the opposite group] will have begun even before the independence of the two states has been proclaimed'.[75] In a similar manner to Cohen, Magnes invoked again Fawzi al-Husseini's call for political equality and cooperation in an independent bi-national Palestine, as part of his plea to prevent partition and establish a basis for joint self-governance. At the same time that he publicly asserted the possibilities of political agreement, privately he acknowledged failure to block the move towards partition, caused in part by strength 'in intellectual resources' combined with weakness 'in organizational and administrative talent'. This called for 'pitiless thoroughness' in analysing the situation and the reasons for Ihud's lack of influence.[76]

Even after the adoption of the UN partition resolution of 29 November 1947, which called for the establishment of two states, Jewish and Arab, Magnes continued to campaign for a unified state. Initially he used the UNSCOP minority report proposing a federal state as a basis. After the termination of the British Mandate and the establishment of the State of Israel on 14 May 1948 he began to advocate a new confederation – the United States of Palestine – which would include Israel and a Palestinian state linked together in an overarching structure. Using the UN partition resolution that insisted on economic cooperation between the two states, he envisaged embedding such cooperation within a political framework. To restore relations to a point that would allow communication and joint action, he called on the Israeli government not to entrench the dispossession of the Palestinian refugees, who were displaced by the war and were in danger of becoming permanent outsiders. This was effectively his last important intervention before his death in October 1948.

Having been in close contact with Magnes during the last few months of his life, the distinguished US-based academic and intellectual Hannah Arendt contributed to disseminating his views and the bi-national idea. Writing in May 1948, she attributed the deteriorating situation to the mood among Jews in Palestine – shared by their American counterparts – which was expressed in the following propositions:

> the moment has now come to get everything or nothing, victory or death; Arab and Jewish claims are irreconcilable and only a military decision can settle the issue; the Arabs – all Arabs – are our enemies and we accept this fact; only outmoded liberals believe in compromises, only philistines believe in justice, and only *shlemiels* prefer truth and negotiations to propaganda and machine guns; Jewish experience in the last decades – or over the last two centuries, or over the last two thousand years – has finally awakened us and taught us to look out for ourselves; this alone is reality, everything else is stupid sentimentality; everybody is against us . . . we count upon nobody except ourselves; in sum – we are ready to go down fighting, and we will consider anybody who stands in our way a traitor and anything done to hinder us a stab in the back.[77]

She expressed support for the notion of bi-nationalism by asserting that

> the idea of Arab-Jewish cooperation, though never realized on any scale and today seemingly farther off than ever, is not an idealistic

day dream but a sober statement of the fact that without it the whole Jewish venture in Palestine is doomed. Jews and Arabs could be forced by circumstances to show the world that there are no differences between two people that cannot be bridged. Indeed, the working out of such a *modus vivendi* might in the end serve as a model of how to counteract the dangerous tendencies of formerly oppressed peoples to shut themselves off from the rest of the world and develop nationalist superiority complexes of their own.[78]

Although Jews could win the war, their conduct would have disastrous consequences:

The 'victorious' Jews would live surrounded by an entirely hostile Arab population, secluded inside ever-threatened borders, absorbed with physical self-defense to a degree that would submerge all other interests and activities. The growth of a Jewish culture would cease to be the concern of the whole people; social experiments would have to be discarded as impractical luxuries; political thought would center around military strategy; economic development would be determined exclusively by the needs of war.

Under these circumstances, 'the Palestinian Jews would degenerate into one of those small warrior tribes about whose possibilities and importance history has amply informed us since the days of Sparta'.[79]

She went on to argue that the partition of such a small country 'could at best mean the petrification of the conflict, which would result in arrested development for both peoples; at worst it would signify a temporary stage during which both parties would prepare for further war'. The only real alternative was a federated state, as advocated by Magnes:

[D]espite the fact that it establishes a common government for two different peoples, it avoids the troublesome majority-minority constellation, which is insoluble by definition. A federated structure, moreover, would have to rest on Jewish–Arab community councils, which could mean that the Jewish–Arab conflict would be resolved on the lowest and most promising level of proximity and neighborliness. A federated state, finally, could be the natural stepping-stone for any later, greater federated structure in the Near East and the Mediterranean area.[80]

In a fitting gesture Arendt dedicated her final words on the topic (written in late 1948 but published a year later) to the memory of Magnes, who had died in the meantime.[81] She repeated his call for a confederal solution for the country, within a regional federation, but expressed scepticism whether Israeli Jews, having won the war, would agree to any major concessions. In particular, she raised questions about the future of an Israeli state that would become dependent on overseas donations and military and diplomatic support in its struggle against its neighbours.

In particular, she lamented the creation of a new group of homeless people, the Arab refugees, who became 'a dangerous potential irredenta dispersed in all Arab countries'. Whether they became refugees 'as a consequence of Arab atrocity propaganda or real atrocities or a mixture of both', their exodus was prepared 'by Zionist plans of large-scale population transfers during the war' and was entrenched by Israel's refusal to readmit them. In this way it made 'the old Arab claim against Zionism finally come true: the Jews simply aimed at expelling the Arabs from their homes. What had been the pride of the Jewish homeland, that it had not been based upon exploitation, turned into a curse when the final test came: the flight of the Arabs would not have been possible' or welcomed by the Jews 'if they had lived in a common economy'.[82] Only one person, she said, raised his voice against making this situation permanent, and it was Judah Magnes. But, all this was to no avail. It was not obvious at the time, but the refugee problem was destined to become the crucial distinguishing feature of the Israeli-Palestinian conflict in its post-1948 incarnation, but discussion of this aspect belongs to another chapter.

CONCLUSIONS

There can be little doubt regarding the importance of the bi-nationalist movement as a dissident force, offering a solid intellectual alternative to mainstream state-oriented Zionism. Yet, it failed in extending its reach beyond small Jewish circles and did not gain any Arab support. Why?

- It operated among people who owed their existence in the country largely to their wish to live independently as Jews: the prospect of compromising on this goal naturally did not appeal to them. Jews who were happy to live together with non-Jews as equals, or were not interested in political sovereignty, usually stayed in their home countries or moved to other destinations, rather than specifically to Palestine.

- On practical grounds, the bi-nationalist case was seriously undermined by the absence of an equivalent force among the Arab population. The call to compromise on the quest for Jewish sovereignty seemed to offer unilateral concessions that were not reciprocated, and therefore were pointless. Pointing out to talks and even tacit agreements with unnamed Palestinian activists or marginal ones, or Arabs from outside of Palestine, could not substitute for the absence of credible Palestinian representatives as partners.

- The mainstream Palestinian leadership rejected compromises along the lines suggested by the bi-nationalists because it feared that any concessions to the legitimacy of Jewish political presence in the country would undermine its own negotiating position, without curbing the forward expansion of the Jewish settlement project. Whatever agreements might have been possible with Jewish bi-nationalists, Palestinian leaders suspected, they would not have been binding on the official Zionist movement, which would move on with its plans for Jewish domination in the country. The bi-nationalists were seen as part of the overall Zionist strategy rather than as dissidents from it.

- Nothing was more disastrous for the willingness to make concessions than the sense that your opponents would continue to attack, regardless of agreements. In particular, armed attacks against Jewish communities, especially the 1929 Arab riots, reinforced internal solidarity in the Yishuv, directed negative attention towards dissidents, and created an atmosphere that focused more than ever on the need to take up arms for defensive purposes and to prevent further attacks, at times by taking the war into enemy territory. This was the case in particular when no clear relationship between the targets and immediate political issues could be found, as was the case when Hebron and Safed with their non-Zionist religious and Mizrahi Jewish populations became prime targets.

- Perhaps the most crucial question to consider, not just in analysing developments in the period discussed here but all the way to the present, is the ways in which responses of the one side shaped those of the other. In a bi-national situation, no movement operated within its own sealed space. But, whereas nationalists could embark on their own course of action without getting approval from others, seeking to realize their agenda by force, bi-nationalists suffered a structural disadvantage because they depended on positive reaction from potential Arab partners. Not only that, but the potential partners responded not only to what the bi-nationalists themselves said or did, but also – perhaps primarily – to what other forces on the Jewish side said and did, over which the bi-nationalists had no control. This reinforced their structural disadvantage: the dominant trends in both camps conspired, as it were, against them by making the environment increasingly polarised. This benefitted those on either side who urged unilateral action and weakened those who argued for mutual consideration.

Ultimately, offering a rational solution based on sharing assets deeply cherished and coveted by both sides was logical because, in principle, it was better to be guaranteed something than to risk everything and – possibly – get nothing. But this logic did not work. For most Arabs a compromise equalled surrender because it forced them to give up their exclusive non-negotiable claim to the territory. For most Jews compromise was fine as a temporary step, as long as it guaranteed their non-negotiable sovereignty on at least some of the territory. The minimum demands of one side were too much for the other side to concede, and the result was increasingly inevitable clash that could be resolved only with the use of force.

2

The Palestinian Communist Party, 1919–48

Alongside the bi-nationalist movement, a radical left-wing trend elevated universal socialist principles above specific nationalist aims, and was concerned with the implications of the Jewish settlement project in Palestine for relations between Jews and Arabs in the country. In a similar manner to the liberal-humanist critique of mainstream Zionism, the left-wing current traces its origins to the very early days of the new settlement in Palestine. In a long-forgotten text from 1886, a Russian Jewish socialist revolutionary by the name of Ilia Rubanovich raised the following questions regarding the new settlement movement: 'What is to be done with the Arabs? Would the Jews expect to be strangers among the Arabs or would they want to make the Arabs strangers among themselves?' If the rights of Arabs were violated through the ability of settlers to have their way through reliance on international powers, local people would defend their rights: 'They will answer tears with blood and bury your diplomatic documents in the ashes of your own homes'. Not only would this doom the prospects of Jewish immigrants, but it would also be disastrous for Jews in Russia, who would become alienated from their fellow Russian masses.[1]

Rubanovich's opposition to the settlement project captured the three main themes of left-wing opposition to Zionism: that it would trample over the rights of indigenous Arabs, that it would force the settlers into an alliance with imperialist forces, and that it would segregate Jews from the masses in their own countries and thus prevent working-class unity. These themes consistently run through the history of the anti-Zionist Left. While working class unity in the Jewish Diaspora is no longer an issue of much concern, the conflict between indigenous Arabs and settler Jews is very much alive today.

In addressing this conflict and seeking possible solutions, the legacy of early attempts to address it from critical perspectives is relevant to our understanding of the shape and direction of current events. Like the liberal-humanist trend, the left-wing critique failed to gain much political allegiance from the Jewish and Arab masses. However, it allows us to examine the tensions between class organization and national mobilization, and explore the difficulties of breaching the boundaries created by nationalism, through the formulation and advocacy of an internationalist perspective.

In what follows, I focus on the pre-1948 Palestinian Communist Party.[2] Its experience can shed light on the historical relations between class and nation as principles of organization, and offer insights regarding the implications of these for activists today. In particular, the question of how to reconcile deep nationalist loyalties with inter-national solidarity, in the context of sharp political conflict, will be addressed historically and with a view to the future.

Having spent its entire existence in the shadow of the Jewish–Arab conflict over the political future of the country, the Palestinian Communist Party was shaped by the same forces that shaped the conflict itself: British imperial policies, Zionist ideology in the Eastern European Diaspora and settlement practices in Palestine itself, and Arab nationalism. In particular, at various intensified conflict periods it found itself torn apart by the pressures of competing nationalist movements. At the same time, in a similar way to other Soviet-aligned parties, its policies were also shaped by the turns and shifts of the international Communist movement and the factional struggles within the Russian political leadership. Both local and international forces need to be taken into account when discussing the Party's evolution during the period.

FROM POALEI ZION TO THE COMINTERN

In its early days the Party sought to reconcile lingering attachment to its roots in the Zionist labour movement with its wish to join the Communist International (Comintern), which was formed in 1919. Operating initially under the name Socialist Workers party – MPS in Hebrew – it emerged from a split off the local branch of the Poalei Zion movement, when most of its members joined other activists to form Ahdut Ha'avoda (Unity of Labour). Headed by David Ben-Gurion and Yitzhak Ben-Zvi, this new party was committed above all to the realization of Zionist constructive principles – conquest of land and labour, settlement on the land through cooperative work – and rejected any attempt to dilute these principles in the name of broad socialist commitments. The MPS, in contrast, adhered to global revolutionary principles and saw itself as part of a vanguard of Jewish socialists with an overall mission not restricted to Palestine. Although settlement in Palestine remained a crucial principle for it, the Party saw the interests of the Jewish proletariat as far-reaching in scope, based on an understanding that the bulk of Jewish workers would continue to live and organize in Eastern Europe for a time to come.

The MPS shared this vision with the left-wing of the world Poalei Zion movement, which went through a split in its 1920 Vienna conference over the issue of affiliation to the new Communist movement. Conflicting approaches led to a break-up of the movement as well as many of its branches – notably in Russia and Poland – mirroring to some extent the earlier divide between Ahdut Ha'avoda and the MPS.[3] The right-wing of the movement rejected the Comintern's conditions of admission and remained focused on settlement in Palestine to the exclusion of anything that may clash with the settlement goals. The left-wing sought to retain a balance between the competing imperatives of Zionism – also referred to as the principle of Palestinism – and communism. This proved impossible, however, leaving the Left torn between the national-territorial focus of labour Zionism and the anti-colonial thrust of the Comintern, with its injunction to members 'to support every colonial liberation movement not merely in words but in deeds'.[4]

Although Lenin's 'Draft Theses on the National and Colonial Questions' from June 1920 contained no reference to Zionism or Palestine, the revised version adopted by the Second Congress of the Comintern in the following month included this:

> A glaring example of the deception practised on the working classes of an oppressed nation by the combined efforts of entente imperialism and the bourgeoisie of that same nation is offered by the Zionists' Palestine venture (and by Zionism as a whole, which, under the pretence of creating a Jewish state in Palestine in fact surrenders the Arab working people of Palestine, where the Jewish workers form only a small minority, to exploitation by England).[5]

Of interest here is that the addition of this clause was due to the intervention of Esther Frumkina, a representative of the Communist Bund, an organization that opposed Zionism but supported Jewish cultural autonomy – with a focus on the Yiddish language – within the broader socialist movement. Eventually it merged with the *Evsektsiia* (Jewish

Section) of the Russian Communist Party. Competing with Zionists over the allegiance of the Jewish masses, it was opposed to attempts to encourage its constituency to leave its Eastern European homeland. The Palestine settlement project itself was attacked for seeking to impose Jewish rule over the indigenous population: 'In Palestine we are not dealing with a population whose majority is Jewish. We are dealing with a mere minority which is trying to subjugate the majority of the workers in the country to the capital of the Entente [British-led allies].' But, this seemed less central to the criticism than Zionism's potential impact on the Jewish masses in Eastern Europe. She added: 'The Zionists are seeking to win supporters in every country, and through their agitation and their propaganda serve the interests of the capitalist class. The Communist International must combat this movement in the most energetic way.'[6]

In response, Michael Cohn-Eber, a representative of the MPS and of the left-wing of Poalei Zion, said that his movement merely demanded the opportunity for Jews 'to emigrate and to colonise this country [Palestine] as long as it is in the hands of the British or any other bourgeoisie'. This was part of the worldwide movement of Jews towards becoming productive and emigrating from their countries of present residence, and intervention was needed 'in order to regulate the emigration and the colonising activity of the Jewish and every other proletariat'. In that way the process would be carried out 'in the framework of the rational use of the natural resources in the lightly populated colonial countries and the appropriate application of the hitherto unused or very badly used human labour power in industry'. The strange choice of language was due to Poalei Zion's theory that Jewish immigration was spontaneously directed to Palestine through economic rather than religious or nationalist motivations.

Cohn-Eber went on to argue that the MPS was 'the only proletarian communist group that fights British imperialism under the most difficult conditions and has the task of leading the working masses of the Arabian Orient in this struggle'. This leading role is due to the fact that 'just as the Jewish bourgeoisie was the first to introduce modern capitalist economic forms of exploitation into the country', so too are the Jewish immigrant workers

the only modern, truly property-less proletariat which is for that reason filled with class consciousness and inspired by the revolutionary will to fight. The Arab masses who work on the estates of Jewish landlords and Arab effendis usually possess their own land and can only be characterized as semi-proletarians. Their natural champion which has to draw them into the revolutionary struggle and fill them with proletarian consciousness is our party there [MPS] which, true to the principles of the Communist International, has carried out very lively revolutionary propaganda among them.

There is little need here to comment on the many problematic assumptions hidden in this text, except to note that they reflect Eurocentric prejudices common at the time, even among socialists, and attempt to use these to appeal to gullible comrades in order to deflect criticism.[7] That was to no avail. Disparaging Arab nationalist forces as reactionary and counter-revolutionary Bedouins and feudal lords who prey on the peasant population, and glorifying the contribution of Jewish activists, who had nothing to do with the Arab masses yet were their 'natural champion', was an attempt to portray Jewish socialists as a revolutionary vanguard. But, it ignored the colonial context within which they operated. The Comintern leaders were not well informed about Palestine, and their approach was indeed critical of nationalist forces that failed to adopt a clear revolutionary programme. Yet, they did know that Jewish immigrants – including the socialists among them – moved there under British protection as part of the Zionist movement's efforts to settle the country. As a result, the Comintern declined to make any distinction between 'bad' bourgeois and 'good' proletarian Zionism.

The aspirations of Jewish immigrants might have been noble, but they operated under the auspices of the British Empire, the enemy of all socialist forces in the Comintern's eyes. As was asserted a few weeks later at the Baku Congress of the Peoples of the East, Britain was 'acting for the benefit of Anglo-Jewish capitalists', and it 'drove Arabs from the land in order to give the latter to Jewish settlers'. It then incited Arabs 'against these same Jewish settlers, sowing discord, enmity and hatred between all the communities, weakening both in order that it may itself rule and command'.[8]

In light of these positions, when the MPS applied for membership of the Comintern, its representative Yaakov Meirson made an effort to distance it from other organizations: 'Our party draws a line separating it from all other parties operating in Palestine, in that it is a territorially-based party which sees no place for national socialist parties.' By relying on the Comintern, the Party could 'distinguish itself more clearly from all the other Jewish and Arab parties that are socialist in name but nationalist in spirit'.[9] In contrast to the ethnically-based Poalei Zion, he claimed, the MPS saw itself as open in principle to both Jews and Arabs who lived in the territory, though in practice its Jewish members were in the majority. For tactical reasons it retained the name Poalei Zion, in order to appeal to its Jewish worker constituency, and cooperated with forces within that movement, but it planned to shed its Jewish identity and sever its remaining links with the Zionist movement.

In fact, Meirson was running about a decade ahead of his movement. In his eagerness to present a radical image that went beyond nationalism, he did not disclose to his listeners that there were no Arab members of the Party at the time and generally inflated the MPS impact as well as the distance it had travelled from Labour Zionism. In his opposition to further immigration and settlement for lack of space in the country, and his contention that the way forward was joint Jewish–Arab class struggle against British rule, he represented a position that alienated many members who continued to focus on Palestine as a destination for large-scale immigration of Jewish workers. They were not ready to abandon Jewish identity and their affiliation to the broad Jewish labour movement, or to commit themselves to territorial politics which would doom settlers to remaining a tiny minority in the country.[10]

The Comintern welcomed the Party's application as 'the beginning of the revolutionary workers movement in Palestine',[11] and agreed to consider financial support for it, but did not accept it yet for full membership. This was due to its continued links to the world alliance of the left-wing Poalei Zion which, at the same time, opened an independent process of negotiating admission to the Communist International.

Already in its 1920 Vienna conference, both branches of Poalei Zion asserted the need of the Jewish proletariat and its representatives to join the global revolutionary movement headed by the Comintern.[12] The left-wing focused on the logic of using Palestine as an accessible destination and the most likely place in which the Jewish immigrant masses could transform themselves into a productive and progressive population, united in supporting revolutionary change elsewhere. The low population density made the country suitable for large-scale Jewish settlement, while uplifting the locals:

> The Arab workers today still are so backward economically and culturally, that it is very easy to make of them a pawn in the hands of feudal and bourgeois nationalist 'liberation movements' of the sheikhs and effendis. In this England has succeeded in creating an atmosphere of chauvinist and religious conflicts, which hampers the development of class society and strengthens the reactionary forces in the country.[13]

Change in Palestine, the argument went, could come about only when led by the radical Jewish workers' movement, and its alliance with the Arab peasant masses will be an important factor in facilitating social revolution in the region as a whole.

The Poalei Zion approach consisted of three components, only the first of which was acceptable to the Comintern: merging into national parties as Jewish sections, extra-territorial representation of Jewish workers, and playing a role in regulating massive Jewish immigration and settlement in Palestine. The last clause in particular gave rise to concern by the Comintern. It wrote to the world alliance of Poalei Zion:

> The idea regarding the concentration of the Proletarian and semi-proletarian Jewish masses in Palestine, which supposedly creates the basis for the social and national liberation of the working Jewish people, is utopian and reformist. Its practical outcome is directly counter-revolutionary, since its goal of settlement in Palestine reinforces the position of British imperialism in the country. The complete dismantling of this ideology [Zionism] is the most important condition that we are forced to present.[14]

Poalei Zion's response included sending a delegation to Moscow in order to explain 'the real Communist essence of our own understanding of the Palestinian clause in the war-plan of the Jewish proletariat, and the revolutionary nature of our proletarian activity in Palestine'. This was part of the overall quest to turn the Jewish masses into productive employment through, among other steps, the 'planned regulation of Jewish immigration and its concentration in Palestine'.[15] Given its previous call to abandon Zionism completely, the Comintern naturally saw this clause as pointless prevarication and insisted on abolishing the Palestinian programme in any form. It also called for dismantling the world alliance of Poalei Zion and for the national sections to join their respective Communist parties, with some degree of autonomy depending on conditions in each country.[16]

While the balance between Jewish autonomy and organization on a national or extra-territorial basis could have been negotiated further, the Comintern was resolutely opposed to the Palestine immigration, Jewish territorial concentration, and settlement focus of Poalei Zion. As the issue was central to their sense of political identity and *raison d'être*, no compromise was possible. In July 1922 the Executive Committee of the Communist International (ECCI) asserted that 'the theme of Palestine, the attempt to divert the Jewish working masses from the class struggle by propaganda in favour of large-scale Jewish settlement in Palestine, is not only nationalist and petty-bourgeois but counter-revolutionary in its effect, if the broad working masses are moved by this idea and so diverted from an effective struggle against their Jewish and non-Jewish capitalist exploiters.'[17]

Interestingly much of the exchange between the two sides, even when Palestine was at its centre, was related to the impact of Zionism on Jewish worker constituencies in Eastern Europe, not so much to issues of colonialism and national conflict in Palestine itself. In this respect the MPS, which remained known by that name although it had changed it in the meantime to the Palestinian Communist Party (referred to by its Yiddish initials as PKP), was different. Its roots in Poalei Zion made some of its activists reluctant to break off with Zionism, while impatience with that legacy led others to side with the Comintern without reservations. The majority of members wanted to keep a balance between these two poles. But, for all sides the crucial point was the implications for their work in the country and their relationship to local forces: Ahdut Ha'avoda and the Histadrut, the Arab national movement, and the British authorities.

Events intervened to place the MPS at the centre of attention. The 1921 riots, which saw attacks on Jewish neighbourhoods and settlements in various parts of country, were triggered by a clash in Jaffa between rival 1 May labour demonstrations. Although it involved Jews only, it was witnessed by Arabs and served to launch a series of attacks on Jewish targets. In the words of the Haycraft Commission of Enquiry:

[T]he disturbance of the peace in Jaffa was in the first instance provoked by the demonstration of the MPS . . . It is our opinion that, taking into consideration the strained condition of Arab feeling, it was unwise to risk trouble by allowing a generally detested, although numerically small body of Communists to carry on any sort of propaganda among this already uneasy population. No one wanted them, and now that the danger has been realized the most notorious have been deported.

The Haycraft Commission was open about its disapproval of the MPS, which they referred to as a 'group of extremists' who 'place the pursuit of class warfare above the claims of race or nationality'. But, they regarded its demonstration as no more than a 'minor provocation', related to the riots as 'a spark igniting explosive material'. It would have amounted to little had it not had for a background serious grievances by Arabs against the British policy of the national home, which threatened to make Palestine fall under Jewish domination. In its fear and resentment of Jewish immigration and settlement,

> practically the whole of the non-Jewish population was united in hostility to the Jews. During the riots all discrimination on the part of the Arabs between different categories of Jews was obliterated. Old-established colonists and newly arrived immigrants, Chalukah Jews [traditional Jews dependent on foreign support] and Bolshevik Jews, Algerian Jews and Russian Jews, became merged in a single identity, and former friendships gave way before the enmity now felt towards all.

This was undoubtedly true but contradicted the Commission's further claim that 'The Bolshevik element in the country produced an effect out of proportion with its numbers, not by the success of its propaganda but by the genuine uneasiness it inspired in the Arabs, more particularly in those of the poorer classes in the country districts'. This situation, the report added, 'conferred upon this handful of agitators an importance that cannot be measured by their exiguous intrinsic numbers, or by their failure to capture the Jewish Labour movement in the country. We consider that the Arabs had a real fear of the Bolshevik element and of its propaganda, a fear which became acute with the less enlightened'.[18] This statement was a gross exaggeration. The notion of 'Bolshevism' may have made some Arabs uncomfortable but they could not have had more than vague knowledge of its meaning and no interest in the factional fights of the Jewish labour movement.

In any event, the role attributed to the MPS/PKP in the 1921 events was used by its opponents to justify a wave of repression against its members. Many were arrested and deported, driven underground, fired from their jobs, beaten up and otherwise ostracized. The British police and Labour Zionist forces cooperated in seeking to get rid of them, and Arab nationalists showed no sympathy for their plight.[19] Rejecting claims that it was involved in attacks on Jewish targets, the Party defined them as pogroms and despicable crimes planned by reactionary Arab landowners who incited the ignorant masses, and worked with the British authorities to cause mayhem and turn ordinary members of the two communities against each other. The British were accused of covering this up by blaming the victims as the notorious Russian Czarist police did with anti-Jewish pogroms.[20] The Comintern did not differ with that assessment, in sharp contrast to its subsequent attitude to the 1929 riots, a crucial landmark in the country's and the Party's history.

The 1921 Jaffa events marked the Party, under all its various names and reincarnations, as the primary internal enemy of the Zionist-led Jewish community (the Yishuv). That was the case for two decades, until it was granted partial 'rehabilitation' when the Soviet Union joined the Allied forces in the Second World War. The intense repression exacerbated divisions among its members and increased its dependence on the Comintern. By mid-1923 it had consolidated its move away from Poalei Zion and its support for an anti-colonial strategy centred on alliance with Arab progressive nationalist forces. At the same time, it did not abandon the quest to make in-roads into Labour Zionism's basis of support among recent immigrant Jewish workers, who became disillusioned with the realities in Palestine.

A few months later, in February 1924, the Party was officially admitted to the Communist International as its Palestine section, using the Yiddish name Palestinische Kommunistische Partei (PKP). The choice of Yiddish was in direct defiance of the Zionist insistence – particularly enforced by Ahdut Ha'avoda – on using Hebrew as the sole medium of public communication. It reflected on-going attachment to the Jewish labour movement in Eastern Europe and thus played a dual role – distancing the Party from the Zionist-led Yishuv, while intensifying its Jewish character and hampering communication with other locals (Arabs and non-Ashkenazi Jews). Both languages were equally unintelligible to the Arab masses, of course.

YISHUVISM OR 'ZIONISM WITHOUT ZIONISM'

The key task facing the Party in the 1920s was the need to re-direct its educational efforts and recruitment drive towards the Arab majority of the population, without neglecting and alienating its Jewish constituency. The Comintern line mandated a shift in focus from the messianic rhetoric of the MPS highlighting the vanguard role of the Jewish proletariat in the Middle East as a whole to the anti-colonial struggle in the country. This did not mean abandoning regional work altogether and Party activists continued to work with sister organizations in Lebanon, Syria and other countries. The one consistent theme throughout the decade was that of setting roots among the indigenous workers and peasants and aspiring to lead their national movement against British rule and the Zionist political project.

The Party's work among Arabs was hampered by the low levels of literacy, class organization and consciousness in the country, lack of familiarity with local culture and language, and above all by the foreign origins of its members. In their vast majority they owed their presence in the country to Zionism, even if they had renounced much of its principles after having arrived there. They joined the Histadrut which quickly became the main institution of Labour Zionism after it was founded in 1920. It combined trade union, cooperative, and land settlement functions, and the Party campaigned for a focus on the former (union activity), opening it up to Arab members, while discarding functions associated with the national home policy. Despite their opposition to the 'national' nature of the Histadrut, it was very difficult for Party members to find jobs and receive social protection without becoming members. Thus, in important respects, the Party joined the organized Jewish community, which remained its main constituency for much of the period under discussion here.

Since the Arab national movement regarded ongoing Jewish immigration and consequent demographic shift as the main threat to its quest for independence, the Party faced a critical dilemma in relation to that. To oppose immigration and settlement would have undermined the position of its Jewish members and its own existence. To accept them as Jewish national rights, with or without the consent of the majority of current residents, would have alienated it from the Arab movement. The Party was an anti-imperialist force, drawing support from a community which existed and grew thanks to the same imperial force the Party regarded as its main enemy. Further, the Party grew largely through the same process – Jewish immigration – that allowed the entire Jewish community to grow and thereby weaken the position of Arabs in the country.

The way out of the dilemma was the approach that became known as Yishuvism, developed by the Party's foremost leader in the 1920s, Wolf Averbuch. It rejected Zionism as a nationalist ideology and political movement that called for concentration of the Jewish masses in Palestine and the eventual formation of a Jewish majority state there. At the same time, it accepted the Yishuv as a legitimate community, which would continue to grow and develop due to ongoing immigration, independently of the Zionist project, in the same way that Jewish communities in the USA, Argentina, South Africa and elsewhere developed at the time. The practical implication was a strategic combination of two crucial components. The first was participation in Yishuv activities – elections to municipal councils, cultural events, union membership and cooperative life, activity in the Histadrut under the name of Workers' Faction (known as the Fraktzia, the Party's own name presented legal difficulties). This was supplemented by campaigning against the exclusionary aspects of Zionist policies, as expressed in particular by the notions of Conquest of Labour (replacing Arab with Jewish workers) and Conquest of Land (displacing Arab tenants from recently-bought land and replacing them with Jewish cooperatives). The goal of the strategy was to radicalize Jewish immigrants and push them beyond Zionism, while demonstrating to Arabs that dissident Jews could become allies instead of enemies. This was meant to serve as a basis for joint Jewish–Arab struggle against British imperial rule.[21]

The analysis behind this approach was an interesting combination of some elements inherited from the Poalei Zion approach together with new structuralist Marxist insights. It argued that Jewish immigration was driven by large historical forces that made social existence in Eastern Europe insecure. This was a result of the undermining of traditional Jewish economic activities and growing anti-Semitism. Palestine was merely one destination for the impoverished masses, most of whom were motivated by survival needs rather than by religion or nationalism. There was no point in encouraging or opposing immigration or emigration; socialists regarded these forces as given. The movement of people and capital into the country contributed to its modernization and development along capitalist lines, but Zionist ideology put a break on such development due to its exclusionary practices. It was therefore in the interest of different class forces (workers, capitalists, farmers – both Jewish and Arab) to collaborate across ethnic-national boundaries, and jointly fight foreign rule and its local allies – the Zionist movement and Arab feudal landowners.

The Zionist labour movement's emphasis on cooperative work and land settlement made sense only if the task was to replace Arab workers with Jewish immigrants, but that was a narrow approach that undermined the interests of the same Jewish workers in whose name the movement spoke. They subjected themselves to exploitation to advance 'national' goals instead of joining with Arab colleagues to fight their common exploitation. The labour movement had to defend workers' interests instead of engaging in the build-up of national institutions and creating isolated 'socialist' enclaves within the capitalist economy.

British imperialism advanced its strategic interests and promoted the products of its own industries at the expense of both Jewish and Arab producers. Its divide and rule policies aimed to increase tensions and open hostilities between the two communities, which were meant to allow it to intervene to keep the peace. The way to overcome this strategy was embarking on a joint struggle against foreign rule, for national independence and political equality. That one of the national groups in the country was indigenous to it while the other arrived there as part of a settlement project (and very recently so), did not seem to play a major role in the analysis.

The strategy of Yishuvism – which Nahman List refers to as 'anti-Zionist Zionism' or 'Zionism without Zionism'[22] – and the Party's predominantly Jewish membership and leadership, which changed little in the course of the 1920s – helped the Party gain support in the mid-1920s, but were at odds with the overall thrust of the Comintern line. That line increasingly focused on support for 'every national revolutionary movement against imperialism', and on mobilizing the colonial peasant and working masses in an 'anti-imperialist united front' for national liberation. Communists of European origins were supposed to assist the locals without forming their own parties:

> European communist workers in the colonies must try to organize the indigenous proletariat and win their confidence by concrete economic demands (raising the wages of native workers to that of European workers, labour protection, social insurance, etc.). The creation of separate European communist organizations in the colonies (Egypt, Algiers) is a concealed form of colonialism and only helps imperialist interests. The creation of communist organizations on this national basis is incompatible with the principles of proletarian internationalism.[23]

How this injunction applied to Jews in Palestine, who were neither native to the country nor citizens of the colonial power, was not obvious. They did not enjoy privileged political status as individuals and did not control the indigenous population. Jews in Palestine thus differed from equivalent groups in 'normal' cases of colonial rule, such as Algeria or South Africa, which informed the Comintern policy. They enjoyed a higher standard of living because they were subsidized by Zionist settlement agencies, not by colonial authorities. Their legal position as a community was recognized within the framework of the national home policy, but as residents they had no special privileges compared to the 'natives', nor were they aligned with (non-existent) settlers from the colonial mother country. They had no formal say in the way the country was governed nor could they call on state power to gain access to natural resources. The government did not act directly at their behest or on their behalf.

Conceptualizing their role could not be done with standard formulas. The bulk of them were recent immigrants of European origins but not from any of the main colonial powers. Their settlement project was made possible due to British Mandate, but it started before it and – as we know now – continued after it. They were new to the country but claimed ancestral rights. They acquired land but did not have the coercive capacity needed to take it by force. Unlike in most cases of European settlement elsewhere, employing the cheap labour power of indigenous people was not a prime goal of their project. In fact, opposition to it was a major source of conflict within the Jewish community and between it and Arab workers. They sought political power at the expense of the locals, but wished to do that independently of imperial frameworks. In their own eyes they were redeeming the land of their ancient forefathers while bringing modern benefits to its present-day residents. In all that they exhibited some of the features of colonial-type conquest but not others.

For Arab nationalists, though, these fine distinctions were immaterial. From their perspective all Jewish immigrants were foreign to the country, having arrived there through a colonial process aimed at establishing a Jewish national home at the expense of the true owners of the land. They had no legitimate political rights in the country, which was Arab in essence.[24] The modern, socialist, progressive credentials of the settlers were of very limited interest as were their internal disputes. Faced with this rejection, the Party had to change its orientation and image fast, and radically distance itself from the Yishuv, if it wished to gain support and recruit members from the Palestinian-Arab community. This imperative was the foundation for a decade-long debate over the contentious policy of indigenization, known in the local context as Arabization.

THE QUEST FOR INDIGENIZATION

Since its earliest days the Party was made acutely aware of the discrepancy between its anti-colonial approach and its settler origins and membership. All its leading Jewish members came from Eastern Europe, with its vibrant labour movement and familiarity with socialist theory and practice. Some of them took part in the Russian Revolution and were seasoned activists. It was natural for them to assume they could play a leading political role both in relation to the local Palestinian-Arab population and the broad Arab masses of the Middle East. Not having been exposed directly to issues of colonial domination before, they found it difficult to grasp the gap between their self-image as a revolutionary vanguard and the way they were perceived by local people. In their view, no other group of experienced socialist cadres similar to themselves was to be found in the entire region. And yet, they were new to the place, did not speak its dominant language – Arabic – and were regarded with suspicion as intruders. Although they tried to make up for some of these deficiencies by studying the language and history of the region, and made important gains in this respect, they were still outsiders.[25]

A change in the demographic composition of the Party – membership and leadership alike – alongside a change in orientation became essential. The first resolution of the ECCI on Palestine, in 1923, started with a positive mention of the Party's activity among Arab workers, highlighting its work 'in circumstances of a semi-feudal backward country, under a unique form of Zionist colonization, promoted by imperialism', which allowed the Arab national movement to unite the indigenous population behind it in opposition to Zionism. The united Arab national front will inevitably fracture due to contradictory class interests.

The Comintern called on the Party to play a role in this process by exposing 'mercilessly the traitorous role of the feudal, land-owning elements, who seek to compromise with British imperialism', and fighting their influence in the movement. It urged work among the peasantry to create an independent movement for agrarian revolution, together with the radical urban and rural intelligentsia, support the 'nationalist elements of the urban and rural bourgeoisie' who took part in the struggle, but also expose their inherent 'lack of consistency and hesitation'. The first practical task outlined for the Party was 'to intensify its activity among the urban Arab proletariat and peasantry', and help them organize and become effective in a mass struggle against Zionism and imperialism. This meant operating within the national movement and all its structures, but also continue to campaign among Jewish workers in Europe and America.[26]

The focus on working with the Arab population did not mean neglecting the Jewish workers constituency. Specific tasks regarding class organization were outlined for them, though not national liberation tasks. Participation in the Histadrut, despite its active Zionist role, was considered essential in order to reach the Jewish working masses. The tendency to boycott it was reversed and the Party was expected to campaign for its excluded members to be re-instated within the Jewish-only unions.[27]

In response, the Party made repeated assurances regarding its efforts to recruit Arab workers, but recognized that progress was slow and difficult; lack of knowledge of Arabic was an important obstacle. Of great concern was the conditions of Arab workers who were 'divided and dispersed in settlements and are mostly illiterate and under the influence of Muslim sheikhs [traditional leaders], who encourage among them fatalism and resignation to their difficult conditions, passivity and apathy. Jewish workers fall under the influence of the national-chauvinists [Labour Zionists] and are exceptionally rigid and conservative'.[28] The frank recognition of difficulties was accompanied, however, by inflated assertions of the Party's success in 'overcoming the conservative loyalties, obtuseness and submissiveness of the Arab toiler, burning the poison seeds of national hatred and hostility out of his soul and consciousness', and thus turning itself into 'a real territorial Communist centre in the country, attracting and binding to itself all the honest and revolutionary forces from among the toilers of the country's peoples'.[29]

It is clear from this correspondence that both sides regarded national liberation as a crucial part of the anti-imperialist struggle, and that Jewish workers had a role in it, albeit not a leading one. Regardless of their recent immigrant origins, Jewish workers were seen as legitimate recruits, subject to organization by the Party and participants in the struggle for socialism. But, the divide remained clear: Arabs were expected to combine nationalist and class tasks, while Jews were to stick to class issues, at most rendering assistance to Arabs in their own struggles.

Reporting on the progress made in working with the Arab national movement and recruiting Arab members became a regular component of the Party's communication with the Comintern. Another recurrent theme in the early years (mid-1920s), was the relationship with Communist parties in the region, Lebanon, Syria and Egypt. With a bit of hyperbole, List refers to Averbuch as an aspiring 'Lenin of Arabia', whose quest to play a role in revolutionary developments in the Middle East had messianic tones. At a more mundane level, the PKP sent emissaries to assist the emergence of sister parties, forged links with other forces (Druze rebels in Syria), and published Arabic-language newspapers and educational material targeting Palestine and neighbouring countries, serving 'without exaggeration, as the sole revolutionary arena in the entire East'.[30] It went further and proposed in a 'top secret' memorandum to create a centre of communications that would serve the Comintern in its contact not only with Palestine itself but with the Arab revolutionary national movement and the labour movement in Syria, Egypt, Arabia and Iraq.[31]

Although the Comintern continued to use PKP members for missions involving relations with various movements in the region, it did not put them in charge of other communist organizations. It was bad enough from its perspective that suspicions were raised inside Palestine about Jewish domination, without extending these to other countries. Regional ambitions were not allowed to distract the Party from the urgent need to transform itself from within. A 1926 ECCI resolution opened with the notion that 'the centre of gravity of the PKP's activity must be among the Arab toiling masses'. At the same time, the PKP 'must help increase the discontent of the toiling Jewish population [with British policy]. It must pay particular attention to increasing its ideological and organizational influence among the Palestinian proletariat and linking its struggle with that of the Arab people, against imperialist oppression'.[32] These tasks, the Comintern suggested, should be related to activities with a broader focus: strengthening contacts with Arab nationalist organizations, forming left-wing factions within them to intensify their revolutionary character, collaborating closely with progressive nationalist movements and connecting with other nationalist forces in Syria and Egypt – even India! – by organizing joint media and solidarity activities, and so on.

But all this faced a crucial obstacle. The Comintern formed 'a firm opinion' that the party suffered from 'hypertrophy and expansion of energy in one pole, namely the Jewish one, and atrophy in the other pole, that is: weak development of activity among the Arab proletariat and peasantry'. Things have not improved since the PKP was admitted to the Comintern, and it continues to dedicate '99% of its work' to activity among Jews, and is a territorial party 'only on paper'. The Comintern acknowledged that the Party propaganda consistently addressed Arab workers – in written and verbal forms – but it failed to recruit them as members.[33]

The Party was praised for its successes among Jewish workers, but also scolded for failing to direct 'maximum attention' to Arab workers. The task set for it was to reach, within a year, equality in the number of Jewish and Arab members, if not an Arab majority. This target clearly was unrealistic and the Comintern knew that. Further, shifting attention from Jewish to Arab workers, when deep divisions existed between them, of necessity meant squandering some of the gains made in previous years, as limited number of activists and organizational resources were available for the recruitment and retention of members. Of greater concern was the shift in focus of political campaigning. Yishuvism facilitated making inroads among Jews by focusing on their concerns (jobs, housing, working conditions, unions). A shift to a focus on Arab national goals helped the Party gain Arab support but inevitably meant alienating many Jewish activists.

Throughout the period, the Party's fortunes among Jewish workers experienced ebb and flow based on the visibility of the national conflict.

Although it served as a permanent background, in workers' consciousness the conflict did not invariably occupy a central position. There was an inverse relationship between its intensity and the extent to which the Party managed to appeal to Jews on a class-based agenda. The Party experienced loss of support after waves of nationalist violence (1921, 1929, 1936), and some success in periods of relative calm (the mid-1920s, the early 1940s). To enable legal operation and deflect association with its anti-Zionist positions, the Party formed front organizations that provided it with some space to shield its activists from confrontation. The Workers' Faction was its vehicle when formed in 1923, but in April 1924 it was expelled by the Histadrut Council, which declared that

> the group of people disguised as 'the Workers Faction within the Histadrut' has proved in all its tricks and shenanigans that it is an enemy of the Jewish people and the working class in Eretz Israel. The Council condemns its incitement against immigration and its smears against the Jewish labour movement in the country, aimed to deceive the international labour movement. The Council decides to abolish 'the Workers Faction within the Histadrut' on all its different names and reincarnations.[34]

The Party's campaign in solidarity with Arab tenants in Afula in the Jezreel Valley, dispossessed after the land was bought by Jewish companies, increased the hostility towards it. Its support for the resistance of the tenants, which resulted in bloody clashes with the police, which was assisted by prospective Jewish settlers, targeted the 'Jewish bourgeoisie' which was 'dipping its hands again in the blood of Jewish and Arab workers', and the Zionist Organization, which was 'using Jewish workers as cannon fodder' to rob Arabs of their land. The Party called on workers not to play a role in evicting tenants but rather side with them in a common struggle against Jewish and Arab exploiters and the British police. In response, many communist activists were physically attacked and evicted from Histadrut institutions, some lost their jobs, were arrested and deported from the country. This kind of reaction by the organized Jewish community, and in particular the labour movement, was typical. It made the prospect of gaining support and building alliances with other forces, based on common class positions, very difficult to sustain.

This was the case even with the movement closest to the PKP, Left Poalei Zion, with its common historical roots as well as shared acceptance of the Comintern as a revolutionary leader. They stood on a similar class programme but were divided on the question of Palestine, which was the reason they split up to begin with. Efforts made in 1925 by the Red International of Labour union, Profintern, affiliated to the Comintern, to encourage the two movements to cooperate on the labour front failed, due to one central issue: 'Their [PKP's] negative attitude to immigration, the concentration of the Jewish masses in Palestine.' In their proposed platform for labour unity, Poalei Zion insisted that 'the immigration of Jewish workers is the most important factor in strengthening the working class', and that the labour movement must fight for 'free and unlimited immigration to the country'. In addition, they agreed to cooperation only within sector-specific associations, and excluded all other matters dealt with by the Histadrut as a national structure: cooperative work, settlement, immigration, culture, politics. Profound distaste for working with the PKP/Workers' Faction on anything other than narrow union matters was clearly expressed by Left Poalei Zion. Even such limited cooperation was only due to its wish to work with the Profintern internationally rather than to any desire to collaborate with its local section.[35]

The attempt to juggle Yishuvist and anti-Zionist positions led to inevitable complications, but there was no real alternative to it. Views put forward by internal opposition groups, to the effect that a consistent anti-colonial approach required leaving the Histadrut and perhaps leaving the country altogether, remained dissident minority positions. In fact, the task of turning immigrant workers against their leaders, by working with them and their organizations, was repeatedly re-asserted as central to the Party's efforts. Working with and within Zionist structures was not the same as being Zionist, however. Even Gdud Ha'avoda (Labour Battalion), a national commune of urban and rural workers who moved towards communism in the mid- to late 1920s, rejected the anti-Zionist position. They regarded the historical process of Jewish immigration to Palestine as progressive in essence, enabling Jewish proletarianization and industrialization of the country, thus creating the preconditions for a social revolution and healing of the Jewish economy. This meant that the Battalion took 'an active and conscious part in the class struggle against the capitalist regime', and at the same time undertook 'special pioneering tasks to prepare the internal foundations of a communist society and create a Jewish workers' centre in Palestine'.[36] Although the Battalion's memorandum noted as one of its tasks that of forming a united Jewish–Arab front against British imperialism, it also recognized that it differed from the Comintern (and the PKP) regarding the role of Jewish immigration and Jewish population in the country.

More than a year later, Menahem Elkind, speaking for the left-wing of the Battalion, submitted another memorandum, outlining their position that 'the PKP underestimates the value of the Jewish population in Palestine, including its Jewish workers, as a real political force that must be considered in the struggle against British imperialism in Palestine, and that its attitude to the Arab nationalist movement is too one-sided'. This was a self-defeating attitude, Elkind argued: 'as long as the PKP upholds its position regarding the Jewish national question in Palestine, not only can it not expect to become a mass party enjoying the support of Jewish workers, but on the contrary, it would be seen by the vast majority of Jewish workers as a hostile party', dooming it to isolation from the masses. If the Battalion were to adopt the same positions, it could expect to be isolated in the same way. However, it was willing to cooperate with the PKP on other issues – related to union activities – on which they agreed, provided the PKP refrained from undermining the Battalion's operations.[37]

The Party dismissed this criticism as reflecting the residual legacy of colonial Zionist attitudes, but could not itself escape from criticism that its own practices also reflected just such a legacy. Oppositional forces from within raised the concern that the Party deviated from the official line by failing to condemn Zionism. In their view, 'Zionism was a special type of imperialism', and Zionists were occupiers and colonizers of the country. There was no sense in which Jewish immigration into the country and settlement in it could play a progressive role. Participating in institutions such as the Histadrut and taking part in elections to Jewish communal institutions compromised the Party's position and aligned it with the Zionist colonization process.[38] In response, the Party said that this critical line amounted to a loss of class perspective, regarding all Jews as counter-revolutionary and all Arabs as revolutionary. Motivated by despair, the Party's representative argued, the opposition lost all hope in working among the Jewish masses, who were the bulk of the working class in the country, and it was dismissive of the Party's actual and potential work among Arabs, offering no way forward except for narrow sectarianism.[39]

Although the opposition did not gain much direct support from the Comintern, by the late 1920s the notion that the Party needed to transform itself had become ever more persistent. The Comintern kept noting its weak presence among the Arab masses and called on the Party to intensify it but without weakening its work among Jewish workers. This could be done by 'active participation in the struggle for national liberation and close contact with the Arab national-revolutionary movement'. At the same time, the Party was to keep political and organizational independence from the national movement, condemn the reactionary traitorous elements within it, campaign among peasants, the intelligentsia and workers to build mass organizations for national liberation, form secret communist factions within these organizations, and push the movement leftward 'by relying on the most revolutionary elements in these organizations'.[40]

Interestingly, despite the criticism of insufficient work among Arabs within the country, at that point in time – 1927 – the Comintern still regarded the PKP as a key vehicle for revolutionary intervention in the entire region and set for it far-reaching tasks with regard to communist and nationalist movements, all the way from Iraq to North Africa, working with the Italian and French communist parties in their respective colonial territories. Given the Party's very limited resources, these could have been little more than flights of fancy, perhaps early indications of the onset of the Third Period with its unrealistic revolutionary expectations.

In theoretical terms, the calls for intensified activities among Arab workers and nationalists did not mean abandoning Yishuvism altogether or giving up on the revolutionary potential of Jewish workers. The Comintern explicitly rejected such calls as defeatist, threatening to make the party a narrow sect by using ultra-leftist rhetoric. But, it argued that the PKP must not 'underestimate the importance of Zionism as an instrument of the imperialist subjugation of Palestine, with the support of the Jewish working masses'. It urged a course that involved 'linking the interests of the daily struggle of Arab toilers with the interests of the daily struggle of the Jewish proletariat, while waging a systematic campaign against Arab and Jewish chauvinism and pooling Jewish and Arab workers into a joint organized fight against the class enemy'. Since the Jewish masses were a substantial part of the Palestinian working class, it was important to realize how British imperialism relied on Zionism by exploiting 'the nationalist prejudices and the political backwardness of Jewish proletarians in order to strengthen its influence in the country'.[41]

The Party's role was to expose the true nature of Zionism and the way it served imperialism in subjugating the masses. It could do that by 'removing the best elements in the Histadrut from the influence of Zionism', and 'transforming the Histadrut into a true class-based trade union'. That is, by making it into 'an organization whose doors are open to all proletarians, and particularly Arab workers'. Strengthening existing Arab unions was another essential task to be carried out through 'uncompromising struggle against Arab nationalists' and their influence among Arab workers. Crucially, all this work must be undertaken with the realization that Jewish workers were *not* a hopeless 'uniform reactionary mass', as Party dissidents claimed, thereby reflecting their own lack of confidence in their ability to expose reactionary Zionist ideology and fight its influence among the masses.[42]

These formulations, variations of which guided the Party for the first decade of its existence, adhered to an overall anti-Zionist position and yet maintained a careful balance between potential Jewish and Arab constituencies. It was not neutral between Zionism and Arab nationalism, clearly siding with the latter against the former and prioritising the struggle against British rule. But, it sought to do so without abandoning the quest for an independent position from either movement. Working with Left Arab nationalist elements, and at the same time with progressive Jewish workers and within their organizations, was seen as a way to combine an anti-colonial agenda with a socialist class perspective. The two were seen as theoretically compatible, even if in practice the Party frequently experienced difficulties in reconciling them.

In summary, going back to the question of the role of 'European' workers in colonial situations, the Party and the Comintern regarded the Zionist movement – including its labour wing and radical elements such as Left Poalei Zion – as political allies of British imperialism. Thus it was an obstacle to the liberation of the country from colonial rule. In this sense Zionism was similar to settler-colonial movements and institutions in South Africa and colonial outposts in Africa and elsewhere. There was also a crucial difference between these situations. White workers in South Africa, French workers in Algeria, Portuguese workers in Mozambique and so on, directly benefited from the exploitation of indigenous labourers, as employers themselves (of domestic labour), as holders of skilled supervisory positions in the process of production, and as citizens with privileged access to social and political rights. Their class interests were thus incompatible with those of their black counterparts.

In Palestine, in contrast, Jewish workers did not exploit Arab labour directly, nor did they occupy a privileged social and economic position either in the workplace or in the society and polity at large. Potentially, they could become allies, if only they were liberated from the impact of exclusionary nationalist ideologies and separatists practices. This potential basis for cooperation across national lines was the foundation for the strategy of Yishuvism, and for the Comintern's continued faith in the prospects of recruiting progressive Jewish workers to the anti-colonial cause and turning them against their reactionary leadership.

But faith alone was not enough. The balancing act which sought to reconcile the ideological rejection of Zionism with political work within some of its institutions, and among its adherents, could not be maintained for long. It had collapsed by the end of the 1920s, as events in Palestine, combined with shifts within the world communist movement, forced the Party to modify its positions and move in a different and more contentious direction.

THE 1929 UPRISING AND THE DRIVE TO ARABIZATION

Increasing tensions between the organized Jewish and Arab communities over access to and control over the holy places, resulted in the outbreak of country-wide violent clashes in August 1929, in which hundreds of civilians were killed.[43] The Party was caught unaware by these events, which exposed its isolation from the growing nationalist sentiments among the masses of both groups. The Comintern, which was experiencing at that time the fervour of the Third Period with its expectation of revolutionary insurrections in the colonial world, used that opportunity to push forward Arabization in a decisive manner. The relatively civil debate over strategies gave way to more acrimonious struggles, accusations and splits during the 1930s.[44]

The Third Period was conceptualized as coming after the period of relative stability in the mid-1920s, and it reflected accentuation of the 'contradiction between the growth of the productive forces and the contraction of markets', inevitably giving rise to 'a fresh era of imperialist wars among the imperialist States themselves; wars of the imperialist States against the USSR; wars of national liberation against imperialism; wars of imperialist intervention and gigantic class battles'.[45] Growing antagonisms in the world system were expressed in acute contradictions in capitalist countries, a swing to the left and intensified class struggle, as well as colonial revolts in Asia and the Middle East.

This opened up a period of 'insurrectionary outbreaks', triggered 'by the weakening of European imperialism as a result of the war, by capitalist development in the colonies, the influence of the Russian revolution, the centrifugal tendencies in the premier maritime and colonial power in the world, the British Empire'. It was expressed in revolutionary events in China, 'making a tremendous hole in the entire edifice of imperialism', and 'continuing revolutionary ferment' in India. This 'revolutionary process in the colonies' reflected 'the profound general crisis of capitalism'.[46] Overall, the edifice of world imperialism is being undermined from a number of directions, and the partial stabilization of capitalism shaken, by the contradictions and conflicts among the imperialist powers, the rising of the colonial millions, the struggle of the revolutionary proletariat in the mother countries . . . Against this revolution imperialism is mobilizing all its forces . . . This is bound to release all the forces of the international revolution, leading inexorably to the downfall of capitalism.[47]

Palestine was mentioned in the context of North Africa and the Middle East, where 'the rise and growth of the urban proletariat' due to 'the greater penetration of foreign capital into these countries', is followed by the peasantry, which 'gradually, but very slowly . . . is also being drawn into the struggle'.[48] Communists must 'give a revolutionary character to the existing peasant movement',[49] and 'attract into their ranks in the first place the native workers, fighting against any negligent attitude towards them', in order to become 'genuinely based on the native proletariat'.[50]

From this flowed the tasks of the PKP as outlined by the Comintern in early 1929. A united Arab–Jewish union movement with a solid class basis would allow the Party to organize a joint struggle against imperialism, and 'link-up with the Arab peasantry and arouse it into revolutionary struggle'. In the process, the Party should transform from being 90 per cent Jewish into a force uniting the Arab majority of the working class and the peasantry together with the Jewish proletariat, 'in a common struggle against imperialism, against the feudal and reformist Arab nationalists, and against the Jewish bourgeoisie and the Zionist and Poalei-Zionist agents of British imperialism'.[51]

This analysis may serve as a background against which we can evaluate the 1929 events, and the clash between the PKP and the Comintern. In line with a long-held distinction between the Zionist movement and the Jewish population, the PKP rejected all armed attacks against civilians. This was particularly appropriate in that case, since most Jews attacked and killed in the 1929 riots – in Hebron, Safed and Jerusalem – belonged to the 'old Yishuv', which pre-dated Zionism and did not form part of the new settlement project. That the Party leadership, together with a high-ranking visiting Comintern official, had to be evacuated from its secret headquarters near Jerusalem, fearing for their lives, and that the events came as a total surprise, may also have played a role in its reaction.[52]

Its initial response was to condemn the killings and point to a tacit collaboration between the British, Zionist and Arab forces, aimed at diverting the masses from the anti-imperialist struggle into bloody inter-communal fighting:

> The religious Muslim masses were used by the imperialist government, with the help of wealthy Arabs, friends of imperialism, and the help of the sheikhs and effendis, to commit slaughter and senseless murder of their brethren . . . this triple alliance – British imperialists, and the Zionist and Arab bourgeoisies – is responsible for the spilt blood.[53]

Although the Party recognized the social needs of debt-ridden impoverished rural people, which were a background to the riots, it criticized the 'terrible savagery' of the massacres and 'pogroms', and attributed them to the incitement by 'dark reactionary forces' of 'uncontrollable peasant-Bedouin' masses. The task of the working class, Jews and Arabs alike, led by the Party itself, was to 're-direct the peasant movement on its pogromist tendencies, remove it from the influence of reactionary leaders', and transform it into a progressive agrarian revolutionary campaign, whose goal was independence and the formation of a workers-peasants government, representative of the toiling people of the country. Blind religious and nationalist fanaticism on all sides was an obstacle to achieving that goal, and served to distract the masses from their just demands. Jewish and Arab workers should have united and resolved the national and social questions together, in a true anti-imperialist rebellion, free of pogroms.[54]

Of particular concern was the responsibility of Zionist parties, especially Ahdut Ha'avoda, that created a monstrous barrier between Jews and Arabs, relying on the Balfour Declaration and British bayonets. The dispossession of Arab peasants, the campaigns for Conquest of Labour and Conquest of Land, the opposition to the formation of elected representative institutions, and the alliance with the British against the interests of the local population, were a constant political provocation, which fed 'the fire of religious and national hatred'. The Arab leadership was also to blame for transforming the revolutionary ferment into a 'tasteless and senseless pogromist chaos', from which suffered not only innocent Jewish victims but also poor Arab peasants. Blind political fanaticism on the Arab side strengthened violent fascist elements on the Jewish side, who pretended to be civilized but were no less bloodthirsty than the ignorant Arab rioters.

This position conformed to the standard approach of the Party, and was not very different from its response to the 1921 Jaffa events. However, the Comintern rejected it as reflecting a right-wing deviation, which in turn was a result of the failure to implement Arabization as demanded all along by the ECCI. The praise given to Party members for their courage and dedication in the course of the events could not offset the devastating nature of the criticism of their leadership. The 'deviation' it was guilty of was expressed mainly in

> an underestimation of revolutionary possibilities, open or hidden resistance to the Arabization of the party, pessimism and passivity with regard to work among the Arab masses, fatalism and passivity on the peasant question, failure to understand the role of Jewish comrades as assistants but not as leaders of the Arab movement; exaggeration of the influence of the reactionary bourgeoisie, large landlords, and clergy on the Arab masses, a lenient attitude towards opportunist errors, failure to understand the need for courageous and vigorous self-criticism of the mistakes committed by the party, a tendency to emigrate without the permission of the CC, that is desertion, resistance to the slogan of a workers' and peasants' government.

Further, 'the evaluation of the uprising as a "pogrom", and hidden resistance to Arabization, are manifestations of Zionist and imperialist influence on the communists'.[55] There was also a 'leftist deviation' at work, expressed in the dismissal of the potential of Jewish workers, and insufficient appreciation of their role in creating a mass labour movement in the country, but that was of lesser importance.

Nothing in the Comintern's resolution constituted a radical departure from its earlier approach. Most of its elements had appeared before then in letters and resolutions, and indeed in the Party's own literature. And yet, their overall thrust amounted to a clear shift of direction. It was not so much the instruction to Arabize the party from top to bottom without delay: adjusting the Party's leadership and membership to the demographic realities of the country made sense as a strategy, even if the removal of the entire leadership was a drastic step. Rather, it was the underlying rationale for it that was controversial: the implied notion that the Arab masses were inexorably moving towards the revolution, regardless of their current leadership and its direction, and that Jews were second-class partners regardless of their personal record.

In addition, there were problems with the analysis. The direct anti-imperialist content of the riots was weak to non-existent (no attacks on government forces or widespread protests against British policies were evident), while the anti-Zionist and anti-Jewish component was prominent. The riots largely bypassed the new urban centres where the bulk of the working class was located. Under these circumstances, calling on the Party to join the uprising amounted to a shift from opposing Zionism as an ally of imperialism to seeing it as the main colonial force in the country. Many members regarded this as an uncritical capitulation to Arab nationalism, and left the Party or were expelled in the aftermath of the 1929 events. Indeed, if the centre of political resistance had moved to the illiterate rural masses, who regarded Zionism and both the old and new Yishuv as elements of the same overall enemy, there was no space for urban Jewish working-class activists in that struggle, nor was Yishuvism relevant any longer.[56]

A year later, a secret letter sent by the ECCI to Party members re-asserted these points, that the 'Jewish bourgeoisie is the main agent of British imperialism in Palestine', and that 'counter-revolutionary Zionism is the main mechanism of British imperialism in the country'. The British made 'the Jewish national minority, which immigrated into the country, into an instrument of oppression of the indigenous Arab population. Zionism, resting on British imperial bayonets, positioned the Jewish national minority, as a privileged layer, against the Arabs. Zionism thus exposed its true nature as an expression of the Jewish bourgeoisie's desire for exploitation, expansionist nationalism and oppression'.[57]

The PKP, the letter said, failed to understand the importance of the national question and its deep agrarian nature. Instead of taking the initiative and presenting a consistent programme of agrarian revolution that would challenge the influence of Arab bourgeois nationalist forces, it left the arena open to the operation of reformist movements. It focused on the Jewish national minority, 'which was in a subordinate position in relation to British imperialism but stood, as a privileged layer, against the Arab masses'. The Jewish working class, as 'a proletariat of a privileged minority', had to 'separate itself firmly and resolutely from its bourgeoisie, which is playing an oppressive and murderous role, move closer to the Arab toiling masses and assist them in their struggle for national liberation from colonial slavery'. A struggle against its own bourgeoisie was the only guarantee that the Jewish proletariat's interests could be protected.[58]

The letter went on to call for 'a consistent and uncompromising revolutionary struggle of Jewish and Arab workers, for the national independence of Palestine as an Arab country, a struggle against imperialism, Zionism and their Arab allies, a brotherhood of the Arab and Jewish toiling masses'. Only on the basis of an anti-imperialist agrarian revolution could 'the victory of the Arab masses, as well as the rights of the Jewish national minority in Palestine, be guaranteed'.[59]

In going ahead with Arabization, Jewish communists, more experienced in the class struggle and members of the oppressive national minority, had to act as assistants of Arab members, not as their nannies or educators. This task could not be evaded with the slogan of 'Arabization plus Bolshevization', which implied that Arab members could not occupy positions of leadership until they proved full maturity. This attitude could serve to rationalize remaining in a Jewish bubble, and was another manifestation of the Jewish nationalist deviation, which was the main enemy at that stage. At the same time, there was a need to be alert to the danger of an Arab nationalist deviation as well, argued the ECCI. Arabization of the Party was the central task, without it leading to a reduction of work among the Jewish workers. There was a need for a 'united front from below' of Arab and Jewish workers 'over the heads of the traitorous Histadrut and the bourgeois nationalist Arab leaders'.[60]

Historians regard the implementation of Arabization from 1930 onwards as a crucial turning point, as indeed it was and felt so at the time: the majority of Jewish members and the entire leadership left or were expelled, or emigrated and eventually were purged in the Soviet Union in the 1930s. At the same time, two new elements were introduced into the Party's discourse, which proved crucially important in retrospect.

First, the focus on Zionism as a colonial force, and thus the main target for revolutionary campaigns, meant firmly grounding the work of the Party in the local realities of settlement and conflict. It did not end its involvement with European and global issues but forced it to pay most attention to Palestine itself in a more resolute manner. Increasingly moving from the use of Yiddish to Hebrew was a corollary of this shift. Second, Jews in Palestine were recognized for the first time as a national minority. It is not clear what prompted the use of this definition. The Yishuv was growing in numbers and consistently acquiring more 'national' characteristics, but 1929–30 was not an obvious cut-off point. Perhaps the logical corollary of having defined the country as Arab was seeing Jews primarily in national terms. This created a lingering tension between seeing the Jewish community as an intruder, in line with the Arab nationalist view, and seeing it as a legitimate minority to be recruited for the struggle, in line with an internationalist view. Musa Budeiri concludes that, with the 1930 Congress, the Party abandoned the goal of 'socialist proletarian revolution' and replaced it by 'a recognition of the national character of the struggle', elevating the task of 'national liberation' above 'social emancipation'.[61] This claim seems exaggerated, though, as the party continued to juggle the two imperatives, albeit with less room in which to manoeuvre effectively.

The December 1930 Party congress emphasized the colonial aspect of the conflict. It criticized the former leadership as having lived in a 'Jewish ghetto', failing as a result to define Jews in Palestine as a 'special dominant minority'. It accused the leadership of having overestimated the role of the Jewish minority as a progressive anti-colonial force and underestimated revolutionary developments among Arabs, whose national struggle acquired 'a special form'. The Party had to 'expose the true aims of the Jewish [Zionist] bourgeoisie and its being, together with the Jewish national minority in Palestine that fell under its influence, the main instrument of oppression wielded by the British occupiers against the indigenous Arab population'. In a thinly-veiled reference to the notion of pogroms, used in its response to the 1929 events, the Party set itself the task of clarifying to Jewish workers 'that anti-colonial revolutions by oppressed people in the colonies have always been accompanied by destructive attacks on national minorities who collaborated with colonialism'. Without mincing words, it added: 'the anti-colonial revolution of the Arab masses in Palestine has been and will continue to be accompanied by a relentless war against the Jewish minority, as long as that minority sides with the British colonialists'. Only by taking part in the struggle against colonialism and Zionism, alongside their Arab counterparts, could Jewish workers expect a positive resolution of the Jewish national problem, realization of their rights as a national minority in Palestine, and the revival of their national cultural heritage.[62]

This radical tone verged on the endorsement of armed attacks on civilians, or at least accepting them as inevitable part of the struggle. It was evident also in discussions of activity among Arab peasants, in which calls for armed uprising against government, Zionist agencies and big Arab landowners were made. Harsher positions were adopted on a range of issues, indicating more than a mere rhetorical shift. The need to put Yishuvism finally to rest seemed paramount. Thus, Jewish immigration to Palestine – previously seen as a spontaneous movement shaped by harsh social and political realities in Eastern Europe – was redefined as explicitly political in nature, aimed at relocating a trained Zionist vanguard to seize the country, a process that must be brought to an end. Jewish workers were called upon to provide armed support to Arab tenants fighting dispossession when the land they used to cultivate was sold by the nominal owners to Jewish agencies, and help them expel Jewish settlers who took over such land.

At the same time, Jewish activists were expected to continue their participation in all Zionist institutions – the Histadrut in particular – and take advantage of their membership to campaign against Zionist policies from within. The goal was not to take over such structures but rather 'influence the greatest mass of Jewish workers and recruit them to the internationalist-proletarian struggle'.[63] This was preferred to a premature campaign to boycott the Histadrut or destroy it from within, which would only have helped its reactionary leadership to isolate communists, thereby denying them access to the Jewish masses.

The logic of the new line was spelled out most clearly, perhaps, in a post-conference document issued by the Central Committee (CC) of the Party early in 1931: 'Inasmuch as the bulk of the Jewish population of Palestine is under the direct influence and leadership of the Zionists, who conduct their imperialist policy in the name of the Jewish nation and for a Jewish state, the anti-Zionist movement emerges in the form of an anti-Jewish movement, and affords an opportunity to the English imperialists and the Jewish bourgeoisie, together with the Arab landowners, to turn the dissatisfaction of the Arab masses into the channel of a struggle against the Jewish national minority as a whole'. However, it was wrong

to regard imperialism, Zionism, and the Jewish population solely as one organic whole (which, for the time being, they are with regard to the Arab masses), among whom there are no internal contradictions which undermine these oppressive forces from within. In their national and social liberation struggle the Arab masses, led by the Communist Party, must give careful consideration to these internal contradictions, hostile to the colonizing forces, and must make use of them on a very wide scale.[64]

The 1930s thus witnessed a decisive shift in orientation towards the Arab population, although Jewish members remained in the majority throughout the decade, and the imperative of working among Jewish constituencies was continuously re-asserted. This shift must be seen against the background of global changes with profound local implications. These included intensifying conflict in Europe, pitting the rising Nazi and fascist regimes against the Soviet Union, and leading to a shift from the Third Period to the Popular Front policies in 1935; growing tensions within the Soviet Union, culminating in the Great Purges of mid- to late 1930s and consequent decline in the Comintern's capacity to maintain control over the international movement; a massive wave of immigration into Palestine, mostly from Germany, which almost tripled the Jewish population to reach 450,000 by the end of the decade and built up its military, industrial and institutional structures, and; a growing sense of desperation among the Arab population, and increased readiness for militant action to address the impending loss of their country. The Arab Revolt of 1936–39, the most sustained campaign of popular resistance in Palestine's history, was the decisive event that marked the decade and, to a large extent, determined the political future of the country.

Given these dramatic events, the radical re-positioning of the Party might have been a wise step if it had prepared its activists to take advantage of new political opportunities. To some extent it did, by promoting a new group of Arab cadres who could immerse themselves in the vibrant Palestinian political environment of the 1930s, in a way never open to their Jewish colleagues and erstwhile leaders. At the same time, the brutal way in which the old leadership was forced to leave office – and eventually the country – and the consequent departure of dozens of experienced members depleted the Party's organizational resources. It was left ill-prepared to deal with events requiring delicate balancing between contradictory imperatives and complex manoeuvres between rival political forces.

A frank 'top secret' evaluation of conditions two years after the Arabization conference showed that most members were new (75 per cent joined in the previous one to two years), with weak links to the working class and the peasantry and limited political education. This hampered their ability to participate effectively and play a leading role in mass mobilization. The Party received attention to its work in trade unions, its contribution to working-class organization such as convening the First Arab Workers Congress in Haifa in 1930. It was appreciated for its active defence of Arab tenants and workers facing dispossession due to Zionist conquest of land and labour campaigns. The Wadi Hawarith affair in the early 1930s became particularly well-known, and the Party warned the Jewish community that by giving rise to such hatred due to Zionist land policies, it was running the risk of bloody revenge similar to the events of August 1929.[65]

This kind of solidarity action rarely translated into sustainable recruitment of members, however. While some progress was reported in modern urban centres – Haifa, Jerusalem, Tel Aviv, Jaffa – the traditional core of the country, with its links to the bulk of the rural population remained off-limits: Nablus, Nazareth, Jenin, Gaza, were particularly highlighted as inaccessible targets.[66]

The Comintern praised the Party for its commitment and achievements but also scolded it for not moving forward with Arabization in a more vigorous manner. The result was that the Party had failed to extricate itself from its isolated position to embark on broad mass action, gain the trust of Arab workers and peasants and recruit the more dedicated activists from among them to its own ranks. The reasons, from the Comintern's perspective, were leadership problems – the ongoing dominance of Jewish members – sectarianism, inconsistent campaigning, and a 'leftist' deviation (dismissal of work among Jewish constituencies). A new leadership was needed, from which the old Jewish cadres who had proved incapable of embracing Arabization meaningfully would be completely removed, to fight both leftist and rightist deviations and allow the Party to benefit from the new opportunities opened up by the radicalization of politics in the country.

A subsequent evaluation report on the Party's work from 1929 to 1934, written by a former emissary who had been working in the Middle East for the previous 15 years, and with the Party directly as its senior guide on behalf of the Comintern in the early 1930s, provided a thorough critical perspective. It noted again the need for an overall transformation in the aftermath of the 1929 events, and pointed out gains in recruitment and spread of influence among Arab workers following the 1930 Arabization conference. And yet, he argued, these gains were squandered:

> The quest for quantity and especially for 'political actions' at all costs, without taking into consideration the political level and readiness of Arab workers for such 'actions', the absence of patient and methodical activity to form basic union cells (workers' committees in factories) and strengthen them, the allocation of all trade union activity to specific party members without any preparation – all this made the work of imperialist agents [seeking to undermine the Party] much easier.[67]

This led to demoralization of activists and collapse of the Party's union work.

Without explicitly using officially-discarded slogans, a very dangerous practice in mid-1930s Moscow, the report effectively reiterated the call for Arabization plus Bolshevization. Pointing out that Arab cadres were recruited too quickly, without proper background checks and training, it highlighted the concerns that had been raised by the compromised PKP leadership after 1929. This identified a real problem, particularly glaring in light of the existing opportunities for radical activism: growth in strike action, unrest in the rural areas, tension in the urban areas due to increased immigration, leading to widespread protests in October 1933. Against this background, the report said, the segregation between Jewish and Arab workers remained the basic weakness of the labour movement: their industrial actions ran in parallel with no linkages between them, and the Party remained isolated from both groups. It identified correctly the revolutionary unrest in the country and the cracks within the nationalist camps (real in the Arab case, less so among Jews), but its limited capacity and sectarian attitudes prevented it from having a real impact.

In retrospect, it is not clear what the Party could have done to increase its support. It expressed its solidarity with the plight of indebted peasants and dispossessed tenants. It tried to organize workers within segregated unions as well as across ethnic boundaries. It defended Arabs against attempts by Zionist labour activists to evict them from Jewish-owned workplaces. It told Jews that sticking to conquest policies would engender violent Arab reaction, and thus endanger their safety. It explained to members of both groups that their nationalist leaderships were sacrificing their interests for the sake of retaining power and resources. But all this was to no avail.

Partly this was due to its highly aggressive rhetoric. Telling Jews that Zionism transformed them into 'an oppressive reactionary minority, supporting imperialism against the national and social liberation war of the Arab people'[68] was not likely to win it many adherents from among them, and neither was their description as 'the wretched slaves of the Jewish bourgeoisie against the Arab popular masses'. Attitudes towards the Party did not improve when it became known that it called on Arabs physically to prevent Jewish immigrants from landing and to force them to turn back (apparently to Nazi Germany from which most of them came).[69] The argument that it was both wrong and dangerous to dispossess Arab tenants and workers, and stand with the British authorities against Arab national aspirations, made analytical sense. But, the language used in making it was so out of touch with the consciousness of Jewish residents of the country, that it could not but alienate them and create a deep sense of anger among its intended audience. It is no wonder that the number of Jewish cadres declined during that period.

When addressing Arab audiences, such rhetoric was more in line with what they were used to hearing from nationalist media and political movements. It was not clear though how to reconcile it with the call for class – rather than national – mobilization, and how some Jews could become part of a struggle that seemed to be directed primarily against all of them. In this sense the PKP's excessive language was self-defeating. It made a distinction between Jewish workers and their leadership, but this helped neither in making Jews feel they had a potential role to play, nor in making Arabs convinced that Jewish workers were potential partners rather than sworn enemies, as nationalist propaganda would have it. In a bi-national society, with two large and hostile camps, it was very difficult to chart out a course that would appeal equally to both. Choosing to side primarily with one group ran the immediate risk of alienating the other. The benefits of doing that were not obvious because other political forces competed for support from the same constituency, and those who offered an undiluted nationalist message gained an advantage over those with a complex and less coherent message.

THE ARAB REVOLT AND THE UNITED FRONT POLICY

An important dimension was added to this dilemma with the new United Front and Popular Front policy of the Comintern, launched at its 7th Congress in July–August 1935.[70] It prioritized the unity of the working class and other democratic forces against fascism as the main enemy. The precise shape of the front was to be decided by local actors, since no single formula could fit diverse conditions in different countries. The Palestine case presented particular difficulties: its Arab national movement regarded the struggle against Jewish settlers as the primary task, and opposed the British authorities to the extent that they facilitated the Zionist settlement project. As a committed anti-imperialist force, the Party supported that struggle. On the other hand, the Comintern regarded fascism as the main global enemy, a position that called for an alliance with progressive Jewish workers. Arab nationalists had no interest in such cooperation. In fact, by the mid-1930s they had established links with Italian and German agents, based on joint opposition to the British-Zionist alliance. The anti-Jewish Nazi obsession must have played a role in these links but was not crucial: other movements facing British domination in Ireland, India, South Africa were interested in gaining German support independently of their attitudes towards Jews.

   An incipient clash thus opened up between the anti-imperialist and anti-fascist imperatives of the communist movement. Having to manoeuvre another set of contradictory imperatives at the same time

– that of implementing Arabization and maintaining a Jewish basis – increased the pressures on the Party. It was torn between the need to demonstrate success in the process of Arabization and the fear of losing its basis of support among Jewish activists. But, the priority of its new leaders was clear: Arabization was paramount, and to enhance it they took part in a campaign to send the old leaders to their political graves.[71] An ECCI committee formed in 1935 to deal with the Party concluded that it had to sever all contacts with the old leadership which continued to exercise 'harmful and degenerate influence'. It had to be 'purified' to get rid of elements that preserved Zionist traditions and disrupted Arabization,[72] and pursue 'broad mass popular mobilization for a struggle against British imperialism and its main support, Zionism, for an anti-imperialist agrarian revolution'.[73] To fulfil that role, the Party had to align itself with national-revolutionary forces within the Arab movement and to support revolutionary agrarian struggles, including militant armed attacks (a reference to the operations of Sheikh al-Qassam).

This was part of an overall effort to link communist parties to the Arab national movement. A regional meeting late in 1935 self-critically asserted that communists had remained out of touch with the masses, due to their 'destructive isolationist positions' in all areas. As a result they were identified with a vague notion of a socialist revolution rather than with the concrete struggle for national liberation. The meeting called on the Party to lead the struggle of the Arab masses against colonialism and Zionism, with a focus on joint action with the national-reformist parties and left-wing nationalist elements. This could be done by organizing popular fronts in relevant places. Fighting against the obstructionist Jewish members who sought to block Arabization was essential to allow the Party to fulfil its role.[74]

What were the implications of this strategic direction for Palestinian Jews? Zionism made them 'a dominant oppressive nation', an ally of British imperialism, rather than a normal national minority oppressed by it. The Party's role, said the Comintern, was to expose Zionist deceptions and make Jewish workers realize they were being bribed to serve as anti-revolutionary cannon fodder in exchange for temporary benefits – higher standards of living. Only by supporting the Arab national liberation struggle, however, could the Jewish minority guarantee its long-term security, and determine its own future 'within a worker-peasant Arab Palestine'. At the same time, despite the focus on the national struggle, it was crucial to continue working within the existing unions (the Histadrut in the case of Jewish workers), regardless of their reactionary leadership.[75]

What this resolution failed to consider though, was the extent to which the Party's work among Jews on union-related matters was compromised by its identification with the Arab national struggle. The two issues were intertwined, and the Party's image as an alien force, hostile to the organized Yishuv, was consolidated among its intended Jewish audience.

This became clear with the outbreak of the 1936 general strike, which signalled the beginning of the Arab Revolt – a sustained campaign of resistance to British rule and Zionist settlement, that combined civil disobedience, boycotts, mass protests and armed struggle. It was waged around the central demands of the national movement: an end to Jewish immigration, an end to land sales to Jews, and the formation of a representative legislative council as a stage towards full independence for the country. The campaign made Jewish and Arab communities, already distant following the 1929 events, even more remote from each other politically and socially. The conditions of growing segregation between towns, villages, and neighbourhoods within mixed cities, could not but have a negative effect on the ability of the Party to operate as the only mixed political organization in the country. Physical communication became almost impossible, movement between different areas was restricted, and intensified nationalist feelings made internationalism very difficult to sustain in practice, even among the Party's own members.

Initially the Party used similar rhetoric in addressing both Arabs and Jews in their respective languages. It called on Arabs to intensify efforts and refuse to pay taxes until their demands were met: in addition to the agreed national demands regarding land and immigration, these included disarming Zionist militias, releasing Arab political prisoners, and returning dispossessed tenants to their land. Jewish workers were called upon to support the Arab strike and campaign for an end to Jewish immigration and settlement.[76]

The Party was involved in armed activities in the countryside and it made plans for Jewish members to join the Revolt by planting bombs at public sites linked to Zionist institutions. But, there was much resistance to that idea and little came of it in practice. Still, this resulted in a rift between the leadership and the Jewish rank and file. Tensions began to build up, eventually leading to the formation of the Jewish Section of the Party in 1937 as a body responsible for work with Jewish members and constituencies. Even before then, differences became visible: the Central Committee (CC) of the PKP called on Jewish workers to support the Arab strike as a national struggle with which they should show solidarity, while the Tel Aviv committee invoked their own interests in a 'common war for the vital interests of all workers, against imperialism and its allies'. It argued that Zionist propaganda was allowing the Arab 'feudal leaders' – a term that had disappeared from the CC's discourse by then – to divert the focus of the struggle from imperialism to the Jewish masses, and thus subvert the joint campaign of all workers for democracy and freedom.[77]

Although created merely in order to enable work under conditions of segregation, the existence of a separate Jewish Section resulted in growing distance between the Party's CC and Jewish members, particularly in Tel Aviv and Jerusalem.[78] Operating among constituencies with disparate concerns inevitably affected the priorities identified by the various forces in the Party, and their positions on core issues. In a country divided between two hostile groups, each with its own array of 'national' forces, the application of the Popular Front policy was bound to lead to different alliances and eventually to divisions within the Party. In a short period of time these divisions were consolidated into two consistent and clearly distinct sets of positions.[79]

While all this was taking place, Soviet politics were going through a period of turmoil and intense conflict, culminating in the show trials and bloody purges of 1936–38. During that time many of the Comintern cadres were arrested or executed and its work was severely disrupted. It could not maintain regular contact with its national sections and largely left the PKP to its own devices, unable to intervene in its internal debates. The Jewish Section solicited its views but in vain. After the demise of the Arab Revolt in 1939, and the restoration of relative calm, the Section sent a long memorandum to the Comintern's Central Control Commission, detailing its differences with the CC, but it never reached its destination.

What was the essence of the dispute between the Party and the Section? Initially they agreed on basic points. Once the Arab general strike was over in October 1936, most efforts were devoted to preventing the British from putting in place a partition plan for the country, with the support of the Zionist movement and against resolute Arab opposition. The Section argued that the Arabs could reach an agreement with Zionists based on: 'Abolition of the Balfour Declaration; full democratic rights for the entire population of Palestine; national, cultural and religious autonomy for the Jewish section of the Palestinian population; observation of the existing numerical ratio between the Jewish and Arab sections of the Palestinian population; protection of peasant and tenant farmers against dispossession.'[80]

The Party adopted a similar formula with one crucial difference: it supported equal rights for Jewish residents of the country but not autonomy for the Jewish community. This set of issues – were Jews in Palestine a distinct national community? What rights did they have? What was the potential for action among them, and the consequences of all that for political alliances across national boundaries? – became a central concern that shaped debate to the end of the period, and has remained central beyond 1948, all the way to the present.

Internal debates plagued the Party since the beginning of the Arabization campaign and they intensified with the Arab Revolt. According to the Jewish Section, the fundamental problem with the CC's position was that it conceptualized the conflict as involving two internally consolidated and mutually exclusive camps: Arab progressives and Zionist reactionaries. Jewish members were supposed to use the same methods of struggle as employed by the Arab camp, in support of the same cause. This included armed attacks on public installations. The result of that strategy was complete isolation from the Yishuv, growing hatred directed at the Party and the Soviet Union by Jews, and desertion of members opposed to that policy. Armed attacks were legitimate when carried out as part of a mass struggle, the Section argued, but amounted to counter-productive terrorism when undertaken by individual Jews, alienated from their own community.

The basic problem with the analysis of the CC, said the Section, was its failure to recognize the internal differentiation of the Jewish community. Instead of identifying issues that potentially could separate Jewish workers from their reactionary leadership, it used slogans and tactics that pushed them into the arms of that leadership. And, in supporting armed attacks on the Jewish community, it did not appreciate how such a strategy gave rise to reaction in kind: growing militarization of the Yishuv and further marginalization of progressive forces within it. What was needed instead was to adjust the strategy to the Yishuv's level of political maturity, based on its own experiences, and to take advantage of its internal contradictions. In that way it was possible to form alliances with progressive Zionist forces. Portraying the Jewish community as a unified reactionary mass was mirrored by the CC's failure to recognize that the Arab camp too was internally divided. It contained reactionary elements in its leadership, with links to global fascist forces. The Party followed that leadership uncritically and thus lost an opportunity to appeal to progressive Arab activists who could not see how it differed from the nationalist mainstream.

The CC's response to such accusations acknowledged both that fascist forces became involved in the Revolt and that the Party underestimated their impact. In its view, the reason for the Arab leadership's cooperation with fascism was the unyielding British-Zionist alliance, which made it impossible to extract concessions from the British. However, this did not change the objectively progressive nature of the anti-colonial revolt. A mass movement fighting against imperialist domination deserved support regardless of its leadership – feudal and clerical in the Palestinian case. The objective situation of Palestinian Arabs, an oppressed and colonized people, deprived them of the political and social basis necessary for the rise of fascism. Therefore their protest campaign was progressive even if the methods they used were not always the right ones (such as the turn to individual terrorism instead of mass armed action).

Differentiation within populations and alliances of progressive forces across national boundaries was a key principle advocated by the Jewish Section, while the CC tended to deal with each group as a solid entity, progressive or reactionary as a whole. This difference in approach was expressed in their attitudes towards participation in Zionist institutions: the Section was in favour of membership in the Histadrut and other communal bodies in order to gain access to the Jewish working masses, form alliances with progressive forces among them, and change these institutions from within. Operating legally and participating fully in the life of Jewish communal institutions was part of the strategy.

In a sense this was a return to Yishuvism but in quite a different historical context, with a Jewish community that was much bigger, better resourced and organized, and more sharply defined than before. The CC, in contrast, agreed to participate in such institutions only in order to undermine them from within. It was opposed to progressive, peaceful Zionism, which aspired to the same goals as mainstream Zionism, in its view, but with the use of different methods. It expected 'progressive' Zionists to revert to aggressive methods of struggle if their peaceful approach failed to produce the desired results.

This issue had implications for bi-nationalism as well, as the Section took part in the activities of League for Jewish–Arab Rapprochement and Co-operation. It participated on the basis of support for democracy and the struggle against fascism (the Zionist Revisionists led by Jabotinsky), and it opposed explicit anti-Zionist demands, such as putting a stop to Jewish immigration, which would have made a popular front with progressive Zionists impossible. Curiously, its assertions made it appear as if it played a major role in the League, although there is no evidence for that from the League's own sources. In any event, the CC was opposed to diluting anti-Zionism in order to form a front with 'progressive Zionists', a term they regarded as an oxymoron. Its logic was simple: If Kalvarisky and

Magnes were Zionists they were not progressive, if they were progressive they could not be Zionists.

Perhaps the underlying point in the entire debate, which became increasingly more important as time passed, was the national character of the Yishuv. Had it become by the late 1930s a full-fledged community entitled to national rights, as the Section argued? For the CC, this was not the case. It recognized that the Jewish people worldwide had legitimate national demands, such as freedom from oppression. But, these were different from Zionist demands in Palestine, which were part of a campaign to conquer the land by dispossessing the Arabs, impose Hebrew by force and undermine the national language of the Jewish people globally – Yiddish. Zionism was anti-national in a dual sense then: it distanced Jews in Palestine from Jews elsewhere, and it separated them from their Arab neighbours. It thus undermined the national aspirations of both groups. Only an anti-Zionist and anti-imperialist movement could satisfy the true national interests of Jews in Palestine and globally, said the CC.

The same set of critical points that had been raised by the Jewish Section in the late 1930s was presented again by its representative in 1942, when regular contact was re-established with the Comintern through a visiting Soviet delegation. It focused on the Party's positions during the Arab Revolt, and its 'uncritical and unconditional support for the Mufti's [Hajj Amin al-Husseini] leadership and its chauvinist programme', which centred on calls for independence and for prohibition on immigration and land transfer to Jews. These positions, which included support for terrorist actions against Jewish civilians, it argued, pushed the Jewish masses into the arms of the Zionist leaders. What the Party should have done instead, the Section said, was focus on the struggle for democratization of the country in the interests of Jews and Arabs alike. Siding with Arab nationalism stemmed from unwillingness to recognize that the objective interests of the Jewish and Arab masses were similar. Thus, the policy of popular front, aimed at uniting progressive forces within each of these internally divided groups, applied to both of them.[81]

The Soviet visitors met with members of the Central Committee and received their report as well. The Party leadership asserted that its position regarding the Revolt was basically correct – with its focus on the struggle against Zionism as mandated by the United Front policy of the Comintern. But, it underestimated the influence of fascist and reactionary bourgeois elements in the Arab nationalist camp and thus fell prey to nationalist deviations. In that way it played into the hands of the Zionist leadership.[82] The Soviets, for their part, criticized the Party for having abandoned the class struggle due to failure to 'position the national question' correctly, and thus leading to confusion within its ranks. This was not the leadership's fault though, as it operated in isolation from the Comintern, in 'complex political circumstances', and under 'conditions of sharp national struggle between Arab and Jewish nationalism' in the country.[83] Needless to say, the Comintern itself was a major reason for such confusion, due to its rapid shifts in policy, loyally following the radical reversals resulting from Soviet factional conflicts. But this, of course, was raised neither by the visitors nor by any of the factions that looked up to them to resolve their disputes.

NATIONALIST CONTESTATIONS

In any event, by the time of the visit (late 1942) the differences between the CC and the Jewish Section (which had re-joined the Party and then split again to form the Emet – Truth – group), had been sorted out to a large extent. This was made possible due to the resolution or suspension of outstanding disagreements, primarily related to internal differentiation among Arabs and Jews. In particular, the principled position of the Party not to collaborate with Zionist forces on any issue was no longer in force.[84] The shared focus on the anti-fascist global war created a new basis for unity. Everything else was pushed aside. The Party instructed its activists: 'We are fighting today not against the Zionist goals themselves, but against their mere consideration. We have no interest currently in fighting Zionism as such, only those political manifestations of the Zionist movement that hamper, in our understanding, mobilization, the war effort, assisting the Soviet Union, and forming a militant anti-Fascist communal [Jewish] front.'[85]

This approach went further to reject attacks on the contracting and cooperative institutions of the Histadrut, which the Party had always opposed as harmful for workers' interests: 'The question of conquest of labour and land is not relevant today, our task is to recruit this large [cooperative] sector of the Histadrut to the general war effort in the country. We must fight the manifestations in that important sector that interfere with the war effort, nothing else.'[86] Among the Arab population, the Party's tasks were more complex, since support for the Allied side was weak. Many people supported the Axis forces simply because they were opposed to British rule. The Party's main role was: 'Liberating the [Arab] masses from fascist influences, inserting anti-fascist and progressive national consciousness into the Arab liberation movement, creating an anti-fascist atmosphere and activating the masses and the national movement in support of Soviet Union and the war against fascism.' This included a struggle against the 'Husseini Fifth Column' and local pro-fascist forces, as well as pro-government forces, with a focus on the labour movement as a centre of gravity for the Party's activities. It was an uphill struggle that was expected to bear fruit later, with the victory of the Soviet Union at the end of the war.[87]

This newly-found unity based on the war effort came at a price, however. With the Soviet-endorsed self-criticism, the Party abandoned one crucial tenet of its programme: the definition of Zionist settlement as a colonial project and the struggle against it. If the Jewish Yishuv was internally differentiated – regardless of its recent immigrant origins – and some of its elements could be drawn into the struggle for independence and democracy, then it was not an oppressive group in its entirety. If the Arab national movement contained fascist elements, then it was not progressive in its entirety. If two national groups fought each other for political control of the country, and the way forward was an anti-fascist democratic alliance of all progressive forces across national boundaries, then the conflict was no longer colonial in nature. That the British imposed restrictions on Jewish immigration and land transfers with the White Paper of 1939, and thus turned against Zionist aspirations, made it easier to consider Arab–Jewish relations without invoking the colonial context. Fighting the British receded to the background in any event, as they and the Soviets became allies in the war against Nazi Germany.

Obviously, the indigenous nature of the Arab population and the foreign origins of the bulk of the Jewish population did not change. The question though was whether this difference should have given Arabs superior rights as the true owners of the country. The bi-nationalist movement equated the national rights of both peoples, regardless of the length of time they has resided in the country. The Arab national movement rejected the rights of Jewish immigrants, though it did recognize native-born Jews as deserving of equality. The Party recognized all along the claim to equality of individual rights of all residents, but did not accept a collective national claim other than that of the Arab majority. Now, with the demise of the Arab Revolt, the strengthening of the national character of the Yishuv, and the Soviet intervention in the debate, it shifted towards recognizing Jewish minority group rights, albeit within the context of national independence for the country as a whole.

This shift in approach alienated the large group of left-wing Arab intellectuals and activists who moved closer to the Party during the 1930s, when it supported the Arab national struggle without reservations. Although many of them rejected the uncritical support granted to the movement's leadership, they continued to identify with the struggle for national liberation. They regarded the Party leadership headed by Radwan al-Hilu as weak and indecisive, constantly shifting between the two national communities. The result was a situation 'where the Party was talking to each community in its own political language and appealing to it in terms of its national sentiments'.[88] That had already been the case with the rise of the Jewish Section, and national divisions within the ranks became sharper with the growing feeling that the World War would force a decision regarding the political status of the country. The 1942 Biltmore programme of the Zionist movement, which put forward the goal of a Jewish state for the first time in explicit terms, made the contestation over the future of the country more acute than ever.

Tensions within the Party came to a head in 1943. Although al-Hilu was the general secretary with extensive powers, his position was being undermined by the Party Secretariat, consisting of four Jewish members who pushed for greater involvement in the Yishuv's affairs. Arab members of the Central Committee, on the other hand, campaigned to become an integral part of the Arab national movement. They regarded association with the Yishuv as an obstacle in their way. Stuck between two opposed camps, al-Hilu was further undermined by the Comintern's dissolution in May 1943. Symbolically and practically this meant greater freedom for local forces to exert their impact and shape their own policies. There was no longer a need for mediators – the role al-Hilu used to play – to convey Comintern directives from the outside. Without such external backing, he was alone in an arena dominated by open expressions of nationalism. His departure from political activity was the logical consequence, signifying the end of the attempt to maintain the unity of the Party across national boundaries.

Out of the turmoil three formations emerged. The PKP continued to be the name of one of them, but it consisted of Jewish members only and thus was not a direct continuation of the Jewish–Arab party of the two previous decades. Another Jewish-only organization was the Communist Educational Association (later re-named the Hebrew Communist Party), led by some of al-Hilu's former CC colleagues, Tzabari and Slonim. In different ways, both of these formations operated on the basis of themes developed initially by the Jewish Section. The most important new organization was the National Liberation League (NLL), with Arab members only, which did not define itself as communist.[89] The split in the movement remained in force until the end of the period and, in a sense, 'foreshadowed the coming partition of the country'.[90]

The NLL was created by activists who became affiliated to the Party in the late 1930s and early 1940s, and were dissatisfied with what the discourse of the time called 'nationalist deviations'. But, there was a crucial difference between the Jewish and Arab deviations: the former had to do with moving closer to core Zionist positions, while the latter was expressed in uncritical support for the nationalist leadership and its methods of struggle. The NLL had no problem with the core Arab national positions: it identified and acted to promote them, but sought to do so with a focus on grassroots popular mobilization, for which Palestinian social relations had to be changed. In that way, its socially progressive orientation was linked to its national agenda. Basing political campaigns on the efforts of workers, peasants, students and intellectuals was the only way, in its view, to overcome the dominance of clerical and feudal elements, who sacrificed national interests for the sake of their personal and class benefits.

The League defined itself as the left-wing of the national movement rather than the Arab wing of the communist movement. This was a subtle but important distinction, which allowed it to claim membership in the nationalist camp. It was also a way of distancing itself from the Jewish PKP, which continued to use the communist label. That label, for the first time since 1919, helped the Party gain legitimacy in the Yishuv, due to the role played by the Soviet Union in the war against Nazi Germany.[91] In this sense there was no symmetry between the two main factions to emerge from the split. The NLL asserted its Arab nature upfront while the PKP did not define itself as Jewish (though it had no Arab members). The NLL was ambiguous in relation to its communist origins – it did not highlight them but neither did it disguise its Soviet sympathies. For the PKP, towards the end of the World War, affiliation with the Soviet Union was helpful as it allowed it to participate in the Yishuv's internal politics. Continuity with the communist legacy was central to its appeal to current and prospective supporters, but incidental to the NLL, which relied on the innovative approach it was bringing to Arab politics – free of family links, tradition, and the corrupting influence of property, power and official connections. In an environment which had seen the dominant parties discredited by their foreign associations, and left politically exhausted as a result of bloody internecine clashes, there was an opening for a refreshing new force.[92]

For the NLL, Palestine was an Arab country fighting for independence from foreign rule. Jews residing there deserved equal rights as a minority group, but had no collective political claim to the country. In line with the old approach of the PKP, the League distinguished between the Zionist movement and the Jewish community. It regarded the former as colonial and reactionary, while the latter was a community with internal class divisions and diverse interests, some of which could be reconciled with those of the Arab people of the country. The struggle was against the leadership of the community, not the masses of its people. An independent Palestine should allow all residents equal participation: Arabs were the majority but the country should be democratic and not grant privileges to members of any ethnic or national group. Although this view clashed with the mainstream Arab position (which regarded Jewish settlers as outsiders, not entitled to rights in the country), the NLL shared the other core demands of Arab nationalism: an end to Jewish immigration and land transfers and independence to the country.[93]

Whether Jews had *national* rights, in addition to *civil* rights, was not clear. On the one hand, the League said in October 1945 that 'in our approach to the problem we accept the responsibility of laying down plans to safeguard the National interests of the Arab people living in the country while guaranteeing at the same time, and not in contradiction, full civil rights and democratic freedom for the Jewish community now residing in Palestine'. This formulation seemed to distinguish between the two groups' rights. But, the statement continued, 'We recognize the right of the Jewish community to develop whatever legitimate just national interests, Jews living under a democratic regime, would be eager to realize'.[94] The content of these national interests and the form they might take were not specified, however.

Uniquely among Arab parties, the NLL understood and empathized with the plight of European Jews, faced with anti-Semitism and genocide. It argued that the national movement failed to grasp the fears that drove Jews to immigrate to Palestine, and lumped all of them together as illegal settlers. It thus drove progressive Jews to embrace Zionism. Only by recognizing Jews as citizens in an independent country could the opposition to Zionism drive a wedge between the mass of ordinary people and their reactionary leadership. For both moral and practical reasons, a distinction between Jews and Zionists was essential. By effectively accepting the demographic consequences of Zionism (the right of immigrants to equal citizenship), albeit without endorsing them, the NLL moved towards abandoning the colonial model. It no longer regarded the Jewish community as foreign, but neither did it recognize it as a national minority with a right to self-determination: 'Zionist slogans for immigration and a Jewish state become non-feasible with the right of the people for self-determination and freedom from all reactionary fetters.'[95]

At the same time, the PKP was moving towards integration within the organized Yishuv. While opposing partition and calling for an independent democratic state, it increasingly upheld a bi-nationalist vision, based on 'the principle of equal right of Jews and Arabs for free national, economic and cultural development, without artificial interruptions and in mutual cooperation and brotherhood of nations, mutual understanding and recognition of each other's rights'.[96] The 10th Congress of the PKP, held in November 1946, was told by Meir Vilner that 'two peoples live in this country and their interests are shared.' Neither an Arab nor a Jewish state was viable: 'Jews and Arabs live together in all parts of the country. Territorial or economic separation is impossible.' Partition or federation would increase the antagonism between them. The only way to solve the national problem was 'the establishment of an independent Jewish–Arab democratic state, in which Jews and Arabs will enjoy full equality'. Unity could be formed on the basis of joint struggle against imperialism and its allies – the Jewish and Arab reactionary leaderships.[97]

On the basis of that position, the PKP sought to re-unite with the NLL. Despite their differences regarding the national rights of Jews in the country, the two parties were not far from each other's positions, as they both rejected the Arab nationalist notion that Jews were an alien group and that a solution would require the departure of their majority from the territory. Opposing partition as unviable and reactionary, and at the same time maintaining separate national organizations, was an obvious contradiction that undermined the quest for a unified solution for the country. It seems that the main reason for the failure to re-unite was the reason the split occurred in the first place: Arab left-wing activists were accepted as legitimate by their national movement only when they ceased associating in the same organization with Jewish activists, regardless of how progressive and supportive of the national cause the latter were.

Having a separate Arab organization was useful not only with regard to the national movement but also in relation to the main constituency of the League, the labour movement. Solidarity between workers, regardless of their origins, is the basic principle of union organization but in Palestine this became complicated by the underlying national struggle over employment. The main organization of Jewish workers played a major role in the Zionist settlement project and was not open to Arab workers, whose unions were also separate. International unions did exist in some sectors, but the bulk of workers did not participate in joint frameworks. Defining its terrain in national terms allowed the NLL and its union activists to focus on what they were strong at: offering a consistent, militant, well-organized and corruption-free leadership, that was solidly based in the national movement but was willing to work with Jewish unions when it was helpful to its cause, putting the welfare of workers and their unions at the centre of its action.[98]

The labour scene provided some opportunities for cooperation between the PKP and NLL. The mid- to late 1940s was a period of militant action and saw numerous strikes of government and private employees. The PKP usually worked in the framework of the Histadrut, but also notably with the NLL in the big state employees strike of Spring 1946, which encompassed tens of thousands of Jewish and Arab workers in the post office, railways, and government offices.[99] Unions aligned with the national movement were more reluctant to work with the Histadrut, and the growing worker struggles in the country did not help in overcoming national boundaries. The gap between class militancy which brought people together, and national identity which set them apart, seemed unbridgeable due to the colonial context of Jewish settlement in Palestine.

There was a clear logic at work here. The emphasis on the separate national identity of Arabs and Jews was shared by all political trends in Palestine, and was recognized by all international forces. The debate was over the legitimacy of that state of affairs and its political consequences. Arab nationalists claimed it was the outcome of a colonial process that could and should be reversed. The NLL agreed that the origins of the problem were colonial, but regarded the process as irreversible and therefore acknowledged that Jews had to be granted equality as individuals, without changing the nature of the country itself. The PKP took an additional step and accepted the legitimacy of the Jewish community, asserting that it had to be accommodated as a national group. Thus, Arab nationalists and Jewish communists were consistent, whereas the NLL was having difficulties reconciling its contradictory political location, between Arab nationalism and democratic equality.

Although the PKP had already ceased referring to Zionism and the Palestine Jewish community as colonial entities, it did not thereby return to Yishuvism, as Ben-Zaken argues.[100] The size of the Jewish community in the mid-1940s was three times that of the 1920s, and its economic and military capacity many times greater. It was no longer a small advanced section of the population, but rather a complete society in its own right, even if its autonomy was relative, not absolute. It was operating from a position of power and coherence vis-à-vis Arabs, who were socially fragmented and politically exhausted by the repression of the Arab Revolt and the exile of their leadership in its aftermath. On the international scene, Jewish claims to statehood in Palestine, no longer disguised by the discourse of a 'national home', were morally reinforced by the Nazi Holocaust and the large number of displaced persons who could not or would not be accommodated within their old countries in Europe.

With all their differences, the PKP and NLL shared an important aspect of their identity: loyalty to the Soviet Union. Its delegate to the UN recognized for the first time in May 1947 'that the population of Palestine consists of two peoples, the Arabs and the Jews. Both have historical roots in Palestine. Palestine has become the homeland of both these peoples'. A just solution therefore had to address 'the legitimate interests of both these peoples', in the form of 'an independent, dual, democratic, homogeneous Arab-Jewish State', which would be based on 'equality of rights for the Jewish and the Arab populations'. However, 'if this plan proved impossible to implement, in view of the deterioration in the relations between the Jews and the Arabs', an alternative plan would be suitable, providing for 'the partition of Palestine into two independent autonomous States, one Jewish and one Arab'. This would be the case only if relations between Jews and Arabs 'proved to be so bad that it would be impossible to reconcile them and to ensure the peaceful co-existence'.[101]

Initially, the PKP emphasized the Soviet delegate's support for a dual Arab-Jewish state, a bi-national state in other words, identical to the PKP's own 1946 position, and ignored the mention of partition.[102] This persisted through the middle of 1947. In his testimony to the United Nations Special Committee on Palestine (UNSCOP), Party general secretary Shmuel Mikunis asserted that 'both the Arab and Jewish peoples of Palestine fight for their just elementary rights for national independence, for an independent, free and democratic Arab-Jewish Palestine'. Rejecting partition, he proclaimed: 'We advocate the plan that Palestine should be constituted as an independent, democratic, bi-unitarian state, which means, a single state inhabited and governed by the two peoples, Jews and Arabs, having equal rights.' Once the British were out of the way, 'Arabs and Jews will be free to decide on the character of the independent state, built on a bi-national or a federative settlement'.

His CC colleague, Meir Vilner, added somewhat unrealistically: 'The problem of Palestine is not the Jewish–Arab antagonism. The Palestine question is the question of a colonial country subjugated by foreign rule and thirsting for freedom. The real issue of the Palestine question lies in the clash of interests between British Imperialism and the population of this country, Arabs and Jews alike.' He attributed the tension in the country to colonial rule, but did not link it to the contradictory interests and aspirations of the two peoples of the country, nor did he mention the role of the Zionist movement in the conflict: '30 years of British rule in our country is the main reason for the present relationship between Jews and Arabs.' Only by abolishing the Mandate and removing foreign troops could a solution be found, involving 'recognition of the right of both peoples to independence in a single free and democratic Palestine, based on the principle of full equality of civil, national and political rights'.[103]

In response to questions, Mikunis agreed that he could not speak for Palestinian communists (the NLL, who boycotted the hearings like the rest of the Arab national movement), but that 'in all basic problems of Palestine, the Communist Party of Palestine and the League for National Liberation are of the same opinion. It means our common fight for independence, for a democratic state, for an abrogation of the Mandate, for evacuation of the troops and against partition of the country'. That they were separate, despite such agreement, was 'a question of organization which has nothing to do with the success or lack of success in cooperation'. This somewhat obscure answer was all that he offered. He was reluctant to provide details of his vision beyond generalities such as 'on the basis of the past, there will be no difficulties between the Jews and Arabs in settling in common vital questions of Palestine' including immigration, overlooking the fact that it was precisely 'the past' that made settling these questions so difficult.

Vilner was more forthcoming and made the point that previous negotiations on immigration showed willingness to reach a solution, relying in his answer on Magnes and the bi-nationalist idea: once issues of political power were removed from consideration, demography would no longer make a difference and all matters would be resolved on the basis of the principle 'equal citizen's rights for every citizen, and equal national rights for both peoples as peoples'. In other words, individual and collective equality. The precise mechanisms – proportional or collective representations, different houses of parliament, unitary or federal arrangements – will be decided in the future. In all that the Party's vision was not different from that of the bi-nationalists, with the exception that the PKP was opposed to any dilution of independence through an extension of the Mandate, UN trusteeship or similar such devices.

Even more than the PKP, the Hebrew Communists (also known as the Palestinian Communist Union) positioned themselves firmly within the Yishuv. They rejected the notion of a united bi-national democratic state, because it ignored the national development of the Jewish community. It was not a minority but an independent society with its own economy, language and national psyche, entitling them to national rights, not merely civil-democratic minority rights. The logical organizational conclusion from that situation was to have separate communist parties, as indeed was the case at that time.[104] This position did not translate into straightforward support for a Jewish state as was the case for Zionist parties, however.

In its presentation to UNSCOP, the Communist Union called for a political settlement that 'will safeguard both peoples against the danger of domination and will solve the problem of majority and minority—and will certainly also guarantee the right of the Jews to immigrate'. A state based on one of the nations in a bi-national situation would inevitably lead to the 'denial of sovereign rights to one of the nations', the mobilization of the excluded nation against the state, and 'economic and political boycott up to armed uprisings, bloodshed and mutual massacres'. Partition was not viable either. In a Jewish state, there will be a large Arab minority, so that 'the difficulty of majority and minority as existing in the non-partitioned Palestine will remain.' This would include unequal distribution of industrial and natural resources, disrupted economic development due to broken relations with neighbouring Arab countries, and continued hostility, leading to 'a typical police State, as it will have to suppress a large national minority'.

The alternative would be based on 'the principle of territorial federalism', which consists of 'the creation of an independent, democratic united State, common to both Jews and Arabs, built on full national and political equality for both its nations and on full democratic rights for all its inhabitants. The form of government ensuring political equality will have to be based on parity'. For that to work 'the fear of domination should be removed, sufficient guarantees against national domination should be given'. This was

inherent in the right of self-determination up to secession, in the right of each nation to create a State of its own. This right can be exercised only on a territorial basis. Therefore, we think that the joint State of

Jews and Arabs should be composed of territorial districts possessing regional authorities of their own; being equally represented at the supreme Government institutions.[105]

The NLL did not give evidence to UNSCOP despite its campaign against boycotting the process. It yielded to the Arab leadership in order to present a united front, but continued to argue it was a mistake to boycott the Committee. When UNSCOP came up with a majority recommendation to partition the country and minority recommendation to grant the two nations autonomy within a united federal structure, the PKP supported the latter. But, in mid-October 1947 Soviet diplomat Semyon Tsarapkin recognized that such an arrangement was no longer viable due to the intensity of the conflict between Jews and Arabs, and therefore that partition – despite its negative impact on economic development – was inevitable and had to be implemented. Within a couple of days the PKP adopted that position and stuck with it through subsequent developments.[106]

The NLL, however, initially rejected the Soviet position and continued to regard partition as an unjust solution.[107] It blamed the Arab leadership for its failure to address the global community by boycotting UNSCOP, and for making support for partition more likely due to its refusal to acknowledge that Arab–Jewish cooperation was essential. In other words, by rejecting the rights of Jewish residents, the Arab leadership made partition inevitable, and ruined the chances of an alternative solution that could get international support, such as a federal state.[108] Both plans – partition and federalism – meant abandoning the colonial model in practice, as they recognized Jewish settlers as equal citizens, and thus were unacceptable to Arab nationalists. But, the NLL was subject to pressure from another powerful source. The Soviet position proved impossible to resist for long, and by December 1947 the NLL had joined the PKP in support of partition, despite ongoing opposition from some of its leading members.[109]

Once the Soviet Union and the United States agreed on a course of action the road was clear for UN General Assembly resolution 181 of 1947, which adopted the majority position at UNSCOP – partition of the country into independent Jewish and Arab states. But, instead of the confederal structure envisaged and economic cooperation, the ensuing military conflict and creation of the State of Israel in May 1948 led to the Palestinian *Nakba* – the massive displacement of hundreds of thousands of Arabs from the areas allocated to Israel, as well as from territories occupied by its forces in the course of the war. The rest of the country that was allocated to the Arab state fell to Egypt (the Gaza Strip, which remained under occupation until 1967) and Jordan (the West Bank, which was annexed formally in 1950 and its residents were granted citizenship).

In its last statement, the Central Committee of the NLL blamed 'the racial hostility in Palestine that was nurtured and deepened by British imperialism with the support of Arab and Jewish reaction' for the war, chaos and destruction resulting from the war. Facing such challenges, the communist movement, 'which always headed the struggle for an Arab-Jewish front against imperialism and for freedom and independence', did not succeed in forming such a united front because it failed itself to unite in one international organization. The League recognized that its 'separate national organizational structure' deprived it of a correct understanding of changing realities in the country, particularly the rise of a new Jewish nationality, which deserved the right to national self-determination alongside the Arab people of the country.

The separate national basis allowed 'right-wing deviations' to shape the NLL policy, and created an 'illusion that the Arab people in Palestine could liberate the country from imperialism, without taking into consideration the revolutionary forces among the Jewish people'. Instead of seeking an impossible national unity between 'the bourgeois and neo-feudal leadership and new popular forces', it should have worked to isolate the reactionary Arab leadership and form a united anti-imperialist Jewish–Arab front. This self-criticism, the NLL said, created a basis for the revival of a unified territorially-based party that would be formed on the basis of the existing institutions of the new Israeli Communist Party within Israel (known as Maki), and on the basis of the existing NLL institutions in the Arab territories of Palestine (including areas such as Nazareth which were temporarily – it was believed at the time – occupied by Israeli forces).[110]

In response, the Central Committee of Maki asserted that it had supported unification since the Party split in 1943, and that the conditions were ripe for merger and the re-integration of all NLL branches and members into the Israeli Communist Party and its leadership.[111] NLL members in the West Bank re-grouped and formed the Jordanian Communist Party in 1951.[112] The Hebrew Communist Party joined Maki in December 1948, but left it again a couple of years later to join the Zionist mainstream. Maki remained united in this form until 1965, when it was split again on ethnic-national grounds, but that is a matter to be discussed in another chapter.[113]

CONCLUSIONS

Over three decades, the Palestinian Communist Party travelled a long way: from the left-wing of the Zionist labour movement to a position outside the Zionist consensus, though still involved with its institutions (guided by Yishuvism). It then broke away from it altogether (as mandated by Arabization), but was torn apart due to the increasing pressures of competing national movements. Eventually it returned to the fold, as a dissident but accepted part of the Israeli Left. Its delegate's signature on Israel's Declaration of Independence in May 1948 became a seal of approval for the circle it had completed. And yet, this is not a story with an ending that could have been foretold. It involved fierce struggles, gains and losses, and radical shifts in the identity of the individual actors: the people that emerged from the process were not those who entered it.

What conclusions can be drawn from that history? The role of identity was crucial. Obviously, in an environment of intense national conflict the ethnic-national background of activists makes a difference, but there was more to it in this case. The positions taken by the Party forced its members to defy the basic expectations of their own community. Jewish anti-Zionist activists in Europe and elsewhere experienced conflicts with their local Jewish communities, at times, but could ignore them. They did not have to live or work in a Jewish-dominated environment or pay attention to the sensitivities of other Jews. This was not possible in Palestine. Not only were Jews there part of a small and tightly-integrated community, which made dissent difficult to sustain, but most of them moved to the country as a result of a choice to immigrate.

This put them in a double bind: as new settlers they depended on their community for a range of essential services, and the cost of dissent was high. At the same time, precisely because they were settlers in a colonial context, their ability to shift allegiances was limited: both because of the psychological difficulty of switching sides a short time after having made a drastic change in their lives, and because they were seen by the other side as aliens who should not have come there in the first place. There was thus an inevitable clash between their 'objective' social position as Jewish settlers and their 'subjective' political stand as anti-Zionist activists, who identified with the Arab national cause but – for the most part – without speaking Arabic or sharing physical space with Arabs or having culture, religion and history in common with them.

This was not the case for Arab activists, whose social and political positions coincided in a way impossible for their Jewish colleagues. They suffered from another difficulty, though, the tension between adherence to particular nationalism and universal socialism. The former tied them to the Palestinian Arab community, while the latter mandated links across the national divide. This was not merely a matter of personal relations but of political agendas: the different imperatives could be reconciled but there was no obvious way of doing that without frictions. Such frictions were shaped – though not determined – by the identity and communal background of Party members.

This conflict-prone situation was further complicated by a unique condition: the Party was part of a global movement. Its course of action was shaped by shifts in policy of the Comintern, which in turn was affected by the constant upheaval and violent conflict that dominated Soviet politics in that period. The Party was not in control over issues of major theoretical and practical interest, such as the relationship between members of settler and indigenous origins, the role of class discourse, attitudes towards competing nationalist movements, the priority of the struggle against imperialism in relation to the struggle against fascism, and ultimately – its position with regard to the future of the country. In all these respects, consideration of the Soviet position was crucial, and frequently of more importance than the Party's own internal deliberations. No other movement discussed in this book was similar in this respect.

Given that class solidarity was nipped in the bud by nationalism, and that even the most radical movement was torn apart by it on many occasions (1929, 1937, 1943, 1965), was there ever a real chance of organizing across national boundaries? It is difficult to answer this question without taking into consideration the global context, which perhaps saw the most violent turmoil in world history. Not only did Palestine see the rise of and increasingly acrimonious clash between two national movements, this was happening while Jews were experiencing a fierce assault on their livelihoods and their ability to survive, Arabs were seeking independence after centuries of foreign rule, the British were facing serious challenges to their empire, and the struggle between Western liberal democracy, fascism, and Soviet-style communism was waged in Europe with intensity not seen before or since. Thus, it was the most politically intense period imaginable, with numerous actors operating in a life or death situation. In this sense it was the least conducive time for reaching out across boundaries, but precisely because of that, also the time when such reaching out was most needed. How feasible that was is a question to which I return in the concluding chapter of the book.

3

Palestinian Nationalism and the Anti-Colonial Struggle

HISTORICAL BACKGROUND

All large-scale historical processes can be divided into periods, characterized by crucial landmark events, developments and dates. These usually play a symbolic role but also serve as indicators of important shifts or new directions. Three such dates stand out in the history of the Israeli-Palestinian conflict:

- 2 November 1917: the date of the Balfour Declaration, which recognized the Zionist movement's claim to a 'national home' in Palestine, and committed Britain to facilitating its realization.
- 29 November 1947: the date of the UN Palestine partition resolution, which led to the establishment of the State of Israel in the following year and to the Palestinian *Nakba* (dispossession of hundreds of thousands who became stateless refugees).
- 5 June 1967: the date of the war that led to Israel's expansion into its current boundaries, incorporating all of historical Palestine within its system of military and political control.

These dates and the events with which they are associated did not create new realities from scratch, of course. Rather, building on existing trends, they served to consolidate pre-existing developments and to open up new historical possibilities. In particular they helped give rise to new patterns of settlement and resistance, and thus reshaped relations between the main protagonists of the evolving conflict.

The Balfour Declaration was issued towards the end of the First World War, after Great Britain had gained control over much of Palestine and large areas of the Middle East that used to be part of the Ottoman Empire. It followed 35 years of organized Jewish immigration and settlement activity in the country, which resulted in the consolidation of a small but growing Jewish community (the New Yishuv), spread over dozens of new rural settlements, towns and urban neighbourhoods. Although it made no reference to that community, its existence was an important contextual factor for the Declaration. It granted international legitimacy to the new Yishuv and facilitated its further growth under the leadership of the world Zionist movement.

Together with the British Mandate for Palestine, officially inaugurated in 1920, it created a new political framework based on boundaries that define the territory to this day. In that way it made the incipient conflict between Jewish settlers and indigenous Palestinian-Arabs more sharply focused on the political future of the country. While Palestinian resistance to Jewish immigration and land settlement preceded the Declaration, going back to the late nineteenth century, the post-1917 period became crucial in shaping the conflict in its current form.

With the demise of the Ottoman Empire and the British takeover of Palestine, two new and related elements were introduced into the country: European imperial rule and a settler political project. The Ottomans governed the country from present-day Turkey but their domain incorporated much of the Middle East and parts of North Africa and the Balkans in a political framework legitimized by Islam rather than by specific national or ethnic principles of organization. The Ottoman ethos saw the empire as the continuation of the great Islamic empires of the past. It did not regard Palestine as a foreign territory nor was Ottoman rule seen as foreign by local residents. There was little room for nationalist or anti-colonial resistance in an environment that saw Palestinian locals represented and governed in the same way as all other Ottoman subjects. Even with the beginning of an Arab nationalist movement before the First World War, the vast majority of the population remained loyal to the Ottoman state and did not organize politically on a separate Arab or Palestinian basis.

All this changed in the post-war period, when the Middle East was divided into different political units. These were administered by Britain and France as Mandatory powers, ostensibly working under the League of Nations to guide the territories to independence, but in practice making their own policies with little outside interference. Struggles against this form of imperial control were waged in many places, including Palestine, usually under an Arab nationalist banner. In this respect Palestinians were similar to their counterparts elsewhere in the region, but with a crucial twist: the main target of their struggle was not Britain's rule in itself, but its role as a facilitator of the Zionist movement and its settlement project. Zionism was increasingly seen as a threat due to ongoing Jewish immigration and land purchases, and consequent fears of dispossession, and also – perhaps primarily – as it embarked on a concerted effort to assert political control over the country as a whole at the expense of local Palestinian Arabs.

These two new components – British imperial rule and the Zionist project – were driven by different imperatives and occasionally came into clash with one another. Yet, from a radical perspective they became fused as forces equally opposed to independence for the country in line with the wishes of its majority Arab residents. How these forces could be disentangled – in theoretical analysis and political practice – was a matter for debate between different orientations. Palestinian-Arab nationalists regarded Zionism as the main opponent, which was able to manipulate the British to do its bidding. Left-wing activists regarded the British as the main culprit, using the Zionist movement to enhance their control of the region and its strategic resources – oil above all, but also transport routes, military bases and so on.

The debate between these activist orientations was expressed in various forms throughout the period discussed here. It divided those who directed most attention to the national conflict from those who adopted a broader framework of analysis and action. The former focused on the struggle against the Zionist settlement project in Palestine before 1948 (and the State of Israel after that), and the latter focused on the struggle against imperial control of the region, including Palestine, exercised by Britain at first and taken over by the USA from the mid-1950s onwards. These two approaches were not always clearly distinct, however, and some overlaps between them existed at times. Still, for our purposes they can be distinguished both in their different emphases and in the courses of action that flow from the analysis.

The nationalist approach conceptualized the question of Palestine as a clash between indigenous Arabs seeking independence and foreign Jewish settlers acting to take their place and realize their own independence. The solution therefore consisted in restoring the rights of the indigenous population by reversing the process of settlement and colonization. This should be carried out for the entire country or, if impossible, for a part of the country at least. The left-wing approach conceptualizes the question as a struggle for economic and territorial control between the global forces of imperialism and local populations. Although settlers frequently joined imperialist forces, under the mistaken belief that they would thus enhance their security, their survival could be guaranteed only by local anti-imperialist movements. Settlers could become allies of liberation forces, even without being aware of that necessarily.

The nationalist and left-wing approaches presented above are best seen as ideal types, that is to say analytical benchmarks rather than empirical realities. In practice, the picture is more complex since the boundaries between foreign and local populations are not always clear, the alliances between imperial powers and settlers may take different forms with different political implications, and indigenous people are internally divided on social and political grounds. Some indigenous groups may enter relationships of cooperation but also of conflict with some settler groups, and benefit or suffer differentially from imperial policies.

This diversity of conditions leads, in turn, to diverse political strategies: a conservative nationalism opposed to the settler project but willing to collaborate with imperialism; radical nationalism that incorporates elements of left-wing rhetoric; socialist movements that form popular fronts with one type of nationalism or another, and so on. Nationalism itself has assumed partly overlapping and partly contradictory forms: the local-territorial nationalism (*wataniyya*) of Palestinians co-existed with the broader but less structured pan-Arab nationalism (*qawmiyya*), and it was never completely separate from the religious Islamic identity of the majority of the population. At different times one or more of these forms of identity assumed a dominant role in popular consciousness but without ever displacing the other elements permanently.

To provide a historical framework for the discussion, serving to place it in a global context, I will introduce notions of colonialism and apartheid, and the struggle against them, into the chapter. This is not meant to offer a solid comparative angle throughout but rather to enable a different vantage point (or a benchmark) from which to examine the case of Palestine and some of its unique features. That the South African liberation struggle is frequently mentioned these days as a useful analogy for the Palestinian struggle makes this vantage point particularly interesting. But first, let us define these terms: apartheid was a South African system based on the classification of people into distinct racial groups, each of which was allocated specific territories and sets of social and political rights that went with them. The relationship between the groups was hierarchical: whites had access to most resources and were in charge of the system as a whole, including the definition and monitoring of the boundaries between groups. The system was in place between 1948 and 1994 but many of its features had been evident for decades if not centuries before it was formalized as an organizing principle of government policies. Despite several changes during that period, it retained its essence until the end.

The struggle against apartheid was based on opposition to the unequal allocation of resources between groups and, more fundamentally, opposition to the very logic of classification into groups. Rejection of the notion that racial boundaries were natural and obvious, and therefore could serve as a basis for social and political arrangements, was a central feature of the anti-apartheid struggle in South Africa, even if such race-based ideas did creep into it at times. Crucially, in its later stages the anti-apartheid campaign was consolidated around the notion of non-racialism, implying the removal of race altogether as a legitimate consideration, rather than calling for equality of people organized on a racial basis. The extent to which this idea dominated popular consciousness varied over time: we must not confuse official rhetoric with massive support by the grassroots, and we need to recognize that to some extent at least there has been a revival of a more explicit racial thinking in the post-apartheid era.

Of relevance here is that both apartheid and the opposition to it were ways of organizing internal relations within a single unequal society. Commonly-used rhetoric about separation, segregation and the literal meaning of the term apartheid (apartness) must not obscure the incorporation of all groups of people within the same social and economic frameworks. Attempts by the state to entrench separation through influx control laws, forced removals and fake independence for the 'homelands' were important, but ultimately failed to reverse the processes of migration from the countryside to the urban areas and from the black townships into the 'grey areas' in city centres. And of course, the anti-apartheid movement was based on the recognition that indigenous people had been conquered and there was no going back to pre-colonial independence: the only political alternative was full integration on a basis of equality in the same society and state.

Beyond the details of South African history, apartheid in a generic sense – unbounded in time and space by the specific case that gave it its name – exists when a system is based on principles that enshrine and entrench social and political inequalities between collective groups, defined in racial, ethnic or national terms. An anti-apartheid movement seeks to overturn such a system and undermine the rationale for existing inequalities. The problem tackled in this way is not nationalism or national identity in themselves, nor foreign rule and the need for independence from colonialism. Rather, it is the idea that group membership defined by shared ancestry is the main criterion used to allocate or deny political and civil rights – such as citizenship, free movement, and access to land. Such rights should be granted to all residents as members of the same political community regardless of their origins.

Using this understanding of apartheid, the argument in this chapter is that the Palestinian nationalist paradigm is an anti-colonial but not anti-apartheid perspective: it does not break away from racial or national group identifications as the basis for social and political rights, but rather seeks to reinforce boundaries between groups. Largely it has failed to offer a vision of a shared future within the same framework in order to overcome ethnic or national distinctions. Of course, this does not make it illegitimate or invalidate its cause. But, it is important to recognize that transcending nationalism is essential to the anti-apartheid orientation. Radical left-wing perspectives are closer to the anti-apartheid ideal type but usually unable to extricate themselves from nationalism and from thinking in group terms.

In what follows, the chapter examines the extent to which the nationalist perspective dealt with issues such as definition of group membership and boundaries, distinctions between internal and external forces, relations to colonial and imperial powers, and alliances within and between groups. This allows us to consider the relevance of the anti-apartheid paradigm as a global term for liberation movements in other parts of the world. The focus is not on direct references to South African apartheid – which was unknown or attracted little attention until the 1970s – but to broader issues of colonialism, imperial rule, settler control and indigenous resistance.

The three dates noted earlier (1917, 1947, 1967) are used to divide the discussion into periods which saw radical changes in the physical and political configuration of intergroup relations. The focus here is on the discourse and terms of debate rather than on practical on-the-ground political campaigns and organizational structures.

THE BRITISH MANDATE PERIOD

Palestinian-Arab Nationalism

One of the early exchanges about the positioning of Palestine within the broader imperial system, addressing the political relations between different groups in the country, is found in correspondence between the British Secretary of State for the Colonies (Winston Churchill) and the visiting Palestine Arab Delegation. The Delegation arrived in Britain in 1922 to contest the terms of the Mandate for Palestine. Speaking as 'representatives of the Arab People of Palestine', it called on the British government to abandon the Balfour Declaration and change its course: 'revise their present policy in Palestine, end the Zionist *condominium,* put a stop to all alien immigration and grant the People of Palestine . . . Executive and Legislative powers'. Failing to do that would mean British policy would be used rather 'to smother their [Palestinian Arabs] national life under a flood of alien immigration'. Only the creation of 'a national independent Government' would 'command the respect of the inhabitants and guarantee peace and prosperity to all'.[1]

In response, Churchill rejected the Delegation's claims to represent 'the whole or part of the people of Palestine', and asserted that the government had 'no intention of repudiating the obligations into which they have entered towards the Jewish people.' This meant that 'the creation at this stage of a national Government would preclude the fulfilment of the pledge made by the British government to the Jewish people.' Churchill acknowledged that 'the non-Jewish population of Palestine are entitled to claim from the Mandatory not only assurances but adequate safeguards that the establishment of the national home, and the consequent Jewish immigration, shall not be conducted in such a manner as to prejudice their civil or religious rights.' But, he did not recognize that they constituted a group with national – not merely civil and religious – claims, or that their claims were equal in importance to the commitments made to the Zionist movement.

In countering Churchill's approach, the Delegation's main argument did not dispute Britain's overall position in the region or its imperial role. Rather, it dealt with the contradictory commitments made by the British to their Arab allies in 1915 (the Hussein-McMahon correspondence, which pledged support for Arab independence), in 1916 (the Sykes-Picot agreement, a plan to divide war spoils between Britain, France and Russia), and 1917 (the Balfour Declaration with its concessions to the Zionist movement). These were examined in light of post-war international conventions. Without going into the details, which have occupied many volumes of historical and legal analysis, it is clear that the British government secretly made conflicting promises to different parties in order to win their support for the war effort, and started worrying about resolving the inevitable mess only later on.

British attempts to assure Palestinians that Jews were not expected to make Palestine as a whole their national home, but rather merely build it *in* Palestine, were dismissed by the Delegation: 'It is an incontrovertible fact that public security in Palestine has been greatly disturbed by those Jews who have been admitted into the country from Poland and Russia, that arms are continually being smuggled in by them, and that their economic competition with the Arabs is very keen . . . nothing will safeguard their [the Arabs'] interests but the creation of a National Government'. The country witnessed

> division and tension between Arabs and Zionists increasing day by day and resulting in general retrogression. Because the immigrants dumped upon the country from different parts of the world are ignorant of the language, customs, and character of the Arabs, and enter Palestine by the might of England against the will of the people who are convinced that these have come to strangle them . . . it is not to be expected that the Arabs would bow to such a great injustice, or that the Zionists would so easily succeed in realising their dreams.

Palestinian opposition to the Jewish national home was consistent throughout the period. In particular, the Palestinian-Arab national movement rejected two of its aspects: immigration of Jews into the country and land transfer to Jewish institutions. It urged the British to ban both practices. Together with the call for a representative government, these three demands formed the core of nationalist resistance to the Mandate. As argued by Emile Ghory, secretary of the Arab Higher Committee, during his 1936 visit to Britain, 'the Arab sees that day by day he is being driven into the position of a minority, and perhaps into a situation where he could be easily ousted from the country'. The Arab Revolt that started in that year was motivated by Jewish immigration and land purchases which increased landlessness among the Palestinians rural masses. The absence of representative institutions aggravated the frustration of elites and masses alike:

> We have been appealing to the British people and the British Government for eighteen years. We have had no justice . . . The people became desperate and hopeless. They foresaw their fate, and decided on April 19th last [1936] to declare a general strike. That strike has developed into a revolution. It is not the act of terrorists or marauders or snipers: it is a revolution. It is not a revolution designed to threaten the power of Great Britain, nor to force its hand, but to ask for justice. The Arabs have been forced to choose the path they have chosen, because they would not have been heard otherwise.

Speaking in the midst of the Arab general strike – the most radical and persistent act of mass action during the period – Ghory added:

> The disturbances in Palestine are not fomented by any foreign propaganda, and they have no foreign finance [a reference to suspicions that the Axis powers were behind the Revolt]. They are not religious. Moslems and Christians are together in this. They are not racial, because we are not anti-Semitic. We have nothing against the Jews as Jews. We have lived with them on the best of terms when they were persecuted in every Christian country. And we are prepared to live with them again provided their political aims do not go any farther.[2]

It is clear from the discussion that British imperial rule was not the object of concern in itself – the Jewish national home policy was. Arab residents of Palestine might have been content with the British presence if they could have seen a clear way to eventual independence of the country as an Arab state. But, the continued growth of the organized Jewish community made the prospect increasingly remote.

Was it possible then for the Arabs to drive a wedge between the British and the Zionist movement? This would have required of Palestinians to use the British offers of limited representation in government in order to strengthen their own national institutions and thereby block the demographic growth and geographical expansion of the Jewish community. Initially, the British offered Palestinians advisory powers within the Mandate framework and the national home policy. But, by the late 1930s, faced with growing Arab resistance, they had moved to impose limitations on Jewish immigration and land purchases and to open the way for Arab majority rule and independence. The MacDonald White Paper of 1939 was an important move towards meeting Palestinian national demands. However, the Palestinian-Arab leadership, headed by Hajj Amin al-Husseini, consistently rejected the British proposals, though not without internal dissent. It seems the refusal to make any symbolic concession to the notion of a Jewish national home was seen as more important than the potential of the proposals to undermine some of the practices associated with it.

We do not know if willingness to compromise on symbols would have resulted in substantive gains for the Palestinian national movement. Going along with the British proposals of 1939 – as well as earlier less generous proposals – might have provided them with an opportunity to build up representative structures, organize on a mass scale, match their Zionist opponents' institutional capability and confront political challenges from a solid basis. In retrospect, it is striking how Israel was established on the foundations of the 'state within a state' created during the Mandate period, while Palestinians were unable to mobilize in a similar manner. There were several reasons for this gap between the two communities, and failure to take advantage of political opportunities due to dogmatism most likely was one of them.[3]

With the outbreak of the Second World War, the prospect of political independence for the country was suspended, though the Zionist movement adopted for the first time the goal of statehood as its official position in 1942. By the end of the war, much of international opinion had switched to support that position, in large part due to the Holocaust and the resulting large number of Jewish displaced persons in European camps. A Jewish state was seen by many as an obvious solution to this problem. In a last ditch attempt to sway international opinion, distinguished Arab-British academic Albert Hourani outlined the case against a Jewish state in Palestine. In a presentation to the 1946 Anglo-American Committee of Enquiry he asserted 'the unalterable opposition of the Arab nation to the attempt to impose a Jewish State upon it'. Such opposition was 'based upon the unwavering conviction of unshakeable rights and a conviction of the injustice of forcing a long-settled population to accept immigrants without its consent being asked and against its known and expressed will; the injustice of turning a majority into a minority in its own country; the injustice of withholding self-government until the Zionists are in the majority and able to profit by it'.

At the same time, Hourani acknowledged that Jewish residents were there to stay and had to be accommodated as equals within an overall Arab national framework: 'the only just and practicable solution for the problem of Palestine lies in the constitution of Palestine, with the least possible delay, into a self-governing state, with its Arab majority, but with full rights for the Jewish citizens of Palestine'. He promised further that Jews would have 'full civil and political rights, control of their own communal affairs, municipal autonomy in districts in which they are mainly concentrated, the use of Hebrew as an additional official language in those districts, and an adequate share in the administration'. In other words, they would gain 'membership of the Palestinian community' which is one with an Arab character. The Arab nature of the state – an essential part of its identity – stemmed from 'two inescapable facts: the first that Palestine has an Arab indigenous population, and the second that Palestine by geography and history is an essential part of the Arab world'.[4]

While Hourani offered a reasonable balance between majority rule and minority rights, based on liberal political principles, it is doubtful that his position reflected public opinion among the majority of Arabs in the country. He was speaking as a diplomat and a British citizen rather than a popular Palestinian leader, and his attention to possible future arrangements within the framework of a joint state was unusual. He conceptualized the conflict as involving the degree of control and power wielded by the different communities – and thus as capable of being resolved through rational means. In contrast, the foremost Palestinian leader of the time, Amin al-Husseini, was far less conciliatory. He regarded the conflict from its inception as a fight between irreconcilable opposites, part of a Zionist–British conspiracy to take over Palestine and undermine Arab independence and national identity in the entire region. Unlike other colonial clashes, he argued, 'The enemies' plan concerning Palestine is based not only on colonialism; rather there are other dangerous factors – religious, national and strategic – aimed at replacing one nation with another, completely eliminating the existence of this [Arab] nation by putting an end to its nationalism, religion and history, and erasing its traces, so that it can be replaced by the other nation'.[5] Under these circumstances, it was impossible to contemplate conceding any ground to the enemy to conspire with foreign forces against the local population and the Arab world more broadly – an inevitable result of the expansionist dynamics of Zionism, in his view.

And indeed, Palestinian Arabs were displaced by Israeli forces in 1948, while those Jews already residing in the country were joined by hundreds of thousands of new immigrants from Eastern Europe and the Middle East. Their main national project became to replace Palestinians and exclude them (physically and figuratively) from the scene. The ways in which these forced population movements made the Israeli–Palestinian conflict intractable is a matter for another study, as is the extent to which the attitude displayed by al-Husseini and his colleagues became a self-fulfilling prophecy, reinforcing the dominant Zionist view of 'us or them', with no prospect of living together peacefully within the same political framework.

In any event, it is clear that there was a big gap between militant rhetoric and the limited capacity of Palestinians to put it into practice, a problem that hampered their campaigns repeatedly. A critical account written by Musa al-Alami, a respected non-partisan activist, outlined the reasons for the outcome, focusing on internal causes and differences between the two sides:

> The fundamental source of our weakness was that we were unprepared even though not taken by surprise, while the Jews were fully prepared; that we proceeded along the lines of previous revolutions, while the Jews proceeded along the lines of total war; that we worked on a local basis, without unity, without totality, without a general command, our defense disjointed and our affairs disordered, every town fighting on its own and only those in areas adjacent to the Jews entering the battle at all, while the Jews conducted the war with a unified organization, a unified command, and total conscription. Our arms were poor and deficient; the arms of the Jews were excellent and powerful. It was obvious that our aims in the battle were diverse; the aim of the Jews was solely to win it.[6]

Although al-Alami did not express that in clear conceptual terms, the crucial difference between the two communities was the self-consciously mobilized nature of the Jewish Yishuv, which emerged and grew as part of a long-term project that included national and institutional consolidation. Palestinian Arabs, in contrast, continued their lives in a more 'natural' form, and were less able to build up the organizational and political capabilities required to confront their opponents. As the majority of the population in the country, whose presence had not been challenged for many centuries – since the time of the Crusades in fact – it was difficult to instil in them the same sense of urgency that prevailed among Jewish settlers, especially acute in light of the Holocaust, which eliminated a large part of their potential resource base but allowed them to mobilize international support for their cause.

Not only was the Jewish settler community better organized than indigenous Palestinians, as could be expected, but it stood out when compared to other groups of settlers in places such as South Africa. The intensity of the transformation process, which saw Jews increasing their numbers eight times in less than 30 years, becoming a third of the population and a decisive economic and political force, is striking from a comparative perspective. The compressed nature of the process made its impact more powerful. To reach a similar position in South Africa it took settlers much longer, in a gradual and uncoordinated process that covered much larger territory. No wonder Palestinians experienced a profound shock and severe dislocation as a result. The impact of their 1948 defeat has shaped the nature of their struggle ever since.

THE POST-1948 PERIOD: FRAGMENTATION AND DISPERSAL

The 1948 war led to the destruction of Palestinian society and the dispersal of many of its members in different countries (a process known as the Nakba). Three different political arenas were created as a result, each with a distinct demographic composition and political status:

- Israel as a Jewish state, including the remnants of the Arab majority now turned into a minority and subject to various legal restrictions but with basic citizenship rights.
- The rest of Palestine, divided into two parts: the West Bank incorporated into Jordan and the Gaza Strip under Egyptian military rule. Their population included the original residents as well as refugees who were displaced from their homes in the areas that became Israel.
- The rest of the refugees, dispersed to various Arab countries and devoid of citizenship rights except for those living in Jordan.

While Palestinians retained their overall ethnic identity and continued to regard themselves as members of the same national community, of necessity their organization started reflecting the different political frameworks within which they found themselves. From 1948 onwards we cannot refer to a unified Palestinian struggle without differentiating between its diverse settings. Of most importance in this context is the need of all sections of the people to create new political structures and design new approaches, in order to address the challenges of dispersal and fragmentation and to cope with the new conditions.

Palestinians – and Arabs broadly – were affected by the events of 1948 and the need to learn their lessons and to prepare for new challenges. An important role in this process of reflection was played by a book written in the midst of the war by the Syrian historian Constantine Zurayq. The book's title, *The Meaning of the Nakba*, was the first time the term was used for the 1948 defeat, and it caught on as the standard term for it.[7]

Zurayq bemoaned the absence of national unity, dedicated leadership, public commitment and willingness to sacrifice all for the sake of victory. The remedy, in his view, consisted first of all in heightening the sense of danger represented by Zionism, worse than imperialism or neo-colonial domination. The latter were a temporary evil, while Zionism was 'the greatest danger to the being of the Arabs', threatening 'the very center of Arab being, its entirety, the foundation of its existence'. All media resources needed to 'intensify in the souls of all Arabs an awareness of the danger . . . so that every thought which we have and every action which we perform will be influenced by this feeling', reinforcing the will to struggle as that 'of one ready to die'.[8]

In addition to such psychological preparation, there was a need for mobilization of military and economic resources, increased efforts to unify the Arabs politically, and gain diplomatic support, and involve the popular masses in the process, all in readiness for 'total war, not confined to troops in the field of battle, but involving all the people; not content with some of the resources of the nation, but demanding the mobilization of all of them in their totality'. If such mobilization forced the Arabs to halt projects for reform and hamper 'building up our countries internally', and it resulted in using up resources meant for public works, education and agriculture, 'in fact all the income of the Arab states – above the minimum necessary for living – so be it!'. Nothing was of any value if the Zionists won and were allowed to 'sink their fangs into the body of the Arab nation'.[9]

The way forward then, according to Zurayq, was for the Arabs to match the success of the Zionists by using their example and adopting progressive, modern, scientific, technologically advanced, committed, participatory and united attitude towards the national struggle. The extent to which these ideas served as a basis for Arab and Palestinian nationalist mobilization in the post-1948 period will be explored in the following sections. It is important to look at Zurayq's contribution on both of its contradictory aspects: a call for modernization and against tribalism, dynastic rule and religious prejudices on the one hand, and a call for militarization and sacrifice of development for the sake of nationalist gains on the other.

The 'Internal' Palestinians

The smallest part of the Palestinian-Arab people remained within Israeli state boundaries, approximately 15 per cent of the total population of Palestinians and a similar proportion of the Israeli population. Left after the war bereft of leadership – most officials of the national movement had fled the country before or were expelled during the war – it lived through the first decade of statehood in a survival mode, seeking to safeguard its existence and avoid expulsion. Initially, its electoral representation consisted largely of government-sponsored lists of 'notables' who did not challenge the discriminatory and oppressive policies to which Palestinians were subjected.[10]

The only legal expression of protest politics was through the Israeli Communist Party (Maki). Former leading members of the NLL – Emile Touma, Tawfiq Tubi, Emile Habibi – joined the Party and made it a prominent voice for the concerns of Palestinian citizens. They could play that role in Israel because Maki never identified as an Arab nationalist party: the majority of leaders and members were Jews, though the proportion of Arabs increased over the years to become a majority by the mid-1960s. Even then the Party retained a Jewish–Arab identity and never considered itself as part of an Arab national movement. It did not openly challenge the notion of Israel as a Jewish state nor did it offer a radical conceptualization of the relations between different groups, although it called for equality to all citizens. It raised the social and civil concerns of Palestinians, and bravely confronted the regime on their behalf, but it worked more to reform the ideological and political system than to transform it (a task that was far beyond its capacity in any event). This caused tensions between Maki and other dissident forces.

Arab regimes and nationalist movements in Palestine and elsewhere in the Middle East suffered a humiliating defeat in 1948. For at least a decade after that the shockwaves of the defeat were still felt, leading to a series of military coups and popular uprisings, and shaping the contours of politics in the region for decades to come. Palestinians were affected in a differentiated manner, depending on their geographical and political position. The one factor uniting all of them in the region was the rise of a new strand of Arab nationalism associated with the leadership of Egypt's president Gamal Abd al-Nasser. The manifestation of this regional movement within Israel emerged in the second half of the 1950s, independently of the Communist Party and at times in opposition to it. It became consolidated as the *al-Ard* (The Land) movement.

While Maki had to reconcile the global Soviet policy imperatives with the local concerns of its constituencies, Arab nationalists could pursue the ideal of Arab unity in a single-minded manner, as the key to the liberation of Palestine. Opposition to Western attempts to form military alliances with friendly Arab regimes – especially the Baghdad Pact of the mid-late 1950s – provided a common political denominator for pro-Soviet and Arab nationalist forces in the region. This proved a short-lived affair, however. The growing influence of Nasserism, with its quest for national unity under Egyptian hegemony, led to the formation of the United Arab Republic (UAR) in 1958 as a result of a merger between Egypt and Syria. Attempts to extend the union to Iraq under a new government led by General Abd al-Karim Qassem were not successful. Restrictions on the activities of the Communist Party in the UAR contrasted with the openness of the new Iraqi regime to the local Communist Party, and gave rise to conflict on a regional scale that affected Palestinian politics as well.

Nationalist activists cooperated with Maki to create a broad Popular Front (initially named the Arab Front) in order to defend Palestinian citizens' rights. They agreed on a programme of demands that included return of internal refugees to their villages, putting a stop to land confiscation and returning land to its original owners, abolition of the military government, equality of rights and end to official discrimination, making Arabic an official language, and acknowledging the right of return of external refugees. However, the Front split in 1959 when the nationalists left to form a new movement.[11]

Operating under the name of al-Ard, the movement aimed to provide an undiluted voice for Palestinians in Israel and assert their links to the rest of the Palestinian people and the Arab nation. It saw the solution to the Palestinian issue within the framework of broader Arab unity, under Nasser's leadership. Like the Communist Party it called for civil equality, return of or compensation for refugees, and Palestinian self-determination, and there was little to tell them apart in this respect. But, it operated without relying on internal Jewish or external Soviet support. This independence from any source of 'legitimate' authority (from the Israeli state's point of view) doomed its chances to work legally and grow as a party competing with Maki for the support of Palestinian citizens. The intense repression it faced from state agencies forced it to close down its operations but its legacy continued to inspire younger activists.

Although the movement published little by way of programmatic guidelines, two documents allow us to identify its key positions: a memorandum to the Secretary-General of the UN and a submission to the High Court of Justice, appealing the state's decision to prohibit its registration. The UN 1964 letter asserted that 'the Arabs in Israel are part of the Palestinian Arabs who are an integral part of the Whole Arab nation'. They demanded 'total equality for all citizens' and an 'end to discrimination and oppression', within the context of the UN Palestine partition resolution of 1947. Israel was called to adopt 'a policy of non-alignment, positive neutralism and peaceful coexistence' within the

region, and to recognize the Arab national movement and its quest for
unity and socialism as 'the most progressive and reliable force on which
the future of the region depends'.

Two issues were of specific concern: the systematic campaign of
land expropriation, which led to Arab villages losing the bulk of their
possessions, and the policy of political oppression – directed at activists
as well as the general population – which made it difficult for people to
organize and fight for their rights. Military rule and the use of Emergency
Regulations (a relic from British times) were particularly harmful. The UN
was called upon to intervene, since neither the legal system nor Jewish
public opinion and the mainstream press offered assistance in fighting
inequalities of that nature. This was needed because 'The authorities
are waging an uncomparable mean and violent campaign of terror,
persecution and discrimination against the Arabs who are, in spite of all
false allegations, the first legitimate owners of the country'.[12]

In its articles of association, al-Ard's key goal was

> To find a just solution for the Palestine question, considering it a whole
> and indivisible unit, in accordance with the wishes of the Palestinian
> Arab people; a solution which meets its interests and desires, restores it
> to its political existence, ensures its full legal rights, and regards it as the
> first possessor of the right to decide its own fate for itself, within the
> framework of the supreme wishes of the Arab nation.[13]

Other goals included support for liberation, unity and socialism in the
Arab world, and support for all progressive anti-imperialist movements in
the world, and the oppressed peoples fighting for their liberation.

Looking at these goals, the High Court rejected the appeal against
the State's refusal to register al-Ard as an association. It ruled that the
movement's goals amounted to opposition not only to government
policies but also to the mere existence of the State of Israel and the Jewish
national presence in it. The Court argued that national minorities had a
right to equality, and to maintain cultural and ethnic identification with the
broader Arab world. But, the insistence that a solution had to realize the
wishes of Palestinians as the sole group with the right to determine their
own fate and the future of the country was code for denying the rights of
the Israeli state and its Jewish population. In addition, the Court claimed,
Arab national unity and socialism were another code for support for the
Nasser-led Arab national movement denying Israel's existence. In other
words, in the Court's view, both the local and regional meanings of the

movement's programme were a disguise for its wish to destroy the state rather than change its regime.[14]

It must be recognized that the positions of al-Ard were indeed ambiguous regarding the core issues of the Israeli–Palestinian conflict. It chose a legal course of action, shunned violence and sought to operate through the established political channels. At the same time, it challenged the foundations of the Israeli state ethos and its dominant Jewish identity. It aligned itself in an unqualified manner with regional Arab nationalism and local Palestinian-Arab identity and, unlike Maki, made no attempt to dilute these with talk about class or other possible bases of commonality with Jewish groups. Its aim was to uplift a specific segment of the population, an oppressed minority that was part of a large regional majority and itself had been part of a local majority before 1948. There was little possibility of a meaningful Jewish–Arab front at that time, before Palestinians re-established their identity and organization on an independent basis. In our terms, it was premature to form an anti-apartheid perspective due to the prior imperative of resurrecting the political existence of Palestinians from the passivity and despair into which they had been thrown as a result of the 1948 defeat.

To understand all this we must consider the historical context. In contrast to the national leadership during the pre-1948 Mandate period, al-Ard operated from a position of weakness and marginality, acting as a voice for a community constantly under threat. Although Palestinian citizens survived the Nakba by staying put in their communities, they knew their status was not secure, and that elements of the Israeli political and security establishment wanted to subject them to intensified oppression, bordering on the expulsion of 'subversive' elements. They were cautious to avoid arrest and other forms of harassment by state agencies, and the 1956 massacre of dozens of civilians in Kafr Qassem was probably still fresh on their minds. Their approach was defensive in nature; they realized they stood no chance against state power on their own. The rest of the Palestinian people were recovering still from the 1948 defeat and the only force that could potentially come to their help – the Arab national movement – was beyond the borders, not in a position to intervene directly in Israeli affairs.

The 'External' Palestinians

Arab nationalism was the dominant political trend also among other segments of the Palestinian people, refugees and residents of the West

Bank and Gaza. They did not wait for Nasser to raise the banner of the movement. In fact, the most important organization – like al-Ard, more for its legacy than for its concrete achievements – was the Arab Nationalists Movement (ANM, *al-Qawmiyyun al-Arab*). Formed by students at the American University of Beirut in the early 1950s, inspired by Zurayq's teachings, it aimed to create a revolutionary alternative to the parochial movements that failed to defend their people against Zionism and liberate them from Western domination. It was pan-Arab in composition and orientation but, not surprisingly, Palestinians played an important role in it: as stateless activists they found it easy to identify with a movement that organized across states and national boundaries.

The activists most associated with the movement were George Habash and Wadi' Haddad, Palestinians who found themselves in exile after 1948. Particularly in Lebanon and Jordan, the movement enjoyed substantial support from refugees, appealing to them with its focus on return and vengeance. But, although the liberation of Palestine was the main concern of its founders, they focused more on the broad Arab scene: they regarded Arab unity and independence from foreign rule as a precondition for waging a successful campaign against Israel. In the words of Haddad: 'The way to Tel Aviv is through Damascus, Baghdad, Amman, and Cairo'.[15]

Initially, in the early to mid-1950s the ANM repeated themes to be found in Amin al-Husseini's rhetoric. The cause of conflict was defined as 'the constant aspiration of the Jews to conquer Palestine and establish their own government', representing 'a danger equivalent to absolute extermination', which 'will not stop within its present borders but will fight a fierce battle against our people'. Although imperialism was clearly a problem in the region, the main danger was the Jewish political movement, which enjoyed the support of many countries and the wealth and resources of International Judaism. To fight it effectively, the problems that caused the 1948 defeat had to be overcome: 'the deterioration and corruption of our national conditions, represented in the fragmentation of the homeland, the dominance of imperialism and its allies, the weakness and disintegration of our social existence, and the predominance of the reactionary conceptions among Arab individuals.'[16]

Subsequently the movement became involved deeply in the question of Arab unity, expressed through merger attempts between different countries, and the question of Palestine receded to the background. At the same time, an internal debate started pushing it to the left, leading to a new emphasis on social issues:

The age in which the movement of Arab nationalism was separated from the progressive social revolution has ended . . . There is no longer a political national question standing separately and posing against a specific social question called 'the workers question' or 'the peasants question'; or 'the question of social progress'. The Arab question has come to mean an overall revolutionary concept which is the melting-pot of the national, political, economic and social ambitions of the progressive Arab masses.[17]

The debate was not directly related to the Palestinian struggle, but it was the beginning of greater concern with global issues within Arab activist circles, heralding the rise of a political trend that saw links between local, regional and international struggles.

By the mid-1960s, a renewed focus on Palestine had become evident, although it was seen, as before, within a broader regional context: 'Our struggle for Palestine is at the very heart of our struggle for the realization of the [Arab nation's] objectives: unity, liberation, socialism, and the redemption of Palestine.'[18] Yezid Sayigh characterises this approach by saying 'Palestine was now the means, Arab unity the end', but as it turned out, Palestine increasingly became prominent as an end in itself while Arab unity faced irreversible decline. It is no coincidence, of course, that the ANM's shift towards Palestine came at the same time that al-Ard intensified its activities inside Israel, the Palestine Liberation Organization (PLO) was established by the Arab League and *Fatah* launched its first military operations, all in the early to mid-1960s.

The generation of 'The Children of the Nakba' came of age in those years, having recovered from the defeat of its elders and rediscovered Palestinian local patriotism embedded within pan-Arab nationalism. Different organizational forms manifested themselves in its various arenas, all sharing an assertion of an overall Palestinian-Arab identity, a rejection of Zionism (usually without distinguishing it clearly from Judaism), and a focus on mass mobilization as essential to the restoration of the homeland. All this was accompanied by new analyses of Israel as a colonial phenomenon.

The establishment of the PLO in 1964 symbolized these concerns. Although it was part of an initiative from above, driven by Egypt as a leader of the Arab League, it reflected a growing demand by Palestinians in the West Bank and Gaza, and the Arab Diaspora, to take charge of their own affairs and embark on a struggle to reclaim their rights. Even forces sceptical of the Arab states and their power politics saw in the event an opportunity to galvanize the masses, and gain support for the Palestinian cause in the region and globally.

The founding document of the PLO, the Palestinian National Charter, outlined the consensus existing at the time in the Arab world. It spoke in the name of the 'the Palestinian Arab people', who struggled against 'the forces of international Zionism and colonialism', which sought to 'conspire and worked to displace it, dispossess it from its homeland and property'. The principles guiding the Organization were that 'Palestine is an Arab homeland bound by strong Arab national ties to the rest of the Arab Countries and which together form the great Arab homeland', and that it was an 'indivisible territorial unit'. The Palestinian Arab people had 'the legitimate right to its homeland and is an inseparable part of the Arab Nation'. It would determine its country's destiny 'when it completes the liberation of its homeland in accordance with its own wishes and free will and choice'.[19]

The Palestinians were 'those Arab citizens who were living normally in Palestine up to 1947, whether they remained or were expelled'. There was a place for 'Jews of Palestinian origin', if they were 'willing to live peacefully and loyally in Palestine'. While the Palestinian people firmly believed in Arab unity, 'in order to play its role in realizing this goal, it must, at this stage of its struggle, preserve its Palestinian personality and all its constituents. It must strengthen the consciousness of its existence and stance and stand against any attempt or plan that may weaken or disintegrate its personality'. Arab unity and the liberation of Palestine were 'two complementary goals; each prepares for the attainment of the other. Arab unity leads to the liberation of Palestine, and the liberation of Palestine leads to Arab unity. Working for both must go side by side'.

The rejection of Zionism had to be total since it was

> a colonialist movement in its inception, aggressive and expansionist in its goal, racist in its configurations, and fascist in its means and aims. Israel, in its capacity as the spearhead of this destructive movement and as the pillar of colonialism, is a permanent source of tension and turmoil in the Middle East, in particular, and to the international community in general. Because of this, the people of Palestine are worthy of the support and sustenance of the community of nations.

There can be no doubt that this was a document thoroughly steeped in nationalism, undiluted by any class or social concerns, and asserting Palestinian and Arab exclusive rights to the country and region. The

Charter did not approach the issue from a potentially universal recognition of individual rights but from the standpoint of a national group denied and dispossessed of its particular historical rights, and now seeking to restore them. The contrast with the guiding principle of the Freedom Charter, adopted by the 1955 Congress of the People – 'South Africa belongs to all who live it, Black and White' – is striking.

The Palestinian Charter rejected explicitly the notion of common ownership of the country, and protagonists were defined only in collective terms – 'the People', 'the Nation', seen as entities moving through history in an unchanged form – rather than as people who may be clustered into groups but derive their rights as individuals. Of course, such discourse is common to all nationalist movements; it is the non-racial South African anti-apartheid movement rather that stands out in this respect. Palestinian-Arab nationalism was not unique in giving priority to the nation as a collective actor, but its attempt to regain a country from which the majority of its adherents had been physically excluded was indeed very unusual.

Precisely this distinct feature of the Palestine issue was addressed in a landmark study in the following year, Fayez Sayegh's *Zionist Colonialism in Palestine*, perhaps the first serious scholarly discussion of Zionism from a Palestinian perspective: 'Though they have openly disdained the "natives", ruthlessly suppressed them, and methodically discriminated against them, European colonists have as a rule deemed the continued presence of the indigenous populations "useful" for the colonists themselves; and, as such, they have reserved for the "natives" all the menial functions and assigned to them inferior roles in the settler-dominated societies.' Jewish settlers in Palestine 'have found it necessary to follow a different course, more in harmony with their ideological system', a course followed 'nowhere in Asia or Africa – not even in South Africa or Rhodesia'.

As long as they were 'powerless to *dislodge* the indigenous Arabs of Palestine (the vast majority of the country's population)', settlers focused on '*isolating themselves* from the Arab community and instituting a systematic boycott of Arab produce and labor'. But, '*boycotting* the Arabs of Palestine instead of *evicting* them from their country was, however, only a tactical and temporary suspension of the Zionist dogma'. The aim remained evicting Arabs from Palestine to enable 'the incarnation of the principle of racial exclusiveness'. This was put into effect with the 'racial elimination' of 1948 (the Nakba). The remnants of Palestine's Arabs under Israeli rule were subjected to racial discrimination 'of the kind already made famous by other racist European colonists elsewhere in Asia and Africa'.[20]

The eviction of the bulk of the indigenous population in 1948 was the unique predicament of Palestinians and it shaped their strategy ever since. It was responsible for their reliance on the Arab world, as a territorial and logistical resource, and for their adherence to pan-Arab nationalism. With Nasserism on the ascendancy, in the 1950s and early 1960s, it was possible to hope that a powerful Arab front could challenge Israel from a position of strength. But, the collapse of the UAR in 1961, and subsequent intra-regional clashes, forced a rethink of that strategy. Nasser's reluctance to confront Israel militarily before the Arabs were ready, made many young Palestinian activists feel they had to take the initiative themselves. Discussions in the Arab League over the issue of a Palestinian Entity seemed a lip service to the goal of liberation, and an attempt to exploit the plight of Palestinians to further narrow Arab political interests. Even the creation of the PLO was seen in large part as manipulation by Arab states. As Abu Iyad claimed in 1969, 'the purpose of the Organisation was to absorb the discontent which had begun to permeate all sections of the Palestinian people and to give expression to the Palestinian people's unrest and its determination to build a Palestinian national revolutionary movement . . . at first an attempt to circumvent this true revolutionary unrest'.[21]

Against this background emerged the most important movement of the period: Fatah – the Palestinian National Liberation Movement (which was not part of the PLO at the time).[22] What made Fatah distinct were three principles:

- First, its single-minded focus on Palestine. Arab unity, socialism, Islam, class struggle, and other issues were of interest only to the extent that they served the Palestinian cause.
- Second, its aim to mobilize the Palestinian masses and involve them directly in the process of their own liberation. In this sense it was different from the PLO, which was primarily a diplomatic structure within the Arab state system, and the ANM which was self-consciously an elitist organization. Fatah was particularly concerned not to let Arab regimes manipulate the Palestine issue to serve their own goals.
- Third, it advocated armed struggle as its core strategy, the only way to liberate the country, drawing primarily on the Algerian, Vietnamese and Cuban examples.

In all these respects Fatah put forward a new approach that quickly gained ground and eventually became the dominant force in the national movement. It appealed to Palestinians to take control of their own affairs: the movement must 'originate directly with Palestinians and not be linked to any particular Arab country . . . it must be a comprehensive movement that would start operating from all Arab countries simultaneously in order to engage the enemy on all fronts'. It was interested in practical activities, not empty rhetoric, because 'the Palestinian people no longer believe in talk and speeches. All they want is to see action'.[23]

And action had to be radical: 'The only way to regain the robbed homeland is an organized revolutionary movement, unaffiliated, a movement that flows from the heart of the Palestinian people, that will spring from all the territories surrounding the occupied land simultaneously.' It aimed to realize one goal: 'For us, the Arabs of Palestine, this is the primary goal above all others. Every revolutionary group in the Arab homeland must recognize the revolutionary significance of the willingness of the Arabs of Palestine to stand at the forefront of the Arab struggle for the liberation of their homeland.' In their actions, the Palestinian vanguard would open the way to liberation and unity of all Arabs.[24]

The model for the struggle was regional as well as global:

Revolutions all over the world are inspiring us. The revolution in Algeria lights our way like a bright torch of hope. When the Algerians took up their revolution in 1954, they were only some hundred Arabs facing 20,000 French troops and well-armed settlers . . . The revolution in Algeria proved to us that a people can organize itself and build its military strength in the very process of fighting.[25]

Frequent references to Cuba and Vietnam appeared in Fatah's publications, as it saw itself as a militant alternative to the PLO's sedate style of action, which was coupled with bombastic rhetoric (for which its leader – Ahmad Shuqeiri – was notorious). Having opened an office in Algiers in 1962, Fatah used it to establish links with other liberation movements and militants, such as the Vietcong, Che Guevara, and the forces fighting Portuguese colonialism in Africa.[26]

The specific question of how the Algerian example could help in dealing with the question of settlers was not raised at the time. In his classical study of Israel as a colonial state, written just before the 1967 war, French Author Maxime Rodinson argued that 'the colonial origins of the Algerian *Pieds Noirs* did not prevent the FLN from recognizing their rights'. They were not expelled but left the country because of their refusal to adapt. And, 'no one speaks of chasing the whites out of South Africa because of their colonial origins. They are asked simply to coexist with the Blacks as equals'.[27]

How this attitude applied in the Israeli case was a question not answered by Fatah. Like all Palestinian organizations it did not follow the course taken by the ANC in South Africa, making a distinction between the apartheid regime, seen as the enemy, and the settler population, some of which members were allies in the struggle against the regime. As Nelson Mandela said in 1964:

> Above all, we want equal political rights, because without them our disabilities will be permanent . . . It is not true that the enfranchisement of all will result in racial domination. Political division, based on colour, is entirely artificial and, when it disappears, so will the domination of one colour group by another. The ANC has spent half a century fighting against racialism. When it triumphs it will not change that policy.[28]

Rodinson pointed out that 'the relations between the Israelis and the Arabs have in fact been less relations of exploitation than of domination', but that fact did not diminish their colonial character. This raised a crucial issue, which had little to do with theoretical definitions of colonialism. When indigenous people were not exploited by settlers, they became redundant, and therefore targets for dispossession and dislocation. Palestinians in 1948 were displaced from their homes and replaced by new Jewish immigrants. This situation gave rise to two strategic questions: how would Palestinians gain re-entry into the territory from which they had been physically excluded, and how they would deal with the people who took their place. These questions became even more critical in the period opened in June 1967.

THE POST-1967 PERIOD: RESISTANCE, OCCUPATION AND CIVIC STRUGGLE

The June 1967 war was a turning point in more ways than one: it created Greater Israel, which has retained its boundaries to this day. It re-unified Palestinian citizens of Israel with residents of the West Bank and Gaza, but subjected them to different legal systems with the latter living under military occupation. It separated the refugees in Arab countries from their counterparts remaining within the pre-1948 boundaries. It dealt a death blow to Nasserist Arab nationalism, which was proven unable to follow up on its stated ideological commitments with action in the battlefield and, at the same time, gave rise to a new wave of armed opposition to Israel in the shape of a large number of Palestinian resistance organizations. Following in the footsteps of Fatah, these organizations gained mass support as a fresh and viable alternative to the incompetent and corrupt Arab regimes. Within a few months they managed to take over the PLO leadership.

It seemed that once again – as in 1948 – a huge gap opened up between the verbal threats and promises made by the Arab regimes and their actual capacity to act upon them. Particularly notorious in this respect was the PLO leader, Ahmad Shuqeiri, blamed by many including Palestinian activists for playing a major role in the defeat of 1967 (termed Naksa – setback – as opposed to the 1948 Nakba). In a series of interviews, speeches and press conferences, Shuqeiri used fiery rhetoric, bordering on threats of genocide against Jews in Israel, which helped mobilize international public opinion on the side of Israel and legitimize its military actions. Voice of the Arabs, an Egyptian state radio station, played a similar role, inciting for war and celebrating imaginary victories in the battlefield.

As the Syrian poet Nizar Qabbani put it in his celebrated poem written in the immediate aftermath of the war, 'Footnotes on the Book of the Naksa':

> Stirred
> By Oriental bombast,
> By Antartic swaggering that never killed a fly,
> By the fiddle and the drum,
> We went to war
> And lost.

> Our shouting is louder than our actions,
> Our swords are taller than us,
> This is our tragedy.

> In short
> We wear the cape of civilization
> But our souls live in the stone age.

> You don't win a war
> With a reed and a flute.

> Our impatience
> Cost us fifty thousand new tents.[29]

The wave of self-reflection that opened up after the war included an essay by Constantine Zurayq titled 'The Meaning of the Nakba Revisited', in which he reasserted the need to adopt modern civilization, forge internal unity and increase the role of science and education, as well as enhance democracy and freedom of expression – at the expense of blind obedience to authority and religion – as the basis for a national revival. He highlighted the morale and fighting spirit of the Algerians and Vietnamese people that allowed them to overcome their military and technological inferiority and win against far more powerful colonial forces. A similar kind of popular war could defeat the Israeli enemy, he argued, but for that the focus of struggle had to shift back from Arab regimes to the Palestinian masses themselves. Accurate and detailed knowledge of Israel was essential, to avoid moving constantly between the two self-defeating extremes of Arab propaganda: dismissal of its capacity as an artificial entity and exaggeration of its world power and influence to the point that it seems invincible.[30]

Perhaps of greater interest was the contribution made by another Syrian scholar, Sadik Jalal al-Azm, based in Beirut at the time, who offered a thorough critique of Arab society. Al-Azm saw a need for a radical re-evaluation that was not merely technical in nature but dealt with fundamental issues of culture, morality and politics. This included distaste for terms such as Nakba and Naksa that implied the operation of forces of nature beyond human control, and thus deflected attention from the responsibility of social and political actors. Without mincing words, he was scathing in his criticism of self-serving myths that prevented the necessary self-reflection: the notion that Israel acted in stealth, that imperialism and colonialism were to blame, that Arabs were individually brave but faced unfair challenges, that the Soviets were not helpful, that world Jewry was too powerful, that it was God's will or punishment for secularization, and so on. For him, these were excuses for failure to deal with the sources of defeat: a culture that was not modern and rational, that was unable to look at its problems critically and rely on its own resources to solve them.

Defeat in battle was due to the underlying characteristics of Arab culture: '[W]e adhered during this war to the greatest extent to the pattern of our life, a pattern that still essentially employs tradition and custom rather than dynamics, mobility, and ingenuity. Thus we entrenched ourselves in fortified positions out of fear of a mobile and fluid war.' In other words, 'we, as usual, bragged about appearance and form', but 'abandoned the kernel and core', and kept clinging to 'formalities, proprieties, appearances, and established routine'.[31] Instead, Arabs must adopt the methods of a popular war of liberation, like the Vietnamese but in a different context: the Palestinian *fedayeen* will be the vanguard, but there is need to go beyond their actions in the occupied territories and mobilize the Arab masses, and this calls for a thorough socialist transformation of Arab societies: 'The required response entails not only equipment, machines, experts, and aircraft, but also a particular kind of mentality, psychology, cultural background, and physical reactions that the industrial revolution implanted in modern man and the scientific revolution confirmed in him so that they become part of his nature.'[32]

Beyond developments in the Middle East, the war was a global event with far-reaching implications. The radical anti-Zionist Israeli organization Matzpen provided the first analysis setting the war in such a context. It identified the 1950s as a decade of progressive victories: 'Anti-imperialist forces came to power in many countries in Asia and Africa, and the direct presence of the colonial powers was considerably reduced in these continents. The forces of imperialism were retreating.' In the Middle East, this was reflected in the outcome of the Suez war of 1956, the rise of Nasser to global prominence and the retreat of European colonial powers. However, the 1960s witnessed a backlash: 'American imperialism became a "world gendarme"; in many countries reactionary coups d'etat took place – inspired, instigated and financed by the United States Central Intelligence Agency – which succeeded in overthrowing anti-imperialist governments.' Recent and ongoing attempts to replace anti-imperialist regimes took place in Congo, Cuba, Vietnam, the Dominican Republic, and so on. As a part of its 'global offensive', the US tried to overthrow the left-wing Ba'ath regime in Syria, and Israel went along with it for its own interests. Nasser fell into a trap of defending Syria and found himself pulled, against his better judgement, into a war for which Egypt was ill-prepared. The result was a massive defeat and a great victory for the USA/Israel (though it must be recognized that the overlapping interests of the two parties were not identical).[33]

The Armed Palestinian Resistance

Few people anticipated at the time that the discrediting of Nasser, the Arab regimes and Shuqeiri would open the way to new modes of resistance, locally as well as globally. The right-wing backlash against liberation forces, which included growing repression in South Africa, with thousands of anti-apartheid activists imprisoned or driven underground and into exile, achieved success but unleashed a counter-backlash of its own. The mid-to late 1960s witnessed the rise of the New Left and student rebellions worldwide, campaigns in opposition to the US war in Vietnam, the rise of the Third World as a force challenging Western hegemony, and intensification of the struggle for racial equality in the West and against authoritarian regimes in Latin America and Eastern Europe. Both the South African anti-apartheid campaign and the Palestinian resistance fitted into this growing trend.

From a conceptual perspective, the two most important innovations introduced by Palestinians in the post-1967 period, somewhat in contradiction with one another, were the assertion of the role of armed struggle and the identification of a new goal for the movement, that of a secular democratic state that would grant equal rights to all its citizens, Muslims, Christians and Jews.

The revised Palestinian National Charter, adopted by the PLO in 1968, after it had been taken over by the resistance organizations, introduced a new notion: 'Armed struggle is the only way to liberate Palestine. Thus it is the overall strategy, not merely a tactical phase. The Palestinian Arab people assert their absolute determination and firm resolution to continue their armed struggle and to work for an armed popular revolution for the liberation of their country and their return to it.' Resistance organizations (also referred to as commandos or *fedayeen*) called for a popular liberation war, which required 'escalation, comprehensiveness, and the mobilization of all the Palestinian popular and educational efforts and their organization and involvement in the armed Palestinian revolution'.[34] In this move, reflecting realities on the ground, the PLO aligned itself conceptually with other armed liberation struggles, Algeria and Vietnam above all. How to implement the strategy under geographical, demographic and social conditions that were very different from those other struggles remained an unresolved question and a challenge never met successfully.

The second innovation was perhaps even more important potentially. It opened the way to a re-conceptualization of the goal of the struggle and its agents. For the first time in its history the Palestinian movement recognized Jews residing in the country as legitimate members of the national community. That the definition regarded local Jews in religious terms rather than as a separate national group made it unappealing to Israeli Jews. Still, it was an important development that brought the Palestinian struggle closer to the anti-apartheid movement.

At the same time, there were lingering ambiguities that marred the prospect of change. A Fatah document, *Towards a Democratic State in Palestine*, from September 1970, maintained that 'All the Jews, Moslems and Christians living in Palestine or forcibly exiled from it will have the right to Palestinian citizenship'. This applies to all Israelis, 'provided, of course, that they reject Zionist racist chauvinism and fully agree to live as Palestinians in the new Palestine'. In support of this position, senior leader Abu Iyad was quoted to the effect that 'not only progressive anti-Zionist Jews but even present Zionists willing to abandon their racist ideology will be welcome as Palestinian citizens'.[35]

Setting ideological criteria for citizenship, especially under conditions in which 99 per cent of the target population would fail, was not an encouraging sign, and neither was the statement that 'the process of the revolution will inevitably increase the tempo of [Jewish] emigration, especially of those beneficiaries of a racist state who will find it very difficult to adapt to an open, plural society'.[36] Even if the statement were meant merely as a prediction, it was likely to serve as a self-fulfilling prophecy. We must recognize though, that this was the beginning of a shift that had been unthinkable for Arab opinion only a couple of years earlier. Fatah attributed the legitimacy of this new approach to the credibility it had gained from its armed struggle, which shielded it from criticism for being too conciliatory towards Israelis: 'Had this approach been made before *Fateh* had resorted to arms it would have been received under the then existing circumstances of recession by a strong attack from Arab opinion in general and Palestinian opinion in particular. Thus, this strategic approach has been made possible by the force of *Fateh* as a national liberation movement and political and military strength'.[37] Still, the expectation that if only Israeli Jews – especially those of Arab cultural origins – were offered the option of living as equals in a re-born Palestine, they would abandon Zionism, and sever the supposedly artificial bonds between Jews of different origins, was delusional.[38]

After Fatah, the biggest Palestinian organization was the Popular Front for the Liberation of Palestine (PFLP), a successor organization to the Arab Nationalists Movement. Its founding document asserted that 'the revolutionary masses must take their responsible leadership role in confronting the forces and weapons of imperialism and Zionism, which history has proved is the most effective weapon to crush all forms of colonial aggression and to give the initiative to the popular masses to formulate the future according to their will and interests'. The armed resistance was 'the only effective method that must be used by the popular masses in dealing with the Zionist enemy and all of its interests and its presence'.

Palestinian resistance was the vanguard of the 'Arab front', and the 'Palestinian fighting masses on the occupied land are actors of the Arab revolutionary march against imperialism and its proxy forces'. There was an 'organic link between the struggle of the Palestinian people and the struggle of the masses of the Arab people', as well as 'the struggle of the forces of revolution and progress in the world'. Imperialism and Zionism were linked to forces of reaction. To confront them there was a need for a 'coalition including all the forces of anti-imperialism in every part of the world'.[39]

In a more analytical mode, the PFLP developed a strategy aimed at confronting the 'organic unity between Israel and the Zionist movement on the one hand and world imperialism on the other'.[40] This could be done by 'the Palestinian revolution which is fused together with the Arab revolution and in alliance with world revolution is alone capable of achieving victory'. This strategy of 'the democratic national revolution in this age has become clear through the Vietnamese experience and before it the Cuban and Chinese experience'. It relied on 'armed struggle to overcome the enemy's technological superiority through a protracted war commencing with guerrilla warfare and developing into a popular liberation war'. This did not simply mean copying the Vietnamese strategy, due to 'the special nature of our battle both in respect of the nature of imperialist presence, represented by Israel, in our homeland, and in respect of the special nature of the land'. How these special conditions would affect the required strategy was not outlined clearly, however.

Similarly, the need for 'full alliance with all revolutionary forces on the world level', to create a 'camp whereby we and all enslaved and anti-imperialist forces will be able to find the force which is capable of defeating imperialism', was asserted in the programme. But, this was done without providing details on how such a venture, involving 'the liberation movement in Vietnam, the revolutionary situation in Cuba and the Democratic People's Republic of Korea and the national liberation movements in Asia, Africa and Latin America', could be put into practice. Supply of weapons and training by China and the Soviet Union was a concrete form of military support, but the rest remained obscure. No specific mention of South Africa and the struggle against apartheid was made in that context.

The PFLP opposed Zionism, 'as an aggressive racial movement connected with imperialism which has exploited the sufferings of the Jews as a stepping stone for the promotion of its interests and the interests of imperialism'. The Front's aim was 'to establish a democratic national state in Palestine in which both Arabs and Jews will live as citizens with equal rights and obligations and which will constitute an integral part of the progressive democratic Arab national presence living peacefully with all forces of progress in the world'. Consequently, a basic strategic line 'must aim at unveiling this misrepresentation, addressing the exploited and misled Jewish masses and revealing the conflict between these masses' interest in living peacefully and the interests of the Zionist movement'. With the growth of armed struggle this would ensure 'the widening of the conflict existing objectively between Israel and the Zionist movement on the one hand and the millions of misled and exploited Jews on the other'.

Similarly to Abu Iyad, the PFLP anticipated that intensification of the armed struggle would open rifts within the Jewish community in Israel. In fact, the opposite was true: the choice of targets and the manner of execution of armed attacks made all Israeli Jews feel threatened and thus consolidated their opposition to the Palestinian movement instead of mitigating it. That the goal of the struggle was defined as 'the liberation of Palestine from the Israeli-Zionist presence', and its replacement by 'a progressive democratic Arab society',[41] did not help attract Israeli Jews to the promise of equal rights for all. They saw it as a thinly veiled threat to exclude them regardless of the precise language used by different organizations. There is no doubt that Palestinian attitudes towards Israeli Jews were indeed changing and becoming more positive – seen against the background of the rhetoric used by Amin al-Husseini and Ahmad Shuqeiri – but not rapidly and clearly enough to effect a change in Israeli attitudes.

The one organization that went further in challenging mainstream Arab nationalist discourse as the foundation for the Palestinian movement was the Popular Democratic Front for the Liberation of Palestine (PDFLP, later known simply as DFLP or the Democratic Front). It emerged as a left-wing dissident faction within the Popular Front, raising themes that had been debated already in the ANM. As part of the Popular Front it was responsible for the notion that 'the Vietnamese–Cuban course of action is the only course leading to victory for under-developed countries against the educational and technical superiority of imperialism and neo-colonialism'.[42] It went on to assert that 'the road to national salvation and liberation of the homeland, together with the solution of the problems of national liberation, requires forces armed with revolutionary arms. These will be capable, in under-developed countries, of defeating the advanced imperialist powers in the fields of military effort and skill'.[43]

The Democratic Front was the first to go beyond standard formulas of individual rights within an Arab national state, by advocating 'a people's democratic Palestine state in which the Arabs and (Israeli) Jews will live without any discrimination whatsoever, a state which is against all forms of class and national subjugation, and which gives both Arabs and (Israeli) Jews the right to develop their national culture'. Due to links of history and destiny, 'the people's democratic state of Palestine will be an integral part of an Arab federal state in this area. The Palestinian state will have a democratic content hostile to colonialism, imperialism, and Arab and Palestinian reaction'. This will liberate 'the Arab and the Jew from all forms of chauvinistic (racist) culture – liberating the Arab from reactionary culture, and the Jew from Zionist culture'. The state will become 'a progressive revolutionary fortress on the side of all forces in the world struggling against imperialism and counter-revolution', and 'encompass Arabs and (Israeli) Jews enjoying equal national rights and obligations – a state in the service of all the forces struggling for national liberation and progress in the world'.[44]

In evaluating the two innovations of the post-1967 period discussed above, both the progress made and the unrealized potential are important. From a fragmented mass of people subject to manipulation by Arab regimes – 'a people in itself' – Palestinians became active agents in the service of their own interests – 'a people for itself'. This was the case in particular for the refugee population in Jordan, Lebanon and Syria, which became the main constituency of the resistance movement. The armed struggle and the publicity campaign around it served to mobilize people and give them a sense of purpose. It generated enthusiasm for a model that presumably worked elsewhere – Algeria, Cuba, Vietnam – and therefore could work again.

At the same time, active participation was restricted to relatively few young men and left most of the rest of the population as supportive but largely passive spectators. The rhetoric of popular mobilization of workers and peasants did not fit with the focus on armed struggle: by definition the militants were not engaged in regular production activities, even if some of them may have come from that social background. Regardless of their own class affiliation, there was little sense in which military action was shaped by class relations, conditions or interests. In this respect there was no difference between Fatah, PFLP, DFLP and others, their different class rhetoric notwithstanding.

This was a symptom of a more fundamental problem. The Cuban campaign was waged from within Cuba itself, and mobilized peasants in support of guerrilla fighters against government forces. The militants came from the outside initially, but their potential constituency were the majority in the country. In Algeria the rebel movement was based initially outside the country but it managed to gain a foothold inside it and recruit the locals to its campaign. Again, they were the undisputed majority although they had to contend with a substantial minority of settlers backed by overseas French forces. Vietnam was similar to Cuba: the Vietcong were a local force fighting against an unpopular government backed by US foreign troops. Working in parallel with military forces from across the northern border provided strategic depth and increased the cost to the enemy. Even the anti-apartheid movement, which was directed at that period from across the borders of South Africa, was a relocated local movement, forced temporarily into exile from the early 1960s to the mid-1970s. But, once the internal front became alive, with the emergence of black trade unions and the Soweto uprising of 1976, the focus of struggle shifted back inside the country and away from the exiles and their military campaigns.

The case of Palestine was different from all these. It was not only militants and leaders in exile but the bulk of their popular constituency as well. This was not a temporary situation but a prolonged one, possibly the only case in modern history of a people fighting to liberate its country from colonial conquest, forced to operate from outside its boundaries. In the process they had to confront not an unpopular regime, a small group of settlers or overseas military forces, but a heavily-militarized and mobilized settler society, which displaced and replaced them. None of the models cited in the literature of the organizations, nor any of the theoreticians of guerrilla and anti-colonial struggle (Mao, Giap, Guevara, Fanon), experienced anything like that. The rhetoric of an 'Arab Hanoi' in Amman or Beirut, and the image of Arab forces marching behind the Palestinian revolutionary vanguard, were trendy and appealing, but did not provide a real solution to the challenge of fighting Israel from beyond its borders.[45]

When confronted with the issue, Palestinian leaders and militants could not provide a clear response. Abu Iyad argued that

> The Palestinian people are revolting under objective conditions which are different and quite distinguishable from those of any other revolution in the world. Why? Because the people is disunited socially, politically and geographically. This situation inevitably imposes new, unconventional techniques and forms of struggle. Nevertheless we do not, in the general concept, constitute an innovation among world revolutions . . . In our Palestinian revolution, we are both inside and

outside, which is normal. On the inside we are in our occupied country because we do not recognise the Zionist Israeli presence. Consequently we are in a perfectly natural situation . . . The external part of our leadership is separated from the occupied territory by a few metres . . . Our bases are located all throughout this land, and many of them are inside the occupied territory . . . Our internal and external bases provide the revolution with continued reinforcement.[46]

This account omitted the fact that it was not only the leadership but also the bulk of the cadres and popular masses supporting the struggle who were external to the territory (not in an ideological or historical sense but in practical terms, being based in neighbouring countries). Palestinians were aware of their unique condition, but it seems as if they operated on the assumption that evocative slogans and the rhetorical solidarity offered by other liberation movements could compensate for the inadequacy of the analogies they used.

The Democratic Front alone, at that stage, insisted on the need to combine armed struggle with political struggle and alliances with progressive Israeli forces. In this vein it started a dialogue with Matzpen. Although they were in agreement on a number of issues, the stumbling block was Matzpen's recognition of the right for national self-determination of Hebrew-speaking Jews, free of Zionism and integrated into a Middle East socialist federation. This principle was rejected by the Democratic Front since it did not regard Jews in Israel as a national collective, although it recognized their individual and civil rights. Subsequent shifts in the position of Israeli anti-Zionist groups, descended from Matzpen, did bring some of them closer to the Palestinian positions, however.[47]

The Struggle Against the Occupation

As noted above, the 1967 war dealt a serious blow to the Arab regimes and facilitated the rise of the Palestinian resistance movement to the forefront of the military conflict with Israel. It is ironic then, that the biggest battle of the movement was waged against Arab forces – the clash of Black September in 1970. It was triggered by growing fears of the Jordanian regime that the country was being transformed into a base for spectacular military operations – such as airplane hijackings – over which the regime had no control. The PFLP was prominent in such operations and its agenda – replacing the regime with a revolutionary state that would embark on armed action against Israel – made the situation explosive. The battle resulted in the ouster of militant Palestinian groups from Jordan and their move to Lebanon. A few years later, Arab regimes took the military initiative against Israel. Their armed forces managed to drive Israel back in October 1973, especially on the Egyptian front. The war ended with a stalemate but it restored Arab pride and the prestige of the existing regimes, an outcome that allowed them to contemplate dealing diplomatically with Israel on an equal basis.

The impact on the Palestinian movement was contradictory. On the one hand, Arab military gains and the consequent turn towards diplomacy served to marginalize the guerrilla forces that played no role in the fighting. On the other hand, Arab prestige – combined with the rising power of the Third World globally – led to a series of diplomatic victories for the PLO. In October 1974 it was recognized by the Arab League as the sole legitimate representative of the Palestinian people, and in December of that year its president, Yasser Arafat, addressed the UN General Assembly. This facilitated the diplomatic campaign that saw the UN adopting in November 1975 a resolution determining that Zionism was a form of racism and racial discrimination. A previous UN resolution from December 1973, condemning 'the unholy alliance between South African racism and Zionism', was invoked there, as well as similar statements by the Organization of African Unity and the Non-Aligned Movement.[48] These developments took place at the same time that apartheid South Africa too was coming under intense diplomatic pressure, leading to its suspension from the UN General Assembly in November 1974.

All this went along with an internal shift in the focus of struggle from the Diaspora to the Occupied Territories. In 1974 the Palestine National Council resolved that the PLO 'will employ all means, and first and foremost armed struggle, to liberate Palestinian territory and to establish the independent combatant national authority for the people over every part of Palestinian territory that is liberated'. But, this was not to be at the price of 'recognition, peace, secure frontiers, renunciation of national rights, and the deprival of our people of their right to return and their right to self-determination on the soil of their homeland'.[49]

The text of the resolution continued to assert the principles of armed struggle, return and self-determination but – for the first time – it did not insist that these applied to the entire territory of Palestine. The prospect of an independent Palestinian state in the West Bank and Gaza was raised as an alternative (at least on a temporary basis) to the liberation of all of Palestine. While the Israeli leadership dismissed the change as merely rhetorical, aimed at destroying Israel in stages, the PFLP-led opposition from within the PLO saw it as a renunciation of the historical goals of the resistance. It formed the Rejection Front, based on the notion that the balance of forces had not changed sufficiently to allow Arabs to negotiate with Israel from a position of strength and make gains. Diplomatic efforts and the creation of a Palestinian state in territories evacuated by Israel would of necessity be conducted in the framework of UN Security Council resolution 242, which advocated peace between all states in the region, including Israel. This might satisfy Arab regimes with their limited territorial demands but would fail to meet the core Palestinian concerns.

In a Beirut symposium held early in 1974, Nayef Hawatmeh of the DFLP made a distinction between the 'American-Zionist-Hashemite [Jordanian] scheme', which would lead to 'a submissive, liquidationist solution of the Palestine question', and 'a concrete, nationalist and revolutionary position' that would guarantee the thwarting of all such solutions. In his view, the use of liberated territories as a basis for ongoing mobilization would be consistent 'with our strategic goal of liberating all of Palestine'. This goal could be achieved by working with the empowered Arab patriotic regimes and liberation movements, and relying on the global role of the Soviet Union.[50] In response, George Habash of the PFLP challenged the inflated evaluation of the shift in the regional and global balance of forces. He pointed out that the Soviet position was that 'a just settlement includes the continued existence of the State of Israel'. Like the Vietnamese, he said, Palestinians had to reject Soviet advice if it violated their national principles: 'Some of our brothers in the Resistance movement conceive of a democratic national authority [in a future liberated West Bank and Gaza] without realizing what it entails: recognition, reconciliation with, and the diplomatic exchange with Israel'. The alternative was the 'continuation of the political, economic, and military struggle in order to change the balance of power'.[51]

The PLO majority was more optimistic. Abu Iyad of Fatah argued that Palestinians could not give up on an opportunity to make gains, even within the limited framework of resolution 242 and the Geneva Convention that was based on it. If they remained united they could ensure their demands were heard and their national authority was formed on the basis of a provisional programme independent of the Israeli-imperialist alliance. A similar argument by Shafiq al-Hout of the PLO rejected the politics of mere denunciation as futile and leading to demoralization rather than mobilization. This was reiterated by Hawatmeh, who maintained that the nature of the Palestinian authority, whether submissive or revolutionary, was not predetermined and would depend on popular mobilization.[52]

Once the idea of an independent state in the West Bank and Gaza was raised, it quickly rose to dominate the political imagination. It became the new international consensus as it was supported by most actors in the region and on the global scene, albeit with the exception of two crucial actors – Israel and the United States. The first US veto of a UN Security Council resolution calling for an independent Palestinian state dates to that period (January 1976). It rejected the call that 'the Palestinian people should be enabled to exercise its inalienable national right of self-determination, including the right to establish an independent state in Palestine in accordance with the Charter of the United Nations', which was based in turn on the demand 'that Israel should withdraw from all the Arab territories occupied since June 1967', and the expectation that the UN would guarantee 'the sovereignty, territorial integrity and political independence of all states in the area and their right to live in peace within secure and recognized boundaries'.[53]

The period of the mid-1970s, then, was a crucial junction in the history of the Palestinian national movement. It did not abandon the quest for a solution that would encompass all the different segments of the people: refugees, occupied residents and Israeli citizens. In practice though, the focus on the establishment of an independent state reshaped the struggle by giving priority to the concerns of people living under Israeli military rule. This effectively 'normalized' the situation as that of a national liberation movement fighting foreign occupation. The unique features of Israel/Palestine – the total exclusion of the refugees and the qualified inclusion of Palestinian citizens – did not disappear from view, but were handled as separate issues. The notion of apartheid, and with it the emphasis on struggle against group boundaries in order to overcome internal inequalities and radically transform society, became less central to the conceptualization of the issue.

Regional developments strengthened this trend by undermining any lingering hopes for a joint Arab/Palestinian military operation against Israel. Two developments were critically important: the Lebanese civil war of 1975–76 involved Palestinians in a disastrous military conflict that fractured the Arab front, sapped their energies and created devastating divisions between them and their Lebanese and Syrian former allies. The 1970 fall of the first 'Arab Hanoi' (Amman) was followed by the fall of the second Hanoi (Beirut). No longer could these places be seen potentially as bases for a coordinated Arab campaign in support of the Palestinian struggle. After a lull in fighting for a few years, with the resumption of Israeli attacks, first in 1978 and then on a larger scale and with more lethal consequences in 1982, Palestinian cadres had to relocate again: this time to places far from the Israeli front such as Tunisia and Yemen.

In the meantime, the biggest and strongest Arab country – Egypt – culminated the diplomatic move it had started in 1973 and terminated its military involvement in the conflict by signing a peace agreement with Israel in 1978. Its initiative was seen by the PLO as 'the greatest blow to the Palestinian cause since it has existed'.[54] All Palestinian factions agreed on a six-point programme in opposition to Egyptian policies and to Security Council resolutions 242 and 338. At the same time, they expressed support for independence on 'any [liberated] part of Palestinian land', without 'reconciliation, recognition or negotiations [with Israel], as an interim aim of the Palestinian Revolution'.[55]

The PLO joined with radical Arab states to form the Arab Steadfastness Front, led by Libya and Iraq (headed respectively by would-be successors to Nasser, Mu'ammar Qaddafi and Saddam Hussein). However, this was an ineffective response to the crucial strategic shift by Egypt, which managed to restore all its lost land while its opponents were left with rhetorical gains but no concrete achievements. This remained the case even after the victory of the Islamic revolution in Iran of 1979, despite its fiery anti-Israel and anti-US symbolism. When the two states leading the regional pro-Palestinian solidarity efforts – Iraq and Iran – entered into a prolonged internecine war, which drained their resources, the dream of liberating Palestine in a military campaign waged from the outside was finally laid to rest.

With Palestinian citizens of Israel renewing their fight for equal rights and share in resources through their own internal political structures, above all the Democratic Front for Peace and Equality formed by the Communist Party in 1977, and refugees in the Diaspora largely removed from the scene, the focus of diplomacy and struggle shifted to the Occupied Territories.

Before 1967, the residents of the West Bank and Gaza had a history of organizing to fight against Israeli incursions and access land that remained within Israeli boundaries. The 1948 refugees – a majority in Gaza and a substantial minority on the West Bank – were particularly keen not to allow the outcome of the war to become permanent. Under Jordanian rule they experienced vibrant party-political life, interspersed with periods of repression, and in Gaza they clashed but also collaborated at times with the Egyptian military authorities over their quest for arms, to repel Israeli raids as well as to enable them to sneak into Israel and their erstwhile property.[56]

The 1967 war changed that. With Israeli forces in control of the newly-occupied territories, no free political activity was allowed. Palestinian resistance organizations and their literature and symbols were banned, and the only legitimate form of expressing dissent was through 'notables' meeting irregularly with military authorities and exchanging opinions and perhaps mild criticisms of Israeli policies. Intense repression, especially in the early post-1967 years, saw thousands of activists driven into exile or underground and imprisoned for long periods. This had the effect of suppressing open manifestations of resistance.[57] It was only years later, in 1973, that attempts at reorganization bore fruit in the shape of the Palestinian National Front. The Front took care not to distance itself or challenge the leadership of the PLO, in order to retain its credibility among the masses, but tensions between the externally-based resistance organizations and local activists were inevitable.[58]

The National Front gained ground quickly on a platform of allegiance to the PLO as the representative of the Palestinian People as a whole. It defined its aims as 'to resist Zionist occupation and struggle for the liberation of the occupied Arab territories', and 'to secure the legitimate rights of the Palestinian people and, in the forefront, its right to national self-determination on its own land'. To achieve that, it was committed 'to reject all plans that aim to dissolve the national question of our people and ignore its rights, be they Zionist (the Allon Plan), Arab (the United Arab Kingdom of King Hussein), American, or any other defeatist and liquidationist solution that resembles them'.[59] In addition, a range of goals that gave more specific content to its activities was listed, including fighting land confiscation, supporting local economic institutions, protecting culture, heritage and holy places, fighting against detentions and inhuman conditions of imprisonment, support for detainees' families, and so on.

By 1976 the Front clearly had become the dominant political force in the Occupied Territories and it managed to win municipal elections with large majorities in most towns. The Israeli response was harsh, no doubt reflecting resentment that its intelligence agencies did not anticipate that their favourite pro-Jordanian candidates would be ousted from power so easily. Some of the new mayors and many activists were harassed, detained, deported and restricted in their activities, culminating in banning the Front altogether, as well as its successor organizations.[60]

Despite attempts to suppress PLO-aligned nationalist organization, and Israeli experiments with creating alternative compliant leadership – the Village Leagues – in the early 1980s, no force opposed to the PLO could emerge in the Territories. The relative order re-imposed as a result of the repressive campaign, reinforced by the PLO's ouster from Lebanon in 1982, did not last long. Tensions continued to simmer under the surface until they broke out with the most sustained expression of mass resistance in Palestine since 1936 – the Intifada of 1987, which lasted six years, and led to the Oslo agreements of 1993.

There is no space here to discuss the Intifada in any detail.[61] It was a massive popular uprising that unified Palestinians in the Occupied Territories and forced the PLO to come out clearly in support for independence and statehood in that limited geographical and political framework. The Declaration of Independence of the State of Palestine, which came within a year of the outbreak of the Intifada, was based on the partition of the territory:

> Despite the historical injustice done to the Palestinian Arab people in its displacement and in being deprived of the right to self-determination following the adoption of General Assembly resolution 181 (II) of 1947, which partitioned Palestine into an Arab and a Jewish State, that resolution nevertheless continues to attach conditions to international legitimacy that guarantee the Palestinian Arab people the right to sovereignty and national independence.

The Declaration owes most to the 'great popular uprising now mounting in the occupied territories', due to which 'the Palestinian conjuncture reaches a sharp historical turning point', leading to 'the establishment of the State of Palestine in the land of Palestine with its capital at Jerusalem'. The state 'shall be for Palestinians, wherever they may be therein to develop their national and cultural identity and therein to enjoy full equality of rights'. Whether Jews living in the country could be included in this definition was not made explicit. It shall be 'an Arab State and shall be an integral part of the Arab nation, of its heritage and civilization'. It rejects 'the threat or use of force, violence and intimidation against its territorial integrity and political independence or those of any other State', implicitly including Israel.[62]

Without renouncing any of its historical claims, the Palestine National Council chose to focus on terminating the occupation of the West Bank and Gaza and using these areas as the territorial basis for the state. It was appreciative of, but also set itself apart from 'those Israeli democratic and progressive forces which have rejected the occupation, condemned it, and deplored its oppressive practices and measures', as well as 'Jewish groups throughout the world' calling 'for

Israel's withdrawal from the occupied territories, in order to enable the Palestinian people to exercise its right to self-determination'. It is the principle of 'separate but equal' statehood that guided the statement, not statehood based on 'one person, one vote', as was the case at the same time for the anti-apartheid movement of South Africa. In essence that has remained the main goal of the Palestinian national movement to this day.

The Internal Democratic Struggle

While Palestinians living under occupation were reshaping their struggle to focus on the goal of an independent state in their territories, Palestinian citizens of Israel were undergoing their own processes of political consolidation. United with a large part of the Palestinian people as a result of the 1967 war, they remained legally separated from them due to their status as Israeli citizens. No longer living under a military government – it was abolished late in 1966 – and with the security services directing most efforts to the newly-occupied territories and their inhabitants, Palestinian citizens were freer than ever to pursue their political agendas.

Not surprisingly, the reunification of all of historical Palestine under Israeli rule did not lead to a unified resistance movement. Palestinians across the Green Line shared ethnicity, culture and family ties, of course, but 19 years of separation created different political circumstances, which resulted in the adoption of radically opposed strategies: residents under occupation focused on the struggle to free themselves from foreign rule, while their Israeli counterparts increasingly aimed to enhance their citizenship rights and enjoy full access to freedoms denied to all other Palestinians. As before 1967, the two tendencies of communism and Arab nationalism were the dominant political forces, usually in a state of tension with each other but also, at times, in relationship of collaboration in the face of the common enemy.

Already back in 1965 the Communist Party split between a minority Jewish faction, which retained the name Maki and was led by Shmuel Mikunis and Moshe Sneh, and a predominantly Arab faction, with a minority of Jewish members, forced to adopt a new name – Rakah (New Communist List). Led by Meir Vilner and Tawfiq Tubi, Rakah retained the dissident positions of Maki, while the Mikunis-Sneh leadership moved quickly towards the Jewish mainstream. This move was expedited by its support for the official Israeli position in 1967 in opposition to the Soviet line. By the end of the 1960s Maki has ceased to operate as an opposition force, and it officially disbanded in 1973. This left Rakah as the sole Soviet-aligned party, and it reclaimed the name Maki in 1989, using it to this day.

As the only parliamentary force that was resolutely opposed to the occupation, Rakah emerged as a critical voice in the post-1967 period, together with the militant Matzpen group. This position enhanced its reputation among Palestinian citizens and it experienced a growth in support among them, but also a loss of most of the limited Jewish support it had retained after the 1965 split. Probably no more than 2–3 per cent of its parliamentary votes were cast by Jews after 1967. The bulk of members and voters were Arab, though the Party never abandoned its Jewish–Arab identity. This combination of factors – its legal existence and bi-national character, alongside its resolute support for equality of rights and opposition to the occupation – allowed it to claim both respectability and dissent, working within the system and on its margins. The result was a rapid rise in its status as the foremost force representing Palestinians inside the Green Line.[63]

A crucial stepping stone in the rise of Rakah to a dominant position was the victory of the Democratic Nazareth Front in the municipal elections of December 1975. Led by Party leader Tawfiq Zayyad, the Front won an unprecedented victory in the biggest Palestinian town in Israel, receiving two-thirds of the vote. This allowed it to establish a basis from which to lead the events of the Day of the Land (*Yawm al-Ard*) that were to follow.[64] Although the rise of the PLO and its diplomatic successes, together with the civic uprising against the occupation, served as a background for these events, they were facilitated above all by local factors: a new wave of land confiscation, part of the state-sponsored campaign for the Judaization of the Galilee. The ongoing centrality of land in the experience of Palestinian citizens since 1948 was displayed in their biggest mass mobilization to date, the general strike of 30 March 1976. As put by Zayyad: 'The battle for the land was, and still is, the basic struggle of the Arabs in Israel for national equality and for coherent development over their lands and in their homeland'.[65]

It is interesting to note how Zayyad carefully linked the overall Palestinian struggle to the specific campaigns waged by Israeli citizens, but also differentiated the two: 'The Arabs in Israel have an important role to play in the struggle for achieving a democratic and just solution of the national problem of the Palestinian Arab people – its right to self determination and to a sovereign national state, and the right of the refugees to return.' A solution to the overall conflict would encourage the internal democratic struggle 'for defeating the policy of racial discrimination and implementing full national equality'. In addition to resolving the land issue,

> the right of the [internal] Arabs to exist and to develop on their land and in their homeland must be recognized. The Arabs must have the right of due respect to their culture and national dignity, the right of full representation in the various official and public institutions, and the right of participation in remolding the general policy of the state and the future relations with the Jewish people.

All this would be done in cooperation with 'democratic and rational Jewish forces'.[66]

There was a clear distinction here between the right of the Palestinian-Arab people to its own state, and the right of Palestinian citizens (referred to as 'The Arabs in Israel') to equality, representation and participation in shaping state policies. In this, the conceptualization of occupied Palestinians as external and Israeli citizens as internal was reinforced. Zayyad's colleague Emile Touma made the same point when he argued that absolute justice could not be realized and partial justice would have to do. This included the right of Palestinians to self-determination in the Occupied Territories, recognition of the right of return or compensation for refugees, and the right of the Arab minority in Israel 'to enjoy its national and civil rights in Israel without discrimination or national oppression'.[67] The PLO's goal of a secular democratic state for Arabs and Jews in the entire country will remain, but only as a 'dream'. In the meantime, both Palestinian Arabs and Israeli Jews would be entitled to their own independent states.

On the basis of these principles, in 1977 Rakah became central to a new electoral formation, the Democratic Front for Peace and Equality (known as the Jabha in Arabic and Hadash in Hebrew). The Front received over 50 per cent of the Arab votes cast in the national elections of that year, the first time that a non-Zionist list gained a majority. Coming on the heels of the successful mass mobilization of the Day of the Land of March 1976, this was another landmark in the rise of internal Palestinian resistance. Other movements emerged at the time but remained on the margins of mainstream politics without ever posing a serious challenge to the dominance of Hadash. Arab student associations and, particularly, the Sons of the Village movement (*Abnaa al-Balad*) called for undiluted adherence to a radical line, in a similar manner to the original al-Ard movement, though this time with a focus on Palestinian rather than pan-Arab nationalism.[68] These movements emphasized the essential Palestinian identity of the Arab citizens of Israel and the shared fate of all segments of the Palestinian people, politically represented by the PLO. But, for obvious reasons they had to tread carefully – state security forces did not tolerate any move to translate abstract sentiments of solidarity into concrete acts of political cooperation across the Green Line, to say nothing of joint Palestinian action beyond the boundaries of Israeli control.

By the late 1970s, then, independent statehood in the Occupied Territories and full citizenship rights inside Israel had been consolidated as two key demands raised by respective segments of the Palestinian people. Although the armed resistance organizations, united in the PLO, were created by another segment – the 1948 refugees – whose concerns were not addressed by either of these demands, they increasingly aligned themselves behind statehood as the key goal, ostensibly as a temporary measure but in practice more and more as the core demand. The quest to realize the right of return of refugees has never been abandoned but has largely fallen out of the effective framework of diplomatic moves and negotiations, which occupied the next decade. With the first Intifada, the first Gulf war, the Madrid Conference and finally the Oslo Accords, these efforts culminated with the forging of a global consensus on a two-state solution. This remains the target to which all players continue to pay rhetorical homage, despite its ever shrinking prospects due to the entrenchment of the occupation and effective Apartheid rule in the Territories by successive Israeli governments.

Palestinian citizens continued to advocate equality of rights throughout the period, with some attempts to forge an explicit link between civil and national demands. In a path-breaking article written in 1993, Azmi Bishara, a former Rakah student leader who became an independent public intellectual, set forward a new agenda: making Israel a state of all its citizens. Bishara argued against the separation of national rights, to be exercised in a separate state, and civil rights to be exercised in Israel. His alternative was a combined struggle: to transform Israel into a state that guarantees equal rights to all its citizens, regardless of their ethnic origins, and to recognize Palestinian citizens as a national and cultural minority, in charge of their own education system, media and development plans.[69] The notion of 'state of all its citizens', in contrast to a Jewish state, quickly caught up and became a standard for Palestinian intellectuals, embodied in a new political movement, the National Democratic Alliance (NDA, known as the Tajamu' in Arabic and Balad in Hebrew).

Over the course of the following decade, activists, academics and intellectuals outlined their vision for Palestinian citizens and their relations with their Israeli-Jewish counterparts, resulting in a series of documents inspired by Bishara's notions. These became known as the Vision Documents.[70] The 2006 framework document, published by the National Committee for the Heads of the Arab Local Authorities, presents its constituency as 'Palestinian Arabs in Israel, the indigenous people, the residents of the State of Israel'. It goes on to state that, as a result of the 1948 Nakba, they became disconnected from the rest of the Palestinian people and Arab world, and since then have been 'suffering from extreme structural discrimination policies, national oppression, military rule that lasted till 1966, land confiscation policy, unequal budget and resources allocation, rights discrimination and threats of transfer', but have managed to maintain their 'identity, culture, and national affiliation'. Israel's definition as a Jewish state excludes them, which is why they call for a 'Consensual Democratic system that enables us to be fully active in the decision-making process and guarantee our individual and collective civil, historic, and national rights'.[71]

Analytically, Israel is identified as executing 'internal colonial policies' against Palestinian-Arab citizens, as part of a process of 'Judaization of the land and erosion of the Palestinian history and civilization'.[72] This made Israel an 'ethnocratic state' that uses ethnicity and religion rather than citizenship 'as a basic principle of the distribution of resources and abilities'. To overcome this system, 'the State should recognize the Palestinian Arabs in Israel as an indigenous national group (and as a minority within the international conventions) that has the right within their citizenship to choose its representatives directly and be responsible for their religious, educational and cultural affairs . . . [and] the State has to acknowledge that Israel is the homeland for both Palestinians and Jews'. The two groups 'should have mutual relations based on the consensual democratic system (an extended coalition between the elites of the two groups, equal proportional representation, mutual right to veto and self administration of exclusive issues)'.

This would lead to the removal of 'all forms of ethnic superiority, be that executive, structural, legal or symbolic', and the adoption of 'policies of corrective justice in all aspects of life in order to compensate for the damage inflicted on the Palestinian Arabs due to the ethnic favoritism policies of the Jews'.[73] A long list of areas in which such policies would apply follows, including land, planning, and housing; employment and service provision; social development; education and culture; institution building. In all these, solidarity with and a sense of common identity and fate with other Palestinian groups and the Arab world would be essential. The precise nature of the relations between them is left vague, however.

In more legalistic vein, Adalah, the Legal Center for Arab Minority Rights in Israel, produced a draft constitution to embody the principles contained in the vision framework.[74] If it were accepted, its area of application would be 'the territory which was subject to the Israeli law until 5 June 1967'. In other words, Israel 'proper'. No clause in the document refers to the Occupied Territories or the Diaspora. The document simply states:

> The State of Israel must recognize its responsibility for past injustices suffered by the Palestinian people, both before and after its establishment. The State of Israel must recognize, therefore, its responsibility for the injustices of the Nakba and the Occupation; recognize the right of return of the Palestinian refugees based on UN Resolution 194; recognize the right of the Palestinian people to self-determination; and withdraw from all of the territories occupied in 1967.[75]

According to the constitution proposed by Adalah, a democratic Israel would be bilingual, with Hebrew and Arabic as official languages enjoying equal status in state institutions. The state would be multicultural: 'each group that constitutes a national minority' would be entitled to 'educational and cultural institutions', and the same would apply to religious minorities. All minorities would be 'entitled to operate their institutions via a representative body chosen by the members of the group', allocated a suitable budget by the state, and given 'appropriate representation' in state structures. Participation of minorities in decision-making is envisaged through a model which requires majority support from 'parties that by definition and character are Arab parties or Arab-Jewish parties'.

Interestingly, the proposed system is premised on indirect ethnic-group representation, rather than universal democracy. It implicitly assumes that people would not transcend their ethnic identity, and therefore would continue to vote and act according to their definition of group interests (the reference to 'Arab-Jewish parties' seems to be a concession to Hadash and the Communist Party, which do not define themselves as Arab, despite the fact that most of their support comes from Palestinian citizens).

Another distinctive feature of the proposed constitution is the notion of 'distributive justice', which aims to compensate 'every group of citizens which has suffered from a policy of injustice and historical discrimination' in the allocation of land, water and in planning. This would enable citizens – potentially refugees as well – to reclaim expropriated private, communal and religious property, and claim compensation for having been uprooted by various pieces of discriminatory legislation. These mechanisms of restitution would apply to settled citizens, internally displaced persons, Bedouins and residents in unrecognized villages. Their purpose is to facilitate a return to the normal conditions expected to apply in a non-ethnic state. That the proposed constitution makes specific mention of various groups of Arab citizens is due to past discriminatory practices. In all other respects, it proposes that equality between citizens must be the norm. Thus, some of the tension between individual and group rights in the document may be seen as a temporary measure or a form of affirmative action.

It is clear that the Vision Documents foresee a future grounded in ethnic identity but, unlike the present ethnocratic system, based on equality between the different groups. Thus, Israel would not cease to be an ethnic state, but would become a bi-ethnic (or bi-national) state. This is clearly different from post-apartheid South Africa, which is supposed to be a non-racial state, allowing racial considerations only for purposes of redress. In Israel/Palestine, the power of ethnic-group identity and historical links to group members beyond the state's boundaries seem too strong to be easily overcome in the immediate to medium-term future.

This sense of history is expressed forcefully in a May 2007 document known as *The Haifa Declaration*, which speaks in the name of

> sons and daughters of the Palestinian Arab people who remained in our homeland despite the Nakba . . . [who] affirm in this Declaration the foundations of our identity and belonging, and . . . [call for] an historic reconciliation between the Palestinian people and the Israeli Jewish people . . . [based on] continued connection to the other sons and daughters of the Palestinian people and the Arab nation.[76]

In doing that, the Declaration rejects the label 'Israeli Arabs' and reasserts Palestinian and Arab affinities. At the same time, the Declaration defines its specific constituency as having been shaped by the 1948 events, 'through which we – who remained from among the original inhabitants of our homeland – were made citizens without the genuine constituents of citizenship, especially equality'. As a 'homeland minority', they are seeking 'democratic citizenship', justice and redress as 'the only arrangement that guarantees individual and collective equality for the Palestinians in Israel'.

The Declaration focuses on Palestinians inside pre-1967 Israel, but within the overall goal of a 'historic reconciliation' between the Jewish Israeli people and the Arab Palestinian people, groups that are not confined to specific boundaries. To achieve this, the state must 'accept responsibility for the Nakba, which befell all parts of the Palestinian people, and also for the war crimes and crimes of occupation that it has committed in the Occupied Territories'. This should be complemented by 'recognizing the Right of Return and acting to implement it in accordance with United Nations Resolution 194, ending the Occupation and removing the settlements from all Arab territory occupied since 1967, recognizing the right of the Palestinian people to self-determination and to an independent and sovereign state, and recognizing the rights of Palestinian citizens in Israel'.

In exchange, the Declaration continues, Palestinians and Arabs must 'recognize the right of the Israeli Jewish people to self-determination and to life in peace, dignity, and security with the Palestinian and the other peoples of the region'. This would require a 'change in the definition of the State of Israel from a Jewish state to a democratic state established on national and civil equality between the two national groups, and enshrining the principles of banning discrimination and of equality between all of its citizens and residents'.

While the Haifa Declaration puts forward an overall vision of a solution to the Israeli-Palestinian conflict, it leaves a few questions without clear answers. It does not address the tension between the quest for a democratic state with no ethnic character, and the notion of equality between ethnically defined groups. Nor does it attempt to reconcile the right to national self-determination with equality at the individual and collective levels. It identifies the role of Palestinians in Israel in transforming the state through their own efforts, but the link between their struggle and that of Palestinians under occupation and in the Diaspora is not addressed. Further, it does not explain how Palestinians in Israel could use their strategic position and familiarity with Israeli Jews to support other Palestinians. These questions require extensive discussion, and the Declaration may not have been the best forum for this, though it could have noted that these issues would have to be examined in the future.[77]

CONCLUSIONS

It is not surprising that the Palestinian movement emerges from this study as a nationalist project to gain recognition and independence for a specific group identified in ethnic and national terms. Historically it was not aimed at abolishing boundaries between groups but rather asserting their rights in relation to each other. The post-1973 shift, from demanding national independence in all of Palestine to only part of it, stemmed from the realization that the larger goal was not realistic under prevailing regional and global conditions. But, it did not change the definition of the struggle as ethnic-national in form and content. In that sense the movement was not an anti-apartheid movement.

Having said that, there were times and trends in that history which saw certain political forces moving towards a conceptualization of identity that could potentially include Jews in Israel in a political framework overcoming ethnic and national boundaries. The Democratic Front for the Liberation of Palestine was perhaps the closest to that idea, but its incipient dialogue with the Israeli Matzpen group was cut short – due to state repression and the civil war in Jordan – and ended up with no tangible results. The debate about the Vision Documents of the 2000s is more promising in this regard as it raises crucial issues of individual and collective rights within the same state framework. It is of most relevance for Palestinian citizens of Israel, however, and its applicability to Palestinians under occupation and in the Diaspora has not been tested in practice, through concrete debates and exchanges – not mere slogans – by the direct stakeholders.

Defining the movement as nationalist rather than anti-apartheid is not meant in any way to discredit it. Rather it serves to position it as part of the great historical trend of the post-1945 period, which saw dozens of anti-colonial movements engaged in struggles for national liberation from foreign rule. That Palestinians have not won that struggle yet (even in part of their homeland) is due not so much to deficiencies in their organization but to the unique conditions of colonial settlement in the country, and the political challenges that faced them as a result. It is only in the last decade that a true anti-apartheid paradigm has begun to emerge among some, mostly foreign-based, activists – with a focus on equal rights for all in the same political framework – but this topic deserves a study of its own, which cannot be taken up in this space.

4

Matzpen: The Anti-Zionist Left in Israel/Palestine

Back in the late 1930s, a young Jewish activist, writing under the pseudonym L. Rock, published two articles on British Policy and the Jewish–Arab conflict in Palestine.[1] He evaluated the relations between British imperialism, Arab nationalism and the Zionist movement, arguing that British policy on Palestine was based on 'a system of divide and rule'. The British incited 'national hatreds between the two peoples in the country in order to assure itself the position of arbitrator'. The feudal Arab leadership and the Zionist movement benefited from this policy, as it strengthened the support of the masses for nationalist leaders, and hampered efforts 'to bring about an understanding between the workers of both peoples'. The basic needs of Jewish workers – for immigration and settlement on the land – did not contradict 'the real necessities of the Arab masses', but due to British provocations the Arabs were 'made to see their national oppressors in the Jews'. Their national feelings were channelled against Jews, in support of feudal leaders, rather than against the real enemy – the British.[2]

In a follow-up article, Rock went on to argue that 'feudal elements' among the Palestinian-Arab population feared 'the modernisation of Palestinian society by the Jews', which would lead to their own destruction, while the Arab capitalist elements took part in the struggle because of 'their exclusive tendencies and their competition with the Jews'.[3] The Arab masses themselves faced 'a basic conflict' between their interests in national and social emancipation and British rule. Their national opposition to Zionism was 'absolutely progressive', due to Zionism's exclusionary tendencies (boycott of Arab labour and produce), but in following the lead of the feudal leadership they played into the hands of the Zionist movement. Only an internationalist leadership could separate the progressive Arab nationalist sentiments from the reactionary anti-Jewish form they tended to take, as well as fight the Zionist chauvinist tendencies among Jews.

Zionism itself was 'a nationalist reactionary conception' because its policy of Conquest of Labour (using only Jewish workers in Jewish-owned enterprises) led to national competition between workers at the expense of class solidarity. The Zionist movement was opposed to the independence of Palestine and to other forms of political democracy, as long as Jews were a minority in the country. In that, it allied itself with imperialism. The Jewish masses themselves were not inherent allies of imperialism, however. Unlike whites in South Africa, they were 'no thin, privileged stratum representing the exploiting interests of the Motherland'. In other words, they could be won to a progressive cause if the right policies to attract them were adopted.

Rock outlined several differences between Jewish workers in Palestine and white workers in South Africa: Jews made up more than half of the entire working class of Palestine, whereas in South Africa whites were only 20 per cent of the working population. Jews were skilled and unskilled, as were Arabs, while in South Africa white workers were skilled for the most part, and 'natives' were common labourers. Whites in South Africa were 'a thin "aristocratic" upper crust', paid five times as much as natives, while in Palestine the Jewish workers were a class. South African whites enjoyed democratic political rights and the natives were 'suppressed colonial slaves'. In Palestine 'both Jews and Arabs are oppressed by an alien government and are deprived of any kind of democratic rights'. Unlike white South Africans, Jews were not privileged in matters of budget expenditures, municipal administration, and labour legislation.

In comparison to other settler groups living under colonial conditions, the Palestine Jewish community presented a unique case. On the one hand, its existence did not depend 'upon the exploitation and oppression of the Arab masses'. This created a potential for solidarity with the indigenous population. However, unlike 'normal' immigrant communities it aspired to become a majority and establish its own state in the new country. This nationalist quest put it in opposition to democracy and independence for Palestine, and set it against the wishes of the Arab population. Jewish–Arab relations thus became a conflict between two mutually exclusive national movements. Under these conditions, the only solution possible was solidarity 'on the basis of the struggle against Zionism, against Arab national exclusivism and anti-Jewish actions, against imperialism, for the democratisation of the country and its political independence'.

Rock's analysis was critical of Zionism and British imperialism, but it had one crucial feature that set it apart from other left-wing perspectives. It looked at the Jewish community and its relations with the Arab population in national terms, and did not regard the conflict between the two groups as colonial in nature. It thus refrained from depicting the Jewish settlement project as illegitimate in its entirety, though it opposed many of its specific practices. This approach – and particularly the contrast with South Africa drawn in the articles – gave rise to a critical response from some South African activists.

These activists, using the name Workers Party of South Africa (Fourth International), and writing in their magazine *The Spark*, focused on the 'fundamental' issue of 'the progressive revolutionary struggle of a colonial people against imperialism'. In their view, Zionism and colonial rule were inseparable: 'British imperialism took up the Zionist cause and Zionism became a servant of British imperialism.'[4] Zionist settlement '*must be at the expense of the native Arab population*' (italics in the original), since 'any colonial development under imperialism means the enslavement, oppression and exploitation of the native population'. Thus, it was not different in essence from white colonial settlement in South Africa: it was motivated by the same quest for 'cheap native labour', the same policy of 'grabbing, of squeezing out the native population from the land, and so the production of a landless peasantry as a reservoir of cheap labour', the same 'greed for more territory', the same 'white, civilized labour policy'.

Given that Palestine Jews seemed united behind Zionism, there was little wonder that 'the Arabs should come to the conclusion that all Jews in Palestine are Zionists and therefore their enemies'. Only when Jewish workers 'break with their chauvinistic leaders, who have chained them to the chariot of Zionism-imperialism', would Arab workers be able to 'free themselves from the influence and leadership of the equally chauvinistic effendis and mullahs'. In this conflict, the moral and political burden was on the Jewish community, to prove that it did not oppose the Arab quest for national liberation. It was not a matter of two national communities with equally legitimate but competing claims – as Rock argued – but of a colonial-type conflict, in which an indigenous Arab group struggled to free itself from British colonial rule that was buttressed by an immigrant Jewish settler group.

In his rejoinder, Rock agreed that the Palestinian Arab national movement historically was 'essentially an anti-imperialist movement', but asserted that Palestine could not gain independence unless 'a unification of the Arab and Jewish masses takes place'.[5] However, Jews would not take part in the struggle if the Arab camp remained unified. Separating the Arab masses from the feudal and bourgeois anti-Jewish leadership was crucial. A genuine liberation struggle had to be waged against the British, not the Jews. Progressive elements within the Jewish population could be won to the anti-imperialist cause, as Jewish workers represented 'by their objective interests, an integral part of the general working class'; they were not a thin privileged layer aligned to the ruling class like white South African workers were. The toiling masses of both groups had to be liberated from the influence of nationally exclusionary leaderships: 'Internationalist socialism in Palestine is the only force that can . . . eliminate Jewish and Arabian antagonism, and link the national liberation movement of the Arabs with the struggle of the Jewish masses for the right to their existence in the country and their growth through immigration.'

The equation between the two national movements made by Rock was at the heart of the debate. The Spark group rejected it: Arabs alone were leading a progressive anti-imperialist struggle; Jews were openly reactionary in their opposition to independence and democratization, and were interested only in establishing their own state. Socialists had no way forward other than support for the Arab national movement in its quest for independence. Jews could gain a place for themselves only by abandoning Zionism and supporting the Arab struggle (though that was unlikely to happen).[6] For Rock, in contrast, Jews and Arabs were internally divided groups – not wholly progressive or reactionary – and the way forward was to incorporate legitimate demands of progressive elements within each group, and remove the reactionary leaderships of both.

Although neither side to the debate discussed South Africa in detail, it is clear that they held very different ideas about its relevance. For The Spark, the Palestine condition was essentially the same as that of South Africa, and all other colonial situations. The solution therefore was the same for both: unconditional support for the native movement as a force fighting colonial oppression, and no concession to settler political demands. For Rock, Palestine was different and unique. With both national groups being oppressed by the imperial power, they were potentially in solidarity with one another. Jews were not essentially an ally of imperialism and capitalist rule as whites were in South Africa. Hence, rather than being vilified they should be recruited to the struggle, at the cost of meeting some of their demands, such as free immigration to the country.

In various ways, this debate continues to rage today, although the historical circumstances have changed. Beyond the specificity of the South African situation, whether the Israeli–Palestinian conflict is best seen in colonial or national terms is a key question for the Left in Israel/ Palestine. Whether there is a South African 'model' that can serve as a guide in analyzing and resolving the conflict is another such question. The discussion in this chapter examines various positions regarding these issues, with a focus on the Matzpen movement from the 1960s to the 1980s.

HISTORICAL BACKGROUND

Shortly before the 29 November 1947 UN General Assembly resolution on the partition of Palestine into Jewish and Arab states, a small group of radical socialists – operating under the name of Revolutionary Communists Alliance (RCA), Palestinian section of the Fourth International – issued a statement on the situation in the country.

In their statement, they predicted that partition would drive a wedge between Arab and Jewish workers, and create political turmoil in the entire region. Against a background of growing labour militancy and emerging unity between Arab and Jewish workers, the group argued that imperialist forces attempted to use partition in order to sow divisions and enhance their ability to rule the region. A 'tiny Jewish state' with 'inevitable expansionist tendencies' would be pitted against a 'backward feudal Arab state'. The resulting chauvinistic atmosphere 'will poison the Arab world in the Middle East and throttle the anti-imperialist fight of the masses, while Zionists and Arab feudalists will vie for imperialist favors'.[7] Addressing Jewish residents of the country, the statement asserted: 'There is only one way: the common class war with our Arab brothers; a war which is an inseparable link of the anti-imperialist war of the oppressed masses in all the Arab East and the entire world.'

In a subsequent statement, the group criticised the two Communist parties (PKP and NLL, which were organized on a separate national basis at the time) for putting the Soviet Union's diplomatic interests above the needs of the working class. In contrast to the Moscow-oriented communists, who initially had opposed partition but changed their position once the Soviet Union had given its support to the UN resolution, the RCA continued to reject partition. The only solution to chauvinism and armed conflict, in their view, was to 'make this war between Jews and Arabs, which serves the ends of imperialism, the common war of both nations', against their class enemies, and to allow 'workers of the two peoples' to unite in a common front against imperialism and its local agents: 'The only way to peace between the two peoples of this country is turning the guns against the instigators of murder in both camps'.[8]

A tension between two fundamental principles can be found in these statements. On the one hand, they refer to two national groups in the country, which are regarded as distinct entities. On the other hand, the solution is defined in class terms, as a struggle of all workers, regardless of national identity, against the feudal and pro-imperialist elements in the region. This tension, between a particular national focus and a universal class focus, has been a constant feature of the radical left-wing analysis of the Israeli–Palestinian conflict. Although the precise terms of the tension have changed over time – the concept of class has lost much of its appeal and has been replaced by a human rights discourse – the tension itself has remained. How to deal with national differences within an egalitarian political framework remains a crucial issue of theoretical debate and strategic exchange among activists.

The Revolutionary Communists Alliance, of which Rock was a founding member, was a small group of a few dozen members, most of whom were Jewish. It was part of the Fourth International formed by Leon Trotsky in 1938, guided by the same set of principles formulated by the Comintern in its early days. They opposed Zionism as

> it serves as a support for British imperialist domination . . . provokes a nationalist reaction on the part of the Arab masses, causes a racial division in the workers' movement, reinforces the 'holy alliance' of classes among both Jews and Arabs, and thus allows imperialism to perpetuate this conflict, as a means to perpetuate the presence of troops in Palestine.

In addition, 'it puts a brake on the participation of the Jewish working-class masses in the class struggle in the rest of the world'.

The way forward relied on progressive Arab forces, which regarded 'the creation of a Union of the Arab countries of the Middle East as the only real framework for the development of the productive forces and for the constitution of an Arab nation'. This goal would be realized by 'the proletariat, which alone is capable of pushing through, by the mechanism of the permanent revolution, the struggle against feudalism for agrarian reform, for the emancipation of the Arab world from imperialist intervention, and for the constitution of the unity of the Arab world'.

In that quest, 'it is the Arab masses, the workers and the poor peasants, who constitute the revolutionary force in the Middle East and also in Palestine, thanks to their numbers, their social conditions, and their material life, which puts them directly in conflict with imperialism'. In contrast to them, 'the Jewish masses of Palestine, as a whole, are not an anti-imperialist force'. As a result, 'unity between Jews and Arabs in Palestine is unrealizable' and could come about only 'through the abolition of all racist ideology and practice on the part of the Jews'. In other words, it required the abolition of Zionist ideology and practices, and 'a split between the [Jewish] workers' movement and Zionism. That is the condition *sine qua non* for achieving Jewish–Arab unity of action against imperialism, and it is the only way to stop the Arab revolution in the Middle East proceeding over the corpse of Palestinian Jewry'.[9]

Partition of the country – as proposed in the late 1940 – was not a solution to the divide between Jews and Arabs:

A Jewish statelet in the heart of the Middle East can be an excellent instrument in the hands of the imperialist states. Isolated from the Arab masses, this state will be defenseless and completely at the mercy of the imperialists. And they will use it in order to fortify their positions . . . The Arabs will also receive 'political independence.' Partition will bring about the creation of a backward feudal Arab state, a sort of Trans-Jordan west of the Jordan River. In this way they hope to isolate and paralyze the Arab proletariat in the Haifa area, an important strategic center with oil refineries, as well as to divide and paralyze the class war of all the workers of Palestine.[10]

As can be seen, the themes of violation of indigenous rights through Zionist settlement practices, imperialist control, and divide and rule policies which reinforce Jewish and Arab reactionary nationalism at the expense of class consciousness and struggle, were repeated here. To all these, the RCA added the role of the PKP and its factions, which were accused of failing to pose a viable working-class-based alternative to the trio of enemies: Zionism, Imperialism and Arab Reaction. Instead of confronting them directly, said the RCA, the Moscow-aligned communists reinforced the reactionary forces' power to manipulate the masses, by supporting the UN partition resolution of November 1947.

But the opposition to partition failed and in the ensuing armed conflict the majority of the Palestinian Arabs residing in the territories allocated to the Jewish state fled or were expelled by Israeli forces. The process, known as the Nakba, completely changed demographic and power relations in the country, and required major adjustments on the part of all political forces.

The RCA ceased to exist as a group, though a few isolated individuals continued to be active politically. One of them wrote a piece in which he argued that 'the Palestinian war has also aided the imperialist powers by strengthening their political position in the Arab East. The general surge of chauvinism created by this war has been very useful in diverting the anti-imperialist mood of the Arab masses all over the Middle East against the Jewish and other minorities in these countries'. In Palestine itself, 'The mass flight of the Arabs from Haifa, the center of the Palestinian working class (oil refineries, railway workshops, etc.), and from Jaffa and the rest of the coastal plain, brought with it the complete annihilation of the Arab working class of Palestine'. As a result, 'The barrier between Jewish and Arab workers built by imperialism, Zionism and Arab Reaction, which had been broken from time to time [by joint activity in Haifa] . . . has now been fortified by political boundaries between belligerent or at least rival states, excluding the physical contact between Jewish and Arab workers'.

What could be done then from that perspective? By Balkanizing the Middle East, 'Anglo-American imperialism succeeded in creating a situation in which it was able to deal separately with each state in the easiest way in order to carry out its economic and political plans'. In response, 'only the concrete action and organization of the workers of Egypt, both parts of Palestine, Syria and the Lebanon and Iraq can succeed in overcoming this suppression, liberate the toiling masses, the workers and the poor fellahin, from the foreign and native yoke and build a new society'.[11] Regional class unity, then, was the way to counter imperialist fragmentation, bolstered by reactionary Arab and Jewish agents. As a slogan, this made sense. How it could be achieved in practice was a question that remained unanswered, however.

Indeed, the conditions created by the 1948 war and its aftermath isolated Israelis – Jews and Arabs alike – from their region, geographically, politically and culturally. Palestinians who remained steadfast in their homeland lost much of their religious, national and intellectual leadership, thus allowing the former activists of the PKP and NLL to occupy new positions of influence. As the only legal party independent of the Israeli-Zionist establishment and its Arab collaborators, the Israeli Communist Party (Maki) served as the focal point around which new politics of identity and resistance began to crystallize. In 1952 it started to publish in Haifa a cultural magazine by the name of *al-Jadid* (the New, in Arabic), edited by two prominent local intellectuals: Emile Habibi of the PKP/NLL and Jabra Nicola who had been linked both to the PKP and the RCA, and was a well-known dissident close to radical Jewish activists.

Nicola's skills as a writer and editor – he had written a few books on Zionism and labour issues in the 1930s, as a PKP member – and his general intellectual stature were too important for the Party to ignore. For his part, despite his critical anti-Stalinist stance, the opportunity to break out of isolation and work in a forum that allowed access to activists and popular constituencies seemed essential to his political mission. He remained associated with the Party until the early 1960s, when he joined the newly-founded Matzpen movement.

Palestinian citizens in Israel focused, of necessity, on efforts to reconstitute their collective identity and regain and extend basic political and social rights. At the same time, the Middle East as a whole was entering a period of great turmoil, from the 1952 Free Officers coup in Egypt, which brought Nasser to power, through the various attempts at Arab unity, the Algerian liberation struggle led by the FLN, to the Iraqi uprising against the Hashemite dynasty in 1958, and the rise of the Qassem regime, aligned with the Iraqi Communist Party. These coincided with the rise of the 'Third World' as a political actor, as expressed in the Bandung conference of 1955. Various attempts to block this radical wave through the formation of the pro-Western Baghdad Pact, and the launch of the tripartite Suez war of 1956, failed. Left-wing forces in the region welcomed these changes but also raised concerns. The international Trotskyist movement took part in this debate through a booklet written by one of its foremost activists, Michel Pablo.

Pablo (whose real name was Raptis), was an Egypt-born Greek, whose 1958 work titled *The Arab Revolution* reflected the perspective of the Fourth International on the global anti-colonial struggle. Arab national unity was a revolutionary goal, he argued. Since the Arab ruling classes suffered from 'organic inability' to achieve it, 'the unity of the Arab nation will prove to be historically the exclusive result of the victory of the Arab revolution under proletarian leadership in its socialist stage'. The commercial bourgeoisie was parasitical in nature and thoroughly reactionary. The emerging industrial bourgeoisie was more progressive, and workers could enter 'temporary alliances for precise goals, which do not alienate the autonomous objectives and policy of the class party of the proletariat and the poor peasants', as long as it was clear that the goal of that bourgeoisie was 'co-exploitation of the native masses', not 'a decisive fight against imperialism and against the feudalists' together with the 'revolutionary masses'. The call for 'a national anti-imperialist united front rallying all classes' had to be combined with 'merciless ideological criticism of the inevitable limitations of the national bourgeoisie, and the no less inevitable class struggle against it, in order to complete the bourgeois-democratic revolution and to tackle the socialist tasks'.[12]

Interestingly, little attention was paid to the Palestinian question in the document. This was common at a time in which Palestinians, widely dispersed and fragmented internally, seemed to have disappeared from the scene. With them, Zionism also disappeared (conceptually), leaving imperialism and Arab Reaction as the enemies of revolutionary forces. The only reference to Palestinians was in a footnote about self-determination: 'Arab national unification must also include real autonomy and even self-determination for the different ethnic communities that exist in certain states, for example the Kurds in Iraq. It would furthermore have to solve, in the Middle East, the question of the state of Israel and the Arab refugees. These people, 800,000 in number, are still living uprooted and unemployed in camps.' The only solution for 'their painful and explosive problem is their reinstallation in Palestine, the Arab country *par excellence*, the present state of Israel being absorbed as a national minority enjoying a regime of self-government and full cultural freedoms within a United Arab Republic of the Middle East'.[13]

We do not know whether Nicola made any contribution to the document, though he did maintain links with the Fourth International during that period, and joined its International Executive Committee in its 1963 World Congress. Whichever role he played in their resolutions and positions did not receive direct attribution, though as the senior person in the Middle East region it is safe to assume he was responsible for the (rather meagre) attention the topic received.[14] His role received greater attention, however, through his involvement with the Israeli Socialist Organization (ISO), which was formed in 1962 and became known by the name of its monthly publication *Matzpen* (Compass in Hebrew).

THE EMERGENCE OF MATZPEN

Having risen to political prominence in the aftermath of the 1967 war, five years after it had been formed, Matzpen epitomized the radical left critique of Zionist ideology and practices. Its members were few in number but its impact was big. It was the clearest voice speaking against the 1967 occupation, and calling for the restoration of the rights of Palestinians in Israel, the Occupied Territories and the Diaspora. Its voice was fresh and authentic, free of the cumbersome Soviet-style jargon that characterized the rhetoric of Maki and Rakah. It posed a genuine alternative to state

ideology, especially as its formation coincided with the rise of the New
Left internationally, and it embodied the attractive spirit of the youth
rebellion of the 1960s. Still, its support base remained very limited
and it never managed to move beyond the political margins.[15] While its
membership always included Jews and Arabs, the majority of members
remained Jewish.

The initial approach of Matzpen was shaped by its origins in the Israeli
Communist Party. In a book written before they left the Party, the two
'founding fathers' of Matzpen, Moshé Machover and Akiva Orr, reiterated
the position of the Party in favour of mutual recognition of the right
to national self-determination of the two peoples living in the country
(Israeli Jews and Palestinian Arabs). They supported the right of the 1948
Palestinian refugees to return to their homeland or receive compensation
for their land, if they chose not to return.[16] This remained their position
after they and a few other members had been expelled from the Party in
1962 for violating internal discipline. In the first issue of their new journal,
they called for 'recognition of the national rights of the two peoples of
Eretz Israel – the Jewish and the Arab'. The organization acknowledged
that its views were similar to those of the Israeli Communist Party and
the Semitic Action (a liberal movement advocating reconciliation between
the two peoples of the country, led by Uri Avnery), but it differed from
them on other grounds: foreign orientation, attitudes towards democracy
and socialism.[17]

A few months later, A. Israeli (Machover and Orr) asserted that 'The
Question of Palestine' – the entire set of relationships between Jews and
Arabs in the country – had not been resolved: 'The focus of the problem
is that Israel and Jordan divided between them the territory that belongs
to the Arabs of Palestine. Both the private property of individuals and the
homeland of an entire nation were forcibly taken away from them. But
the nation itself did not disappear, and still exists.' They concluded that

> only an Israeli policy that would dare to abolish immediately the military
> government [over Arabs] in Israel, declare publicly that it is ready to
> return to the Arabs of Palestine what was taken away from them in
> 1948, recognise their rights as individuals and as a nation, help them
> acquire political independence and remove Hussein's yoke [Jordanian
> rule] – only such a policy can save Israel from the threatening future.

An agreement between Israeli Jews and Palestinian Arabs, they argued, would resolve the Israeli–Arab conflict and normalize Israel's relations with Arab countries.[18]

The notion that Israel as a sovereign state should accept the right to self-determination of the Arabs of Palestine (which may involve conceding territory) and the right of return of refugees, and in exchange receive recognition of the Arab states, remained the position of the organization for the first two years of its existence.[19] This position placed Matzpen at the extreme left of the Israeli political spectrum, but it was not very different from that of the Communist Party, and did not challenge the existence of the State of Israel or the right of Israeli Jews to self-determination.

A crucial challenge posed by Matzpen, though, was its growing rejection of Zionism. From its initial call for improved relations between Israel and Arab countries, it gradually moved towards a critique of Zionism. It redefined the clash between Jewish settlers and indigenous Palestinians as colonial in nature, and called for Israel to be 'de-Zionized', that is, to cease being a Jewish state and sever its links to Zionist institutions and policies that entrenched the conflict.

The first instance in which Zionism was clearly identified as the source of the Israeli–Palestinian conflict, due to its colonial nature, was in an article discussing the nationalist movement *al-Ard*, which was facing persecution by the Israeli authorities. Matzpen argued that Palestine faced a colonialism of a special type, 'the colonialism of the Zionist movement'. Whereas colonialism in general exploited the labour force of the native majority, 'the Zionist settlement movement was different. Its goal was the dispossession of the original residents in order to establish a Jewish state. The aim of normal colonialism was to exploit the riches of the country; the aim of Zionist colonialism was the country itself'.[20]

In this respect the Zionist movement was different from all other colonial movements, including that in South Africa. Therefore,

> the Israeli-Arab conflict is not a national conflict in essence. It is not a struggle over territory with a mixed population. In the main it is a struggle between the Zionist colonial movement, which sought and continues to displace the Arabs from an ever-growing part of Palestine, and the Arab national movement, which tries to establish sovereign control over all territories inhabited by Arabs.[21]

This point was developed further in a statement from May 1967, a month before the 1967 war. The Palestine question was 'not an ordinary conflict between two nations', because 'the state of Israel is the outcome of the colonization of Palestine by the Zionist movement, at the expense of the Arab people and under the auspices of imperialism'. The solution to the conflict involved 'the de-Zionization of Israel', which would bring an end to the discrimination and oppression suffered by the Arab citizens of the state, and entail recognition of the right of refugees to return or receive compensation. At the same time, 'recognition of the right of the Hebrew nation to self-determination' was essential, because it was the only solution 'consistent with the interests of both Arab and Israeli masses'. It would lead to the 'integration of Israel as a unit in an economic and political union of the Middle East, on the basis of socialism'. Without the prospect of secure existence as equals in the region, Israeli Jews would not free themselves from the impact of Zionism.[22]

This conceptual transition, from regarding the conflict as national in nature to seeing it as colonial in essence, was done largely under Nicola's influence. He joined the organization a few months after it was founded, to be joined a year later by a group of Haifa-based Maki activists, among them his wife Aliza. In their statement, these activists criticized Maki for its lack of internal democracy and its refusal to debate issues of revolution and reform that were raised by the Sino–Soviet conflict of the time. No issues related directly to the Israeli–Palestinian conflict were mentioned in their statement.[23] Notably, Nicola's work in that period did not deal with the conflict either, and focused on developments in the Middle East – Egypt, Iraq, and so on.

In an obituary, Moshé Machover described Nicola's impact:

He was much older than us, the founders of the organization, by 20–25 years. He had gone through the previous 30 years of the history of the world revolutionary movement without being contaminated by Stalinism. He remembered from personal experience things that we knew about only through reading books. In particular, he remembered the crucial period of the Zionist settlement process. Further, he had precisely what we lacked then – a consistent and comprehensive grasp of the Zionist settlement process and especially its impact on Arab society in Palestine. We acquired from him a deeper, more complete conceptualization of Israel as the realization of Zionist settlement. He also grasped the Arab Revolution as one indivisible process. The positions of Matzpen on these issues were adopted mainly under his influence. Some of his arguments we accepted immediately, as they seemed reasonable from the start. Others we accepted eventually, perhaps with some modifications. Of course, it was not a one-sided but a dialectical process. Nevertheless, his impact is clearly visible in all our statements on Zionism and the Arab East.[24]

Along similar lines, Akiva Orr defined Nicola's central contribution as 'the expansion of the political perspective from an approach that is restricted to Palestine to an approach that regards problems in Palestine as part of the problems of the Arab East in its entirety'.[25]

That approach was referred to as the Arab Revolution, a process that was not socialist in itself, but its dynamics pushed it in a socialist direction:

National unification is necessary not simply because the Arabs of the Mashreq [Arab East] share a long common history, a language and a cultural heritage. It is necessary primarily because the present political fragmentation of the Mashreq is a huge obstacle in the way of development of the productive forces, and facilitates imperialist exploitation and domination . . . All these historical, cultural and economic factors are vividly reflected in the consciousness of the Arab masses throughout the region. The aspiration for Arab national unification is one of the most deeply rooted ideas in the minds of these masses. But Arab national unification is impossible without a struggle to overthrow imperialist domination, which is the root cause of the present balkanization. And genuine anti-imperialist struggle means at the same time struggle also against the ruling classes in the Arab countries.[26]

Palestinians played a strategic role in that struggle as they needed to challenge the 'old middle-class and landowners leadership of the Arab national movement' and the new 'petit bourgeois' leadership, both of which showed 'total inability to solve the Palestinian question'. Only 'the exploited masses themselves, under a working-class leadership', could solve their historic problems, but this required 'a subjective factor – a political organisation with a revolutionary theory and a revolutionary all-Arab strategy'.

The only way for the Palestinian people to defeat Zionism was by fighting its allies – Imperialism and Arab Reaction – and 'rally to itself a wider struggle for the political and social liberation of the Middle East as a whole'. A political formula restricted to Palestine was doomed to fail.

Only when the Palestinian Arab and Israeli Jewish masses entered 'a joint struggle with the revolutionary forces in the Arab world for the national and social liberation of the entire region', could the struggle succeed. And for Israeli Jews (and other non-Arab minorities) to participate, their national rights would have to be recognized.[27]

This set of ideas was formulated by Nicola in a more comprehensive manner in a document titled Theses on the Revolution in the Arab East.[28] In line with the Trotskyist tradition, the revolution in the Arab East was defined as permanent revolution, in which even the national and democratic tasks – let alone socialism – could be met only through a campaign led by the working class supported by the poor peasantry. The lack of development of an urban-based national bourgeoisie, and the historical failure of the traditional ruling classes and the new state-oriented petty-bourgeoisie to offer systematic opposition to imperialism, meant that 'the struggle against imperialism – inseparable from all democratic struggles – can only be a struggle against all the existing dominant classes and regimes in the region'. To ensure success, local campaigns and mass mobilizations had to be 'directed by an all-Arab East revolutionary strategy supported directly by mass struggle throughout the whole region ... This strategic unity of the revolution corresponds to the most general national task of the revolution – Arab national unification'. This national task, though, 'cannot be waged under the banner of nationalism'.

A distinction was made here between the progressive quest for national unification and end to foreign domination, and the reactionary nature of nationalism as an ideology. Alongside the realization of national unity, the Arab Revolution 'must recognize and defend the rights of all non-Arab nationalities in the Arab East'. Whereas minorities oppressed by Arabs (such as Kurds) deserved unconditional support, Israeli Jews who oppressed Arabs were different: '[T]heir existence within the borders of this state is the product of a chauvinist colonialist operation, realized by means of oppression and expulsion of the Palestinians from their country.' Yet, they had become a nation distinguished from the world-wide Jewish community and from the Arabs around them. Their current national expression was reactionary and counter-revolutionary, and the main task was to restore national rights to Palestinians, but 'the programme of the Arab Revolution should include a clause on the right of self-determination of the Israeli Jews after the victory of the revolution'. The victory of the Revolution would entail the defeat of Zionism, the liquidation of imperialist domination, and the restoration of Palestinian rights. Under these circumstances, 'Israeli Jews will no longer constitute an oppressive nation but a small national minority in the Arab East. Then it becomes possible to speak of the equality of nations and the rights of every nation to self-determination'. The task of revolutionary activists was to show that the only safe future for Jews in Israel would be to abandon Zionism and join the Arab revolution.

From this perspective, Palestinian independence was not the answer: a Palestinian state never existed and the struggle against Zionism and imperialism before 1948 was part of the struggle of the entire Arab East for national independence and unification. The petty-bourgeois Palestinian nationalist leadership (PLO, Fatah) 'failed to recognise in theory and practice the regional (all-Arab East) scope of the revolution. It separated the struggle for the "liberation of Palestine" from the struggle against all Arab regimes'. That was a mistake which led to its defeat. It neglected the regional dimension of the struggle, subordinated the class struggle to 'national unity' with the Arab regimes (but not the masses), and focused on military campaigns. All this made it impossible 'to politicise the masses in the various Arab countries and mobilise them for a revolutionary struggle' in the entire region. Only such mobilization could combine absolute rejection of all Zionist institutions, with recognition of the national rights of Israeli Jews. This was the only formula that could potentially recruit the Jewish masses to the revolutionary cause.

These reflections, regarding the Palestinian role in the Arab Revolution, were developed after 1967. Before that, the critique of Zionism seems to have taken a back seat to other issues, such as workers' conditions and struggles within Israel, international conflicts (Vietnam, Cuba, the US civil rights movement, the war in Yemen) and questions facing the Left internationally (the Sino-Soviet conflict, Che Guevara's revolutionary expeditions, and the Chinese Cultural Revolution).

The year of 1967 marked an obvious turning point. Growing tensions in the Middle East region, and the rise of the PLO and the Fatah movement, had redirected some attention to the Israeli–Palestinian conflict even before June 1967. With the countdown to war, the issue became more urgent for the organization, and indeed for the entire political scene in Israel, as never before. The centrality that the conflict acquired during that period has not diminished since then. It continues to be the most important fault-line in Israeli politics and culture, serving to divide the Right from the Left to such an extent that in common political discourse the term 'Left' has lost most of its associations with issues of social justice, class struggle and redistribution. It has been reserved for people and organizations advocating a restoration of Palestinian rights and opposing

Israeli military and political domination to various degrees. Using this definition, no organization has been as far Left in Israeli political history as Matzpen and its various spin-offs.

The period of 1967–70 was Matzpen's golden age: its theoretical orientation was consolidated, its fame (and notoriety) reached their height, and it came to occupy a unique niche on Israel's political map. The two components of de-Zionization of Israel (resulting in equal rights and redress for Palestinian-Arab residents and refugees alike), and its integration in a socialist union of the Middle East, had become the foundation of its approach. A third component, added after the war, was of course the struggle against the 1967 occupation and its consequences.

From Matzpen's perspective, the 1967 war and subsequent occupation confirmed its analysis of the inherent nature of Israel, and that 'Zionism is by nature a colonizing movement of settlers . . . [and] its *modus operandi* has always been to create *faits accomplis* – if necessary, by force of arms – at the expense of the Arabs and against the Arabs'. To counter that tendency, 'it is the duty of the Israeli Government to withdraw from all the occupied territories and from the attempt to impose a settlement by force. This demand is the test for every progressive group and person'.[29] Although terminating the occupation was a necessary condition for a solution to the Israeli–Arab conflict, it was not sufficient. An overall solution would require, in addition, 'Israel's withdrawal from the Zionist path and the integration of a socialist, non-Zionist Israel in the region'. The socialist revolution was also the only way to Arab national unification and to ending the Balkanization imposed by imperialism on the Arab world.

But the occupation did not come to an end, and it led to ongoing expansion, political oppression and popular resistance. Palestinians have become 'entirely a conquered people . . . robbed not only of the most elementary political rights, but also of the very prospect for national and human existence'. Their militant response was natural, as

> it is both the right and duty of every conquered and subjugated people to resist and to struggle for its freedom. The ways, means and methods necessary and appropriate for such struggle must be determined by the people itself and it would be hypocritical for strangers – especially if they belong to the oppressing nation – to preach to it, saying, 'Thus shalt thou do, and thus shalt thou not do'.[30]

It is impossible to overestimate the extent to which this statement violated the scared principles of the post-1967 Israeli national consensus, which sought to portray Israeli Jews as a bizarre combination of righteous victims and military superheroes. There was nothing that made Matzpen so distinct politically – and also reviled publicly – as its unconditional support for the right of Palestinians to oppose the occupation. This was regarded as treason, collaborating with the enemy, though the statement added its support to 'only such organizations which, in addition to resisting occupation, also recognize the right of the Israeli people for self-determination'; this with a view to a joint struggle of Arabs and Jews in the region for a socialist future.

Uniquely among Israeli political forces, Matzpen did not succumb to the myth of the 'enlightened occupation' and thus challenged the national self-image of Israel as a liberal democracy practising 'purity of arms'. The Communist Party (Rakah) joined it in condemning the brutality of military rule in the Occupied Territories, but Matzpen alone linked it to the ongoing dominance of Zionist ideology within Israel. The latter was the root of the problem, in its view. What was needed was not merely a withdrawal from the territories, but a socialist revolution that would transform Israel

> from a Zionist state, a tool for furthering Zionist colonization . . . into a state expressing the real interests of both Jewish and Arab masses, a state which can and will be integrated in a socialist union of the Middle East. But in the present circumstances it is impossible even to imagine working for that goal without a consistent struggle against a continued Israeli occupation of the Arab territories. Only through this struggle can the Jewish and Arab masses be mobilized for socialism.[31]

As we can see from this discussion, Matzpen attempted to resolve the inherent tension between national and class discourses by setting the restoration of the rights of Palestinians alongside – not at the expense of – the right of Israeli Jews to self-determination. At the same time, it called for the integration of all groups and states within a socialist federation of the Middle East, perceived as an antidote to local and narrow-minded nationalism. In this way, it hoped, the quest for socialism could be reconciled with ongoing attachment of people to their national identity.

It is crucial to realize, however, that Matzpen never equated the self-determination of Israeli Jews with the existing State of Israel. Its support for the right to national self-determination went together with opposition, not just to the policies but to the very legitimacy of Israel's existence as a

Jewish-Zionist state. In adopting that position Matzpen drew a line that served to distinguish it clearly from the Zionist Left.

In an article published in early 1970, Orr and Machover clarified the meaning of the key notion of de-Zionization: '[T]he abolition of Jewish exclusivity (expressed for example in the Law of Return), according to which a Brooklyn Jew is granted more civil and political rights in Israel and to Israel than a Palestinian Arab born here (whether currently a refugee or a citizen).'[32] From a Zionist perspective, the State of Israel was not a final product but 'an intermediary phase and an instrument for the realization of the full Zionist goal'. Just as a solution to the South African conflict between settlers and indigenous people required the abolition of the racial character of the South African state – the historical source of the conflict as well as the factor that continued to reproduce it – abolishing the Zionist character of Israel, they argued, was necessary to a solution of the Israeli–Palestinian conflict.

In contrast to the Zionist Left, Matzpen rejected the notion of peace and reconciliation between two national collectives (Arabs and Jews) as they existed in the post-1948 period, since that notion entrenched the dispossession of Palestinians in the Nakba. Only a common revolutionary struggle in the entire region, against both the existing Arab regimes and the Zionist regime in Israel, would guarantee true cooperation between people of different origins, and the ability to move beyond national antagonism and, indeed, nationalism itself. Class struggle within Israel was important but was conditional on developments in the region: on its own it would not lead to revolutionary transformation due to the material interests linking Jewish workers – even the most exploited and oppressed among them – to their national bourgeoisie and the Zionist state.[33]

NEW DIRECTIONS POST-1970

The period following the 1967 war saw the consolidation of the anti-Zionist Left position in Israel, with a theoretically elegant synthesis of principled support for legitimate national rights with the struggle for socialism in the Middle East. By 1970, however, the Matzpen formula had started to fracture. It was attacked from two opposing angles: as not being sufficiently resolute in its support for the anti-colonial struggle waged by Palestinians (hence, not national enough), and as not being sufficiently resolute in its support for working-class struggles (hence, not socialist enough). Both attacks came from within, and while neither rejected the original Matzpen formula outright, both stretched it in different directions.

Internationalism and Militant Nationalism

Adopting the name Revolutionary Communist Alliance (RCA),[34] the first group of dissenting activists split off from the ISO in 1970 and moved to assert a distinct identity with a new journal called Ma'avak (Struggle in Hebrew). Among the criticisms of Matzpen, not all of which need concern us here, the following is particularly relevant for the discussion:

> Despite its correct and courageous slogans regarding 'Zionist nationalism' and 'Arab nationalism', Matzpen tends to detract from the typical colonial character of the [Israeli-Arab] contradiction, and to emphasize its national aspects. It therefore refrains from fighting to break the Zionist monopoly on land, and holds an ambiguous position regarding the national rights of Jews in Israel/Palestine and the meaning of the principle of self-determination. This is the reason it sees the State of Israel only as a capitalist oppressive apparatus, which will be destroyed by the revolution as all other states, and not as an oppressive colonial instrument (in addition to its capitalist nature), which is therefore the main tactical enemy of the revolutionary struggle in Israel.[35]

In outlining its political programme, the Ma'avak group re-asserted its view of Zionism and Israel as colonial instruments aligned with imperialism and operating at the expense of the Arab and Palestinian populations. Due to this history, 'Israel is not a society in which internal class contradictions can form the background for an independent Israeli socialist revolution, disconnected from the regional revolutionary process'.[36] At the same time, it was crucial to expose internal contradictions within that society by undermining the power of Zionist ideology over the Jewish masses.

This could be done through the unfolding of three interrelated processes: '1) gradual dismantling of the military superiority of the IDF [Israeli Defence Force]; 2) worsening of the internal economic crisis in Israel; 3) consolidation of an internationalist alternative among the Palestinian liberation movement and the Arab revolutionary movement, and the spread of anti-imperialist consciousness among the masses of Jewish workers in Israel'.[37] Blocking the emergence of such consciousness were Arab chauvinistic trends, which denied the existence of a Jewish national entity in Israel/Palestine and its rights. Without recognizing the political rights of Jewish workers they would not join the revolutionary struggle.

Having recognized the national rights of Jews in Israel/Palestine, the political programme went on to assert that Palestine was a bi-national unit, and that the current territorial concentration of the Jewish population reflected the realities of dispossession of Arabs from their lands. Under these circumstances, territorial separation between Jews and Arabs would serve to entrench the realities imposed by Zionism, and would contradict the right of all citizens to reside and work wherever they wish. The only alternative to the national conflict was joint revolutionary struggle of Jews and Arabs. The struggle against the Zionist regime would have as its ultimate goal the establishment of popular revolutionary rule in the Arab East, as part of the world revolution.

As can be seen from the above, the RCA maintained much of Matzpen's analysis, but it took two steps away from it. The first was greater identification with the Palestinian struggle. It argued that, 'by virtue of its historical position, the Palestinian movement is in the forefront of the struggle not only against Zionism and pro-imperialist Arab reaction, but also against the power and ideology of the [Arab] petty-bourgeoisie, which presents its nationalist reformism as socialism'.[38] This statement, and others like it (equating the Cuban and Vietnamese socialist struggles with the Palestinian nationalist struggle), were criticized as unprincipled concessions to nationalism, albeit that of the oppressed Palestinian people.[39] If the struggle of nationalists received uncritical support, argued Matzpen in its response, what need was there for socialism?

The second step had to do with the notion of Jewish political rights in Israel/Palestine. Although recognized in principle by Ma'avak, these were not formulated in the language of national self-determination. It remained unclear what these rights were and how they could be expressed, if Palestine could not be territorially partitioned. On both counts above, the careful balance constructed by Matzpen between critical support for national rights and the quest for socialist integration seems to have been disrupted, and a more radical rhetoric with a Third Worldist orientation became dominant. Expecting a 'gradual dismantling' of the military superiority of the IDF may have displayed a (misplaced) reliance on the military capabilities of Palestinian resistance organizations, though for obvious personal and organizational security reasons this could not have been stated openly.

It was not only Matzpen members who criticized their departing colleagues. Within a year of its formation, the RCA had itself split and some of its members started publishing a new journal under the title of Hazit Adumah (Red Front in Hebrew). The Red Front attacked Ma'avak for its refusal 'to condemn bourgeois-national ideology in its work among the working class as a whole'. According to this critique, by focusing on workers' struggles and demands, the group failed to target Zionism and Arab nationalism, and addressed the working class on narrow trade union issues only. As a result, the RCA followed in the footsteps of the 'Soviet revisionists and their local representatives' (Rakah) and did not offer a true revolutionary alternative.[40] Ironically, their own call to the 'workers and the exploited' in the first issue of Hazit Adumah, contained no explicit demands of a national nature and ignored the broader context of the national-political conflict.[41]

The Red Front's overall positions regarding Israel and Zionism were not substantially different from those of Matzpen and the RCA,[42] with the notable exception that they included no mention of specific national rights for Israeli Jews, and their language was more blunt than the customary Matzpen formulas: 'The Zionists push the working class in Israel towards a situation that can lead to its destruction. We have to reiterate that Zionism wishes for Jewish workers to become policemen to protect its and its American bosses' interests in the region. If Jewish workers insist on playing this essential anti-revolutionary role they will have to pay a price for it.'[43]

What could Israeli Jews expect from socialism, then? No special treatment, the same as everyone else: 'Jewish workers in Israel, just like workers in the entire world, must abandon nationalism and fight against their own ruling class. If Jewish workers in Israel do that, they would be united with the oppressed people of the Middle East, and in that their security resides. The oppressed people of the Middle East must kick out the Soviet bosses, American imperialists, and their Zionist and Arab nationalist puppets.'[44] It is worth noting here that, in a typical 'Third Worldist' fashion, the Jewish workers were equated with the oppressed people of the region. The latter were not identified by class affiliation, as if their position were determined solely by having been subject to external political domination.[45]

The Red Front had a brief history of just over a year. At the end of 1972 many of its members were arrested and charged with espionage and collaboration with the enemy (Syrian military intelligence), based on a secret trip some of them took to Damascus. In a well-publicized trial in 1973, five members were sentenced to various periods in prison. It is obvious that none of them had any interest in working with the Syrian or other Arab regimes, and their sole interest consisted in establishing links with other revolutionary organizations in the region, primarily Palestinian ones. Statements before the trial, submitted by the leading defendants – Daud Turki and Ehud Adiv – allow us to get a clear idea of their perspective.[46]

Turki, A Palestinian-Arab citizen of Israel, defined their goal as socialism:

> The common goal of all workers, peasants and those who are persecuted in Israeli society. The Jews have a share, and they must have a share, because they are members of the organization on a footing of equality with me, in establishing a new government and a new regime which will allow both the Jewish people and the Arab people to play an effective part in the struggle of the Arab people for liberation.

Turki went on to criticise Zionism, which

> instead of adopting, as it should, a neutral attitude, or one of support for the Arab struggle for national and socialist liberation, it has stood beside this movement's enemies, beside the Americans who are persecuting the Vietnamese people, beside American imperialism which is exploiting the peoples of Latin America and the peoples of Asia and Africa, and setting the Jewish people against the Arab people forever. I think that this attitude amounts to a crime against both the Jewish people and the Arab people.

Turki clearly conflated socialism with national liberation, indeed with nationalism of oppressed people in general (regardless of its class content). Jews should support the Arab struggle for liberation rather than a struggle that supersedes nationalism, although both groups had 'the same future and would live together in a single homeland under the rule of a single state, a state liberated from all foreign influence and all social exploitation'. The criticism that Matzpen directed at Ma'avak – insufficient distinction of socialism from nationalism, albeit of the 'progressive' kind – could have been directed against the Red Front as well.

The same approach was displayed by Adiv in explicit terms. Accepting that 'all trends of Matzpen' had 'a sound theory', he argued that they lacked 'the chapter entitled "what is to be done" to reach the multi-national socialist Middle East they talk of, and in their political activity they restrict their talk to the Jewish state of Israel. That is to say they are preoccupied with convincing the Jews, and completely disregard the Arab struggle, and in particular the Palestinian Arab struggle against Zionism and the state of Israel'. A change of focus was needed to convert the national conflict into a class struggle. This could be done only

> if the Jews will prove to the Arabs, who have been fighting Zionism for dozens of years, that they [the Jews] are on their side, that they are prepared to sacrifice everything they have, to be subjected to the same 'treatment' and to share everything with them. Without this no Arab will have confidence that the sincerest Jewish revolutionary is really revolutionary. No ideology, not even the most equitable and progressive, can convince the Arabs unless it is accompanied by action on the part of those who adhere to it.

While the sentiments expressed in this statement were genuine, they resulted in abandoning the quest for independent analysis and critique of nationalism. They replaced it with personal courage and dedication in the service of a nationalist cause. These were admirable qualities but could not account for how the struggle would be transformed into a socialist – let alone revolutionary communist – political project. With the Red Front, the internationalist programme of the Left ended up being subordinated to militant nationalism. If the principal contradiction between capital and labour was expressed in the Middle East as a contradiction between Zionism and the Palestinian-Arab people,[47] it followed that 'the task of communists is not to present "proletarian alternatives" or to say that they struggle for socialism, but to aspire to lead the national liberation struggle, currently led by Fatah. They can do that by proving to masses that only their leadership can achieve the national liberation they are fighting for. Their communist-led national liberation will be their social liberation as well'.[48] Under these conditions, socialism itself inevitably took a back seat and the link between it and national liberation was severed.

Internationalism and Workerism

In parallel to the move in the nationalist direction above, a move in an opposite direction was taken by another group at the same time. Adopting the Hebrew name Avangard (Vanguard) for its journal, the group also used the name Workers Alliance. Both names were indicative of the group's orientation: it regarded itself as a political and theoretical vanguard standing for a version of 'proletarian' Marxism that tolerated no compromises with nationalism. In its quest to supersede the 'centrist' orientation of Matzpen, which allowed various schools of thought to coexist within a broad radical socialist umbrella, the group aligned itself with a strict sectarian tendency that regarded all other left currents as falling far short of their purist expectations.

Avangard argued that the focus of the pre-1948 Trotskyists on the Palestinian-Arab working class was correct. But, the creation of Israel changed things. With the mass expulsion/flight of Palestinians and their replacement by Jewish immigrants (primarily from Arab countries), a new working class came into being. Jewish workers were no longer a privileged layer of immigrants as they were during the British Mandate period, though the remaining activists from those times continued to regard them as such. They carried their attitude into the ISO, which some of them joined in the early 1960s. Hence, Matzpen showed little interest in the Israeli proletariat as a revolutionary agent; indeed, its interest in the working class in general was limited. Instead, it kept looking for substitutes for the historical role of the working class: petty-bourgeois Arab nationalist forces (Nasserism), rebellious western youth, third world guerrilla movements, alienated intellectuals, and so on. In that it was a typical product of the New Left with its eclectic theoretical approach, which bred opportunism and anti-proletarian tendencies.

For Avangard, it was crucial to understand Israeli society with the use of standard Marxist tools of analysis: 'There is a distinct Israeli class structure, in which the Israeli proletariat produces surplus value (based mostly on imported capital), and is therefore the oppressed and exploited class within it.'[49] The tasks associated with the national or anti-colonial struggle (de-Zionization of Israel, restoration of Palestinian rights) could be achieved only 'through a proletarian revolution in Israel, which is inseparable from the revolutionary process in the Middle East'. These were not separate stages that could be achieved before the victory of the Israeli working class and the establishment of a proletarian dictatorship. The goal of the struggle was an 'Israeli soviet republic', which would use the principle of self-determination to resolve the national question. The task of defeating Zionism was that of the Israeli proletariat – Jews and Arabs alike – and the Palestinian masses would facilitate their own liberation by joining the working-class struggle in each of the countries in which they resided, until a regional socialist federation was established.[50]

In contrast to Matzpen, Avangard refused to acknowledge specific features of Israeli society that would justify treating it as a special case, exempt from what they regarded as the 'normal' mode of political analysis.

Israel had a unique history of course, but so did all other countries, and the task of activists was to organize the working class and work towards a socialist revolution. Zionism and Arab nationalism were manifestations of class rule in the particular context of the Middle East. Their presence called neither for the suspension of class analysis nor for a change in the critique of nationalism.

In particular, Avangard attacked theoretical approaches that blurred the distinction between opposition to Zionism and support for socialism. Whereas for Ma'avak and the Red Front the colonial nature of Israeli society was crucial, and the only way to socialism was through a consistent struggle for national liberation, for Avangard the only way to national liberation was through a consistent struggle for socialism. Matzpen's claims to be fighting for both goals were ridiculed as a typical 'centrist' attempt to avoid having to make clear choices.[51]

Deserving of particular scorn in Avangard's view, was the concept of the Arab Revolution. It was used by Matzpen over the years to refer to a struggle by various 'progressive' forces in the Middle East to unify the region, free it from imperial control, and embark on a process of social transformation that would rid it of feudal, pro-imperialist and 'reactionary' elements. This logic, that national struggle would lead to socialism, because its goals could not be realized within the existing social order, was rejected by Avangard. In their view it inevitably led to accommodation with nationalism and to constant search for substitutes for the revolutionary role of the working class, in the Middle East and elsewhere.

Ironically, due to international pressure which in turn gave rise to internal pressure, the same nationalist 'deviation' gradually began to afflict the group itself. The international organization with which it was affiliated – the French OCI[52] – attacked its positions as being a concession to Zionism. The call for an Israeli socialist revolution and soviet republic was seen by the OCI as entrenching the dispossession of Palestinians by recognizing the State of Israel that was built on its foundation. The 'correct' position rather, was to call for the abolition of the 1948 partition and the creation of a unified state of Palestine to replace Israel and its occupied territories.[53]

Following this criticism, Avangard abandoned the call for a socialist republic in Israel. It started calling instead for convening a constituent assembly in a united democratic Palestine, open to both Jews and Arabs. While this clearly was a move away from the purist class focus, the new position was attacked by other organizations as a continued evasion of the national struggle and an attempt to dilute its specificity, rather than to highlight its importance. It seems that despite the change of slogans, Avangard's origins as a 'workerist' organization meant that its rivals could never consider it as anything different from what it used to be.

These attacks from the outside were echoed by divisions within its own ranks. The French mentors in the OCI continued to reject their Israeli colleagues' positions, and at the end of 1975 expelled them from the international movement they headed. Internal opposition emerged as a result, leading eventually to a public split and the formation of yet another organization, the Palestinian Communist Group, known as the Nitzotz (*Ha-Nitzotz* Spark in Hebrew).

The Nitzotz group started its life in 1976 as a faction which sided with the OCI against the local line pursued by Avangard. It criticised its leadership for not recognizing the colonial nature of the State of Israel, which made it qualitatively different from other reactionary regimes in the region. Palestinian national liberation was pitted against Zionism, imperialism and Arab regimes by its very essence, they argued, and that made 'the Palestinian national interest' crucial to socialism. The centrality of the Palestinian struggle to create 'an independent nation' meant that notions of an Arab nation and an Israeli people had to be rejected. The Jewish population, 'imported by imperialism', had been serving foreign political, military and diplomatic interests against the masses. To avoid a 'death trap', it had to 'join the Palestinian struggle for national liberation' and 'become a component of the struggle to "abolish partition"', which will provide for the consolidation of the Jewish masses as part of the Palestinian nation . . . their class interest consists in joining the struggle for a socialist revolution, which passes through the "abolition of partition" and Palestinian national liberation'.[54]

To clarify the differences between its positions and those of other organizations, the Nitzotz group published another article that focused directly on the question of nationalism and socialism. It put forward a position that was diametrically opposed to Avangard's original stand, and moved close to that of the Red Front (with no mention of armed struggle, of course, and many mentions of Trotsky). The striking point about this article was that it effectively equated the national struggle of Palestinians with the struggle for socialism. Not because the former was explicitly class-based, but because 'the objective needs of the Palestinian struggle for national liberation conditions', and its call for a secular democratic Palestine, position it against imperialist control in the region, by working to destroy its 'fortress', the State of Israel. That struggle – based on the nationalism of 'youth, peasants, women and workers' – was revolutionary in its implications. The task of communists was to participate in the mass struggle and prove themselves as the most consistent and best fighters. They had to reject 'any attempt to counterpose the socialist revolution to democratic demands', avoid raising their own demands, and focus on leading the national struggle to its successful conclusion. In other words, they had to follow the masses' nationalist consciousness rather than become their vanguard.[55]

And what about the Israeli working class that was the centre of Avangard's theory? Its Jewish component was

> a layer enjoying political and material privileges that feed its deep chauvinism and its unwillingness to break out of the Histadrut framework and confront the basic question of the Zionist state . . . any surrender to or accommodation with the reactionary phenomenon of the Jewish proletariat, when the Palestinian masses within and without the Green Line reach the heights of struggle, means lagging behind the class vanguard and following the most reactionary elements of the proletariat.

The proof that Palestinian workers were the vanguard of the working class consisted in their fight against Zionism and imperialism, which Jewish workers obviously did not join. Again, a similar analysis to that of the Red Front, which saw the basic contradiction between capital and labour as expressed by the contradiction between Zionism and the Palestinian people.

The only way forward for Jewish workers, then, was to integrate themselves into the Palestinian liberation struggle. They could acquire class consciousness 'only through confronting the question of the Zionist state, through a defence of the national rights of the Palestinian people, a defence whose most consistent slogan is the right of the Palestinian people to self-determination in a liberated and united Palestine, while granting civil and cultural rights to minorities'. Addressing the fears of Jewish workers could not be done through 'guaranteeing "national rights" after the revolution, or retaining "the right to self-determination of Jews" – these positions justify, even if indirectly, the fears of the Jewish worker of being oppressed after the victory of the revolution, and reinforce his links to the Zionist state'. Only joining the Palestinian revolution would secure the future.

Needless to say, Avangard regarded these positions as surrender to petty-bourgeois nationalism, abandoning the class perspective, and hopeless theoretical confusion, aimed to attract Palestinian militants wishing to fight for national liberation mixed with a dose of Marxism.[56] The split of the Nitzotz group led to the demise of Avangard, although it survived for a couple more years with decreasing membership and output. This signified the demise of the idea that radical transformation could take place in Israeli society on the basis of workers' struggles. The centrality of the Israeli–Palestinian conflict meant that no organization that regarded it as secondary in importance (theoretically and practically) could hope to survive for long. Avangard's belated attempt to jump on the wagon, by changing some of its slogans (support for a united Palestine instead of a socialist Israel), did not rest easily with its continued focus on class struggle and its call for the creation of a workers' party. It satisfied neither those who feared a retreat from a class perspective into nationalism nor those interested in a fuller embrace of nationalism. The outcome was the implosion of the organization, with some members leaving with the Nitzotz and others – including the original leadership – withdrawing from activism altogether.[57]

MATZPEN IN THE 1970s

The departure of two groups in 1970 weakened Matzpen numerically but had little impact on the organization otherwise. Of greater importance was another split, in 1972, which saw it split into two groups, roughly equal in size, both claiming its name and historical legacy. They became known by the location of their main branches, in Tel Aviv and Jerusalem respectively. Matzpen Tel Aviv retained most of the founding members of the group, and its orientation continued to reflect the spirit of the New Left, rejecting rigid organizational structures and tolerating a broad range of theoretical views. Matzpen Jerusalem adopted a tighter structure and theoretical framework, and eventually joined the Fourth International (led by Ernest Mandel). It adopted the name Matzpen Marxist for its journal shortly after the split, and changed the name of the organization to Revolutionary Communist League in 1975, but continued to lay claim to the legacy of Matzpen since 1962 (and to the first 61 issues of the magazine).[58]

Initially, the two groups differed little in their approach to the national question and its relations to socialism. Significantly, the most important compilation of analyses and documents about the Israeli–Palestinian conflict that reflected Matzpen's positions was prepared before the split though published after it, and was regarded by both groups as a crucial resource.[59] Over time, the two groups started drifting apart, though the gap between them owed much more to changes in Matzpen Marxist's approach. Matzpen Tel Aviv retained its analysis almost intact. Possibly, this was due to the fact that its main theorists were based in Europe and thus were less vulnerable to the pressures that arose from practical work within the country.

Its basic principles document, which dates to 1973 (re-affirmed in 1978), reiterated most of the positions discussed earlier: it identified Matzpen's field of operation as the struggle against the existing regime in Israel, and positioned it in an 'irreconcilable contradiction with Zionism . . . a colonial enterprise that is being implemented at the expense of the Arab masses (primarily the Palestinian Arab people), under the protection of and in alliance with imperialism'. It regarded the State of Israel, 'in its current Zionist form', as the product of the Zionist enterprise and also an instrument for its expansion.[60]

Only a socialist revolution would provide a solution to the national and social problems of the region, according to the document, by toppling 'all the existing regimes' and building a political union: 'In this united and liberated Arab East the right to self determination (including right to form a separate state) of each of the non-Arab nationalities in the region will be recognized, including the Israeli-Jewish nation.' In Israel/Palestine itself, Matzpen's task was to topple the Zionist regime by abolishing the institutions, laws, and practices on which it was based. The ultimate goal was the 'integration of the two peoples of the country – the Israeli-Jewish people and the Palestinian-Arab people – in a regional socialist union' on a basis of free choice and full equality.

While Matzpen Tel Aviv maintained its critical attitude to Zionism and Israel, combined with support for Israeli Jews' right to self-determination, Matzpen Marxist began to distance itself from that position. Much of its analysis revolved around the concept of the Arab Revolution. In the concluding chapter of *The Other Israel*, written by the leadership of Matzpen Marxist, they referred to a revolution with 'an objectively socialist tendency', which 'must destroy all the existing oppressive and exploitative structures in the Arab East' in order to succeed. The Zionist state would be defeated, and the only question facing the Israeli Jewish masses was 'whether they will ultimately recognize the Zionist state as their own oppressor and join the Arab masses in the struggle to overthrow it . . . [or] permit themselves to remain a counter-revolutionary force that must be crushed by the Arab revolution'. To move the masses in the right direction, 'the broadest possible democracy in the national question will be especially important'. This implied 'the right of national self-determination for non-Arab nationalities in the region – including the Israeli Jews – so far as the exercise of this right is consistent with defense of the socialist revolution in the Arab East'.[61]

Noticeable in this document, as compared to previous Matzpen writings, was the growing harshness of the rhetoric. This was not just a stylistic change – a real hardening of positions had taken place, and continued, possibly under the impact of contacts with activists from the region. Consistently with that position, within days after the October 1973 war started, the organization asserted its opposition to the war effort and called for the defeat of the Israeli side: 'We see Zionism as responsible for every drop of blood spilled in the region, by Jews and Arabs alike; the Arab masses who wish to regain their territories that are occupied by Israel, and restore the full rights of the Palestinians are not our enemies. Our enemies are the ruling classes in Israel and the Zionist state.' As long as Palestinians were denied their rights, and the Zionist state continued to exist, war was inevitable: 'Only a revolutionary leadership, which combines the struggle against Zionism with anti-imperialist and anti-capitalist struggle against all the privileged and propertied classes in the region, can lead the masses to victory.'[62]

Between 1973 and 1975, much of the theoretical energy of the organization was invested in a document aimed to provide a broad programmatic overview of the 'Arab Revolution' and its implications for revolutionaries operating in Israel and the Middle East. Produced in the name of 'Organizations belonging to the Fourth international in the Arab region', it was written by Gilbert Achcar (of the Revolutionary Communist Group of Lebanon, using the alias Jaber) with help from Michel Warschawski (of Matzpen Marxist).[63]

The document identified the State of Israel as a combination of several elements: it was a product of a movement with 'settler-colonial character', carried out 'at the expense of the original Arab inhabitants, most of whom were expelled.' The immigration process was 'accompanied by the formation of a Jewish proletariat'. The process was distinct from the traditional forms of colonialism which were based on exploiting the original inhabitants, and 'the very nature of the Zionist state – as expressed in its origins and continued reasons for existence, makes it a state that is of necessity directly linked to imperialism. It plays the role of a military bastion in the service of a counter-revolutionary American imperialist strategy for the Arab East region.'

The central task of the Arab revolution was Arab national unity, but there were other national issues in the region (Berber, Kurdish and so on), which generally could be resolved through recognizing the right to self-determination. So far, this formula reiterated the 'classical' analysis of Matzpen. However, that right did not apply to the Israeli-Jewish case in the same way:

> In the present state of Israel, the oppressor majority is Jewish and its oppression has been primarily based on expelling the original Arab inhabitants. In this sense, the only revolutionary attitude is to recognise the complete and unconditional right of the Palestinian Arabs to self determination, that is, their right to return to all the territories from which they have been expelled and to live free of all national oppression.

This presupposed 'the destruction of the Zionist state, which rests on racist foundations incompatible with such a perspective. Only after the achievement of this necessary historical task of the Arab revolution, will it be possible to deal concretely and correctly with the question of the rights of the Jewish national minority in Palestine'.

As part of a successful revolutionary process, there was a need to guarantee 'full civil and cultural rights for the Jewish population, as well as complete equality between Jew and Arab . . . [and] recognising the right to self-administration of the Jewish workers in their regions, within the context of the political and economical centralism demanded by a workers state'. After the destruction of the Zionist state, 'and only after this', could the right to self-determination of Israeli-Jews be recognized, including their right to form an independent state on a part of Palestinian land. But this would be subject to the condition, 'that the exercise of this right in no way affects the rights of other peoples', and it was 'in harmony with the right of the Palestinian Arabs to self determination'.

There were two main differences between the standard Matzpen positions and those found in the Arab Revolution document. The first had to do with the attitude towards the State of Israel: instead of using relatively mild language (de-Zionization, abolition of discriminatory laws, transforming Israel in its current form, and so on), the task was re-formulated bluntly as the 'destruction of the Zionist state'. Coupled with the call for a military defeat of Israeli forces in war, this amounted to a clear rhetorical shift. The second difference had to do with self-determination for Israeli Jews. This right no longer stood on its own but was subordinated to the victory of the Arab Revolution (could only be recognized after the defeat of Israel), and to the prior right of Palestinians to restore their own self-determination.

In these respects, then, Matzpen Marxist moved away from its origins, though it took care to argue that it was not adopting an Arab or Palestinian nationalist approach (unlike the Red Front before and the Nitzotz group after): 'One must distinguish very clearly between revolutionary national tasks and nationalist ideology with its essentially bourgeois character, which forms the greatest obstacle to revolution because it delays the formation of a class consciousness for the working masses.' In its view, supporting national goals was an essential step towards socialism, rather than a way of establishing the 'credentials' of Israeli activists for the Arab masses. In addition, for Matzpen Marxist the practical implication of the Arab Revolution framework was an attempt to coordinate theoretical and political work between Israeli and Arab activists, but without abandoning its organizational independence and class approach.

Adopting that direction was costly, however, as the move encountered resistance from within the organization, and criticism from the outside.[64] Two points in particular were challenged: the notion that there was an 'Arab' revolution, which was neither socialist nor simply a nationalist movement. And, the question of self-determination for Israeli Jews.

The 'proletarian faction', organized within Matzpen Marxist before leaving in 1975 to join Avangard, published a set of documents attacking these positions.[65] For them, the central task everywhere was to form a revolutionary party that would organize the working class and fight their 'own' bourgeoisie. Notions of a regional amorphous pan-Arab revolution were simply 'liquidationist' distortions of the proletarian approach, relying on petty-bourgeois leaderships to play the role reserved for the working class. That role, in Israel, should be played by the 'Israeli proletariat on both its parts – the Jewish and the Palestinian . . . united against the Zionist bourgeoisie'. Palestinian national liberation could be achieved through class struggle, in which the Palestinian masses would be organized together with the working class of each country in which they reside, including Israel.

While this line was predictable, reproducing almost verbatim Avangard's positions, another critique was less expected. In an internal article by a long-serving member of the organization (the only one who survived from the pre-1948 RCA), the document was criticized as reflecting anti-Marxist thinking, expressed in the idea of an Arab revolution (defined in national rather than class terms), instead of a socialist revolution in the Arab region. At the very least, the document demonstrated deep confusion regarding the nature and class character of the revolution, and that was a serious problem.[66] In addition, qualifying the right to national self-determination (subject it to the defeat of Zionism, after the victory of the revolution) is a useless device for mobilizing people at present, on the basis of their current concerns, argued the author.

Notwithstanding these criticisms, Matzpen Marxist stuck to its new positions, and reiterated them in its number 100 issue, which also celebrated its 15th anniversary. It identified the programmatic bases of Matzpen as anti-Zionism, 'opposition to the legitimacy of the Zionist state's existence', support for 'equal co-existence of the two peoples of Palestine in their joint homeland', and the need to mobilize the Israeli working class – on the basis of its contradictory interests – to the struggle against 'Zionist colonialism'.[67] Discussing an impending merger with the Palestinian Communist Group (the Nitzotz), which had split off Avangard by that time, the following were identified as points shared by the two groups: recognition of the colonial nature of the Zionist movement and Israel, unconditional support for the Palestinian liberation movement in its struggle against Zionism, and support for the Arab military forces against Israel.

Other issues remained disputed. Matzpen Marxist asserted that there was an Arab nation, whose quest for unity was progressive; that nationalism – even that of oppressed peoples – was a bourgeois ideology that should be opposed; that the task of revolutionaries was to give a socialist direction to the national struggle, rather than present a consistent nationalist perspective; that Israeli-Jews had national rights, and that workers among them were linked to Zionism not only ideologically but also materially. The Nitzotz group had rejected all these positions but was moving towards accepting them.[68] And indeed, a year and half later, in April 1979, the two organizations merged on the basis of those points.[69] However, the merger proved short-lived, and within less than a year the two groups went their separate ways. As far as can be established, the failure of the merger had to do primarily with personal and organizational issues rather than with programmatic disagreements, though these did emerge later on.

Both of the historical Matzpen factions continued to support a position that attempted to reconcile class analysis with national struggles. The difference between them consisted in that Matzpen Tel Aviv was more 'diplomatic' in its rhetoric while Matzpen Marxist adopted a blunt language that sounded more radical and ran the risk of moving too far in a Palestinian nationalist direction. Ultimately, though, despite their different styles, they retained much in common as compared to Ma'avak, Avangard, and the other offshoots of the original united organization.

HISTORICAL AND POLITICAL CONTEXTS

As the Matzpen story approaches the 1980s, it would be useful to provide a brief contextual analysis of the period during which the developments discussed so far had taken place. The 1960s saw the rise of the New Left and associated movements against the war in Vietnam, in support of racial equality in the USA and gender equality everywhere, against authoritarian regimes in the Soviet bloc and in favour of guerrilla campaigns for social change in Latin America. The rise of the Palestinian resistance in the Middle East fit this pattern, by creating a popular grassroots alternative to corrupt and inefficient Arab regimes. The prevailing sense of worldwide political and cultural transformation during that period, helped Matzpen grow by attracting young activists in Israel, and from among disillusioned Left Zionist immigrants (from France and Latin America in particular). At the same time, this growth also opened activists up to many different ideas and resulted in internal divisions, which were later to cause splits.

The following decade was different in many respects and presented a more mixed picture. The early years of the decade witnessed the American retreat from Southeast Asia, as well as the first serious military setback to Israel in 1973. The rise of Third World forces continued with dispersed developments all over the globe: from the Ethiopian revolution of 1974 through the liberation of the Portuguese colonies in Africa in 1975 and the Soweto uprising of 1976, to the victory of the Sandinista Front in Nicaragua, the Iranian revolution in 1979, and the liberation of Zimbabwe in 1980. Locally, the recognition of the PLO as the sole legitimate representative of the Palestinian people, and Arafat's 1974 speech at the UN general assembly (in which he praised Ehud Adiv of the Red Front), were significant in establishing the Palestinian national movement as a legitimate international player. This was accompanied by growing delegitimation of Israel: most African countries broke off diplomatic relations with it following its 1973 occupation of Egyptian territory, and a 1975 landmark UN resolution defined Zionism as racism and a form of racial discrimination. The growth of resistance in the Occupied Territories and Israel itself, especially the Day of the Land in 1976, provided an impetus to all left-wing forces.

There were counter developments as well during the same period: Black September in 1970 Jordan, which forced the relocation of the Palestinian resistance to Lebanon, and the resulting disastrous civil war in that latter country; the defeat of the armed Left and the installation of military regimes in the Southern Cone of the Americas. Above all, one development proved crucial for Israel/Palestine: the 1977 victory by Likud in the Israeli elections and the subsequent visit to Jerusalem by President al-Sadat of Egypt, leading to the Camp David accords in the following year. These provided the State of Israel with the most important diplomatic breakthrough in its history, and allowed it to embark on the massive settlement enterprise that dominated its policies in subsequent years. Internally, the Black Panthers protests early in the decade which, together with the Ashdod port workers of the same period, were the 'great black hope' of the Left, promising the long-expected uprising of the Mizrahi Jewish proletariat against the state, had given way to massive support of the same oppressed population for the right-wing Begin government by the end of the decade. This trend grew stronger in the 1980s and beyond.

Followed by the rise of the Thatcher and Reagan governments in the UK and USA, the anti-imperialist tide seems to have been halted and even reversed. The Sino–Vietnamese war, the Soviet intervention in Afghanistan and the Iran–Iraq war sealed the fate of any remaining notion of a progressive global alliance of forces opposed to US domination. Internally, the political opportunities that opened up in the mid-1970s allowed for the growth of several Left anti-Zionist organizations in Israel, though the Communist Party (Rakah) was the main beneficiary of that. But all this proved to have been a brief respite from more important political dynamics, clearly seen in retrospect: from the late 1970s onwards, Israel's diplomatic fortunes began to improve, leading to the establishment or renewal of relations not only with the biggest and most important Arab country, but also eventually with most African countries, Eastern European countries, India, China and the Soviet Union.

In that environment, the call for 'the destruction of the Zionist state' began to look increasingly anachronistic. The opposition to Egyptian policy by the likes of the Saddam regime in Iraq and the Qaddafi regime in Libya was a poor substitute for the fervour of the Arab Revolution during the times of Nasser. The shift in the mainstream PLO towards acceptance of a compromise solution, which would see an independent Palestinian state alongside Israel, reflected its recognition that little could be expected from a marginalized rejectionist position. This reality could not have failed to have an impact on anti-Zionist groups in Israel. With an Israeli-Jewish working class firmly aligned with right-wing forces, showing no signs that its 'objective' proletarian status would ever lead it to develop a 'subjective' anti-Zionist class consciousness, and with the demise of the Arab Revolution and its Palestinian component, what was to be done?

The dilemmas facing the Israeli Left were not unique to it, of course, and movements in other parts of the world had to deal with similar conditions. In particular, the viability of an overall political and organizational framework, with set positions on all global and local issues, was in question. The model of a revolutionary party or a nucleus seeking to develop into a full-fledged party, which was adopted by many groups, usually included a written programme starting with grand Marxist theory and culminating in discussion of local concerns, regular publications, selling newspapers and handing out leaflets at universities, factories, and public gatherings, meetings of 'cells', and the issuing of position statements on current affairs. Organizations varied by the degree of formality and regularity of their activities, and by the extent to which they accommodated internal diversity or adhered instead to a strict centralist direction, but most followed this pattern. Each presented its own package and positioned itself as best it could to advance the inevitable revolutionary process.

By the beginning of the 1980s it had become clear that the model was problematic. It relied on the assumption of gradual and consistent expansion, with occasional spurts of rapid growth when conditions allowed for it. This expansion was envisaged as the product of regular work by a small but dedicated group of activists. These activists would take advantage of the unfolding revolutionary process to extend their influence, and use that growing influence to extend the process further. But what happens when the process does not unfold fast enough, or at all, and even suffers a reversal? Only very few hardcore 'professional revolutionaries' would be able to sustain activities on a regular basis, for a prolonged period, under such conditions. The rest would likely become disillusioned and retire from political life – the cycle of intense involvement leading to 'burn-out' feeling and ultimately to withdrawal is quite common – or seek a different mode of activism. Moving between organizations was not unknown, but did nothing to solve the problem. A high turnover rate meant that organizations grew and shrank frequently, though always within narrow limits, shifting between self-proclaimed 'unprecedented growth' and 'deep crisis', interspersed with periods of stability or stagnation.

By 1980, Ma'avak and Avangard had ceased to exist, and Matzpen Tel Aviv had reduced its presence to the point of virtual invisibility – only three issues of its magazine were published in the 1980s, the last one in 1983.[70] Matzpen Marxist alone continued in its mode of operation for another decade, but gradually shifted much of its energy into activities around the Alternative Information Center.[71] The Nitzotz group has remained active – to this day – but moved away from its positions and abandoned its anti-Zionist approach sometime in the early to mid-1980s.

The demise of these organizations did not mean the demise of radical oppositional activity in Israel, however. Instead, they were replaced by a large number of groups and movements, with loose organizational structures and with a focus on specific issues. The Committee for Solidarity with Bir Zeit University, the Committee against the War in Lebanon, Yesh Gvul, Shovrim Shtika (Breaking the Silence), Women in Black, the Committee against House Demolitions, the Committee against Torture, Mahsom Watch, Physicians for Human Rights, Taayush, Anarchists against the Wall, Tarabut-Hithabrut, and so on, are all examples of such movements, which were active at one time or another. In addition, a focus on the dissemination of information has given rise to media agencies such as the Alternative Information Centre, and numerous publications and forums for exchange and debate including News from Within, Between the Lines, Arabs48, Kedma, Haokets, 972mag.com, Mekomit.co.il, Hagada Hasmalit, Challenge and others, many of which are also, and sometimes only, available online.

The new mode of activism has two main features that distinguish it from the preceding mode:

- It is much more focused and modest, mobilizing people around a specific issue that is of direct concern – war in Lebanon, torture, migrant workers' rights, the 'apartheid wall' – instead of trying to cover all issues at the same time within an overall programme.
- It addresses the occupation and related issues from moral, political and human rights perspectives, without adopting an explicit socialist approach.

While some activists may regard themselves as socialist or Marxist, this remains a personal choice with no bearing on the goals and actions of their group. In other words, we no longer have left-wing revolutionary organizations, modelling themselves as miniature parties. Rather these are single-issue movements, which may collaborate with each other, with a focus on the occupation and with no claims to be speaking for – or even about – the working class, or to be using Marxist theory to justify their positions. Abandoning class analysis did not mean abandoning the quest for social justice, however; only discarding one specific and restrictive mode of analysis. Having said that, it is important to realize that we are not looking at a completely new set of activists. Beyond natural generational change, many of the new movements and publications have benefited from the experience, initiative and ongoing involvement of former members of radical Left organizations.

CONCLUSIONS

Two evaluations of the experience of the anti-Zionist Left, written more than a decade apart, are instructive in examining its approach. In 1992, commemorating its 30th birthday, Matzpen Tel Aviv admitted making mistakes, mostly having to do with being too generous in the analysis of other 'progressive' forces. It attributed its inability to grow in size and influence, despite having been correct with most of its positions, to Soviet bureaucratic oppression, which indelibly tainted the struggle for socialism.[72] In a more critical vein, reflecting on the reception of the documentary film *Matzpen: Anti Zionist Israelis* by Eran Torbiner (2003), the former leader of Matzpen Marxist noted two reasons for the failure of the left:

- The expectation that Zionism would be swept away by the rise of a progressive anti-colonial movement has proven false: instead of growing opposition to Zionism, it has gained support, and the anti-Zionist Left was marginalized further as a result.
- The Left's conviction that revolution was always around the corner, if only the masses overcame their false consciousness, led it to focus on attacks on reformist and Stalinist leaderships, rather than on the need to prepare for real social and political challenges.[73]

The fight against Zionism is not doomed, in Warschawski's view. However, new methods must be used, drawing on the lessons of the global justice movement, associated with the fight against capitalist globalization and the World Social Forum, which is conducted by diverse independent forces, civil society organizations, media activists and so on.

With changing organizational modes of action, and the dropping of socialism and class struggle as guiding principles, what remains of the Left's anti-Zionist agenda? There is no single programme, of course, but much of what unites radical Jewish activists was captured in a 2004 statement known as the Olga Document.[74] That two prominent members of Matzpen Tel Aviv and Matzpen Marxist, Haim Hanegbi and Michel Warschawski respectively, were among the six authors is a testimony to the legacy of the ideas associated with the organization.[75]

The document asserts that 'the State of Israel was supposed to grant security to Jews' (but has created a death-trap instead); 'the State of Israel was supposed to tear down the walls of the ghetto' (but is now constructing the biggest ghetto in Jewish history); 'the State of Israel was supposed to be a democracy' (but instead has set up a colonial structure, combining 'elements of apartheid with the arbitrariness of brutal military occupation'). Hence, 'we are living in a benighted colonial reality—in the heart of darkness'.

To counter that, there was a need for an alternative vision based on the principle of 'coexistence of the peoples of this country, based on mutual recognition, equal partnership and implementation of historical justice'. Zionism was based 'on refusal to acknowledge the indigenous people of this country and on denial of their rights, on dispossession of their lands, and on adoption of separation as a fundamental principle and way of life'. Against this 'we are united in the recognition that this country belongs to all its sons and daughters—citizens and residents, both present and absentees (the uprooted Palestinian citizens of Israel in '48)— with no discrimination on personal or communal grounds, irrespective of citizenship or nationality, religion, culture, ethnicity or gender.' Dissolving the Zionist character of Israel, and bringing the 1967 occupation to an end, were essential to the opening of a dialogue about the specific political arrangements to be put in place, in order to put behind us 'the nightmare of apartheid, the burden of humiliation and the demons of destruction' that have plagued the country.

Written in 2004, the document could be read as a summary of the main positions consistently put forward by the anti-Zionist Left since 1967. Socialism was not on the agenda any longer, nor was the building of a revolutionary party a task activists set for themselves today. Yet, the analysis has changed little and the conditions that gave rise to it are still the central focus of debate among the Left, and in Israeli and Palestinian societies in general.

A few years later, in 2007, the Haifa Declaration made many of the same points as the Olga Document, though speaking in the name of 'institutions and members of the Palestinian minority'. The Declaration put forward a vision of 'historic reconciliation between the Jewish Israeli people and the Arab Palestinian people', which required Israel 'to recognize the historical injustice that it committed against the Palestinian people through its establishment', recognize the Right of Return, the right of the Palestinian people to self-determination and an independent state, and the rights of Palestinian citizens in Israel. Palestinians and Arabs, in turn, must 'recognize the right of the Israeli Jewish people to self-determination and to life in peace, dignity, and security with the Palestinian and the other peoples of the region', in a 'democratic state founded on equality between the two national groups'.[76]

Both documents advance a common vision of reconciliation, democracy and equality, but they do that on a separate national basis. The content is similar, and the proposed solution identical, but the power of national identity was too strong to allow for a programme that transcends nationalism altogether. On the positive side, while the Left has failed to gain much public support for its answers, there is little doubt that it posed all the crucial questions. Identifying the problems correctly is one step towards a solution, though the road ahead of us is still long.

5

Conclusions

Three conclusions emerge almost immediately from the historical material in the previous chapters:

- Nationalism has proved more powerful than class in appealing to the masses; class discourse can be effective within national boundaries, not across them.
- The appeal of the humanist liberal discourse, advocating universal values and equality between groups, is limited by the extent to which it is reciprocated.
- Under intense conflict, a range of issues beyond financial and military resources shape the prospects of different parties: internal unity, effective mobilization of people, strategic coherence, tactical flexibility, and ability to manipulate self-images and external impressions.

In order to understand the operation of these factors, I will discuss each one of them in turn, with reference to Jewish settlers, Indigenous Palestinians, and the international context.

NATIONALISM AND CLASS

Class analysis and organization were central to many of the political forces discussed in the book: the Left-wing of the Poalei Zion movement, the Palestinian Communist Party (on all its factions and reincarnations), the Palestinian armed Left (Popular Front, Democratic Front), and Matzpen. None of them used class effectively to overcome the attraction of nationalist ideology, so as to link people up across national boundaries. Some did not even try, either because such an effort was marginal to their constituency's concerns (the Zionist Left) or because it clashed with the nationalist agenda they pursued (the Popular Front). But, particularly for the radical Left which sought an alternative to nationalism, overcoming national divisions was crucial.

The Palestinian Communist Party before 1948 presented the longest and most sustained attempt to bridge over national divisions. Its quest to form a territorial party was the first – and only – such effort during the Mandate period. It was the most serious effort in the entire history of the Israeli-Palestinian conflict. But it failed. In the 1920s it experienced great difficulties due to the Jewish-settler origins of the founding members of the Party. They were genuine and eager, but encountered local conditions that were not conducive for their aim to recruit Arab members and leaders: they did not speak the language, were foreign to the culture, arrived there as part of the project against which they positioned themselves politically, and thus appeared as representing the very forces they were targeting for condemnation and opposition.

Intervention from the outside forced them to expedite the transformation process, but its arbitrary and rushed nature resulted in another problem: the imposition of an inexperienced leadership on a reluctant membership, suspicious of the process as tainted by prejudice against veteran Jews and preferential treatment for Arab newcomers. With the intensification of conflict in the country in the late 1930s, this internal clash led to implosion, with Jews and Arabs forming different factions, eventually destroying unity and establishing separate parties on a national basis. Paradoxically, all factions opposed partition of the country into national units but practised it in their own structures. If the only force ideologically committed to joint political organization could not maintain unity in the face of national divisions, what chance was there for the country as a whole?

And yet, while it is easy to mock the failure to maintain unity among activists working for the same cause, we must not lose sight of their gains. They created a functioning organization that remained unified for 20 years under tough conditions of isolation from their own constituency and repression by British and Zionist security forces. They were the only ones who achieved a degree of solidarity across boundaries though in an uneven manner. In the 1940s activists of the PKP and NLL played an important role in labour struggles in their own communities and occasionally on a joint basis. The NLL in particular managed to become a central force among Arab workers, taking advantage of the absence of a strong nationalist labour movement among them equivalent to the Histadrut in the Jewish sector. It was precisely the NLL's abandoning the quest for an Arab–Jewish organization, and joining the Palestinian national movement, that allowed it to recruit worker activists into its ranks and occupy a leading position in Arab unions. Equally, it was the turn towards the Zionist mainstream that allowed the PKP to gain some Jewish workers' support in the 1940s but not before.

In other words, the success of class-based campaigns was conditional on them staying confined to one national group. There was a trade-off between the class and national agendas. Progress on one front usually meant a setback on the other. This was the case because class realities were framed within a nationalist paradigm, as the campaign for Conquest of Labour showed most clearly. It started as an effort to deny employment to Arab workers in order to provide jobs for existing and potential Jewish immigrants, and ended up being used as a major instrument for consolidating the exclusionary nature of the Zionist settlement project as well as consolidating the dominance of the Labour movement within the Jewish community. Protest action by the PKP was seen as a national treason rather than assertion of class solidarity: Arab workers were defined as competitors, not as fellow proletarians in search of jobs. Their logical course of action was to organize on a similar basis and use nationalism to enhance their own position in the labour market. This usually meant that gains made by the Left in recruiting members and influencing activists did not translate into support for a different political agenda that transcended nationalism.

Matzpen did not experience the same difficulty of reconciling its radical class and dissident national agendas, but that was because it was a tiny organization that never managed to develop mass support. The combination of class analysis and critique of nationalism remained on paper, but even as a theoretical synthesis it led to fierce debates about the balance between the two. In retrospect, most of these internal conflicts and splits seem misguided, resulting from delusions of political grandeur and a permanent sense of impending revolutionary transformation, rather than from sober evaluation of realistic political prospects.

One issue of theoretical interest, involving the intersection of class and national conflict, has remained unresolved since the 1930s. When Tony Cliff (L. Rock) debated the South African radical Left group *The Spark*, he argued that Jewish workers were not inherently reactionary because their existence did not depend on the exploitation or oppression of the Arab masses. The response from his South African colleagues was that Jewish workers were part of a colonial project carried out at the expense of the native Arab population. Hence, they were not potential allies of the revolutionary struggle, which was the preserve of colonized Arab workers. They could join it as individuals by renouncing Zionism, but had no role as a class-based group.

Both sides were right: unlike white workers in South Africa, Jewish workers in Palestine did not exploit Arab workers directly indeed (as Cliff claimed), but they did benefit from land and other material resources confiscated from Arabs in 1948, and ever since.

Matzpen inherited the two parts of the argument. It recognized the material basis – including political privileges of full citizenship which were not valid at the time of the original debate – which tied even the most oppressed and exploited Jewish masses to the exclusionary practices of the state. But, it also recognized that the state treated its own citizens in a differentiated manner and therefore that exploited groups within it were potential dissidents: Palestinian citizens obviously, but also the Jewish working class, consisting largely of Mizrahi immigrants, whose incipient rebellion in the shape of the labour struggles of the late 1960s and the Black Panthers movement of the early 1970s aroused great expectations. But these expectations were never fulfilled, and the Mizrahi proletariat adopted state-sponsored exclusionary nationalism in an enthusiastic manner. To understand why, we need to consider the fate of the bi-nationalist movement.

BI-NATIONALISM AND RECIPROCITY

By definition, bi-nationalism is a concept premised on reciprocity. If it exists in isolation it cannot be effective. This is precisely what undermined the movement before 1948, and what continues to hamper its prospects today, under changed conditions. In the early period discussed in the book, it was a Jewish movement, not just in the sense that all its members were Jews but also in that its concerns, discourse, and mode of operation were shaped in the context of Jewish history, culture, and religion. Its language reflected a through grounding in scholarship and literature confronting the challenges of Jewish modernity. As such, it was not accessible to Arabs and did not provide easy access to Jewish political activists who had limited interest in its spiritual foundations.

Above all, the problem facing the movement was that it did not manage to find an Arab partner and thus appeared to be offering unilateral concessions that were not reciprocated. Why did it not find a partner? Because it ignored the basic asymmetry in the position of Arabs and Jews in the country: the former were indigenous, the latter were newcomers. Veteran activists – Kalvarisky, Smilansky – immigrated there in the 1890s, and the rest later: Bergmann, Scholem and Kohn arrived in the early 1920s. From the perspective of most Arab, sharing power with immigrants who reached the country recently and against their will, was not an equitable arrangement. Given that at the time of the Balfour Declaration only 50,000 Jews resided in the country, less than 10 per cent of the population, the bi-nationalists were seen as demanding much more than their fair share. During the three decades of the Mandate the Jewish population increased its size ten times but remained a minority. Under these circumstances, the most that Arab nationalists were willing to offer was individual equality, but not minority group rights, let alone political parity.

Seen from today's perspective, the Arab unwillingness to share the country – through parity or partition – led to losing it altogether, but that is not the way things looked like before 1948. Palestinians worried that recognizing Jewish political rights as legitimate would undermine their own position without stopping Jewish immigration and settlement. And, in any event, negotiating with the bi-nationalists was not likely to produce agreements that would slow down mainstream Zionists. Concessions to their agenda were expected to enhance the settlement project rather than put an end to its expansion. For reasons of both principle – standing for their own indigenous rights – and tactics – denying the legitimacy of Jewish collective rights so as not to undermine the Palestinian negotiating position – the Arab leadership rejected compromise solutions.

That attitude made sense internally: Palestinians saw no reason to give up territory in negotiations which the Zionist movement had not managed to acquire through the settlement process. But, it was detrimental to the political prospects of Jewish moderates, including the bi-nationalists and left-wing activists. To gain mass support in their community these activists had to show that their approach, which involved making concessions from a Jewish nationalist point of view, would yield results – if not acceptance of the legitimacy of immigration and settlement, at least reduction of the vehemence of the rhetoric directed against it and cessation of armed attacks on Jewish and Zionist targets. But such attacks continued unabated throughout the Mandate period, and gave rise to equally militant and destructive counterattacks from armed Zionist forces. Nothing made Jews less open to internal voices of reason and moderation urging compromises than the total refusal of Arab leaders to consider their claims and the indiscriminate attacks on their settlements, which targeted all Jews, regardless of their affiliation with Zionism.

As noted in the chapter on bi-nationalism, nationalists could embark on a course of action without waiting for approval from the other side, realizing their agenda by force, whereas the bi-nationalists were dependant on acceptance of their claims by Arab partners. These potential partners responded primarily not to them but to what mainstream Zionist forces had to offer, a factor over which the bi-nationalists had no control. The dominant political forces in each of the national camps contributed to making the situation increasingly polarized. This benefited those who urged unilateral action and weakened those calling for mutual consideration.

What hampered the possibility of a resolution of the conflict before 1948 was that the minimum demands of one side were too much for the other side to concede. And, what was being conceded was too little to satisfy the basic demands of the other side. This remains the case today, though the relative positions have changed. Before 1948 compromise solutions – the British Peel Commission of 1937 and the UN partition resolution of 1947 – increased the area allocated to Jews at the expense of that held by Arabs, seeing a large number of Arab residents falling under Jewish rule. Naturally, the Arab side refused to go along with that. After 1967, proposed solutions have been based on withdrawal from occupied Palestinian territories. The Israeli side has been reluctant to give up territory it had acquired in war, while Palestinians naturally are more willing to accept a solution that would see them gaining control over land which is denied to them at present. In other words, compromise is deemed acceptable when your side gains territorial assets but not when it loses them. Under what conditions, then, could a territorial price be seen as reasonable? In other words, what may be a suitable exchange for territorial concessions?

Historically, the answer was legitimacy and recognition. The Zionist leadership before 1948 was willing to reduce the scope of its aims – at least temporarily – and curb its settlement expansion in exchange for recognition of its right to rule part of the territory of Palestine. The Israeli state after 1967 has been willing to concede some of the territory it is occupying in exchange for recognition of its right to rule the rest of the country. This stated willingness has never been put into practice, however. When the Israeli side is strong and feeling secure and confident, it sees no point in making concessions. When it suffers a setback and is lacking confidence, it fears that concessions would make it look even weaker. Constantly torn between supreme arrogance – 'our situation has never been better' – and mortal fear, whereby giving an inch would lead to imminent destruction, the Israeli leadership insists on retaining ultimate military and territorial control, even if indirectly (as in Gaza). In the face of this, all the commitments Palestinians have been making, from recognition of Israel to effective renunciation of the refugees' right of return, are seen as verbal and fleeting in nature, not convincing enough for Israeli Jews, ever on their guard.

This conundrum could be termed *Israel: the whining superhero*. It is founded on a sense that only military might will provide a sustained basis for secure existence. Written agreements may be useful but on the condition that they are always backed up by forceful deterrence, which can be provided by Israel alone and has to be demonstrated repeatedly in order to 'burn' it into the adversaries' consciousness. The reliance on the unilateral use of force is usually accompanied by assertions of extreme vulnerability, and a tendency to equate the mildest criticisms made by anyone, anywhere, with genocidal anti-Semitism. Paradoxically, the greater the gap between Israel's military capacity and that of its opponents (reaching in 2014 its highest point ever favourable to Israel), the more the Israeli leadership reverts into presenting itself as an eternal victim in danger of being 'de-legitimized' and wiped off the map. How can this mental attitude be overcome, to allow a rational solution based on mutual recognition and compromise?

THE BALANCE OF FORCES

To make progress in resolving the conflict we need to learn the lessons of the past. The Zionist movement before 1948 managed to overcome the resistance of its Arab nationalist adversaries by a combination of pragmatism, persistence and effective mobilization of internal and external support. Under the leadership of Weizmann and Ben-Gurion, it pursued a course of action that focused on making steady practical gains that brought it closer to realizing its ultimate aims. It shunned grand proclamations and was willing to make temporary concessions, while holding on to its principles if this ensured achievements on the ground. It paid much more attention to matters that promised daily and gradual progress through the building of material force, than to the constant recitation of lofty principles that remained on paper. And, it used to great effect the superhero/victim duality to attract support from Jews and international powers alike. The superhero image was that of the pioneer and straight-talking 'sabra' who made the desert bloom, holding a plough in one hand and a rifle in the other. The victim was the cowering Jew of the ghetto who needed a safe haven in his historical homeland. Of course, this was not merely an image: the period in question saw the worst persecution of Jews in history, resulting in the physical destruction of European Jewry.

Palestinians pursued a different strategy. They insisted on their rights without making concessions, even tactical and temporary in nature. They were very careful not to endow the other side with any legitimacy but failed to answer its material progress with a strategy for their own achievements on the ground. As indigenous people they had no need to settle the land to enhance their national claim: they already were there and assumed their position could not be challenged. They did not mobilize as a society in the way settler society was forced to, to bolster a claim that was not based on existing presence. Their mobilization was diplomatic and military in nature, but did not involve social and organizational changes along the coherent and self-conscious lines of the Yishuv. Thus they were at a disadvantage despite their numerical dominance.

The global context was crucial as well: the support for Zionism in the Balfour Declaration was motivated by British imperial interests but also by the special place occupied by Jews in European consciousness. As a familiar – but not necessarily liked – group, Jews were visible and interesting in a way Palestinians could never match. Even the frequently hostile Soviets regarded Jewish concerns as important, especially in the post-1945 period. The Holocaust enhanced that importance with the need to address the problem of displaced Jewish survivors. The price was to be paid by reluctant Palestinians. It is not clear that concessions at that point – such as accepting the plea of Magnes to allow the immigration of 100,000 European Jews after the war – would have made a difference. In any event, concessions were not forthcoming, nationalist rejectionism prevailed, the international consensus ignored it, Israel was created, and the battle for Palestine was decisively lost.

It took Palestinians two decades before they managed to resurrect their independent organization and create a new force representing their national aspirations, and another decade or two for them to give up some sacred principles of nationalism to meet a new international consensus that recognized the need for a Palestinian state alongside Israel, based on the 4 June 1967 boundaries. But, by that time Israel had changed. What would have been regarded as a huge victory before 1948 and a welcome achievement before 1967 was no longer satisfactory for Israeli public opinion, euphoric over its conquests. Security, demography, historical rights, holy sites, and strategic considerations were combined in a new discourse and practices of expansion through exclusionary settlement, taking over the land but shunning the population. The resolute anti-occupation efforts of Matzpen and subsequent Israeli movements, the resistance of the armed Palestinian organizations, the popular uprisings and mass civil defiance, have not managed to change this situation. It remains firmly entrenched despite decades of diplomatic efforts and the increasingly futile and self-defeating Oslo 'peace process'.

This is clearly a *bi-national* situation, demographically and socially, but without a *bi-nationalist* solution politically. The reality on the ground has not been translated into corresponding political arrangements that recognize the need to accommodate members of both national communities equally within the territory as a whole or on any part of it. Where does all this leave us? We must examine the actual consequences of the analysis and follow them, with a bit of speculation about future directions.

WHAT IS TO BE DONE?

In Israel/Palestine today there are two ethno-national groups. Israeli Jews are unified by their legal status as full citizens. Palestinian Arabs are divided by their legal status into citizens in pre-1967 Israel, resident non-citizens in the Occupied Territories, and non-resident non-citizens in the Diaspora. The two groups are distinct by virtue of their language, political identity, religion and ethnic origins. Only about 10 per cent of them – Palestinian citizens – are fully bilingual. Many Jews have Arab cultural origins, but their legacy has been erased through three generations of political and cultural assimilation. The delusion that these 'Arab Jews' share any political consciousness with Palestinians – even if in a dormant form – has been laid to rest. On the face of it, this would seem an ideal argument for a separatist two-state solution, but things are more complicated than that.

A solution along South African 'rainbow nation' lines, based on the multiplicity of identities and the absence of a single axis of division to align them all, is unlikely to be replicated in Israel/Palestine. Elements such as the use of English as the dominant medium of political communication, shared by all groups, or Christianity as a religious umbrella for the majority of people from all racial groups, do not exist. At the same time, in pre-1967 Israel people of all backgrounds – veteran Ashkenazi and Mizrahi Jews, new Russian and Ethiopian immigrants, and Palestinian citizens – use Hebrew in their daily interaction and largely share similar social and cultural tastes. In mixed towns, such as Haifa, Jaffa, Acre, there are neighbourhoods in which Jews and Arabs live together with little to distinguish between their life styles except for their home language and religious practices. Without idealizing the situation, it can become a foundation for a new version of bi-nationalism.

Bi-nationalism today is based on the recognition that two groups live together in the same country, separately within homogeneous villages and towns in some areas, but also mixed to varying degrees in other areas. Historical patterns of demographic engineering that resulted in forced population movement and dispersal – most notably the 1948 Nakba and the post-1967 settlement project – have created a patchwork quilt of mono-ethnic and bi-ethnic regions, separated by political intent rather than by natural or geographical logic.

Acknowledging this bi-national reality is not meant as an argument for a particular form of state. Rather it is a call to base any future political arrangement on the need to accommodate members of both national groups as equals, at individual and collective levels. In the words of the radical Jewish activists who put together the Olga Document: 'this country belongs to all its sons and daughters—citizens and residents, both present and absentees (the uprooted Palestinian citizens of Israel in '48)— with no discrimination on personal or communal grounds, irrespective of citizenship or nationality, religion, culture, ethnicity or gender.' It is interesting to note that this formulation draws on the Freedom Charter of 1955, which asserted, 'South Africa belongs to all who live in it, black and white'. The simple elegance of the original formula was changed here into a comprehensive but cumbersome language, a testimony to the difficulty of conveying unity in the face of fragmentation. But, it is not difficult to convey unity – as a first step – among Israeli citizens. Making Israel a state of and for all its citizens equally is both logical and just, and politically feasible though by no means easy.

We must recognize though that people seek incorporation as individuals *and* as groups. In the Vision Documents of Palestinian citizens of Israel, the quest for equality is combined with the call for recognition as a national collective. The tension between a democratic state with no ethnic character, and equality between ethnic groups, is unresolved. Bi-nationalism is compatible with either option: a non-ethnic state, and a state that enshrines equality between individual citizens and provides structured representation for groups in fields such as education and culture. Both must lead to the removal of all forms of ethnic domination. Democratizing Israel in this way is important in its own right and also as a way to reinforce other campaigns. If Palestinian citizens are no longer ostracized as political actors, the struggle against the occupation would receive a big boost by escaping the confines of the shrinking progressive Jewish Left.

Making Israel a state of all its citizens would not change the boundaries of political sovereignty, would have no demographic implications, and would require no negotiation with external forces. It would not challenge 'the right of Israel to exist' but rather seek to modify the internal basis for its self-legitimation. In other words, it would be a process carried out by citizens, over a period of time. Making Israel/Palestine *as a whole* a state of all its residents, by establishing common citizenship, is different. It would mean a fundamental change in the boundaries of citizenship and the allocation of power, requiring a radical re-alignment of the political scene. It is not feasible in the short term as there are no serious political forces advocating it, and it cannot be a substitute for the ongoing struggle against the 1967 occupation and for restoring refugees' rights.

By way of broad conclusion, a viable political strategy would anchor the concerns above in the language of democracy, equality and human rights, instead of that of diplomacy and statehood, thus overturning the Oslo approach. The advantage of this strategy is that it could associate itself with the global justice movement and struggles of diverse independent forces, civil society organizations, and media activists.

What possible form can such strategy take? A thorough discussion deserves a study on its own, and only a brief outline – focusing on campaigns within Israel – is possible here. First, we must recognize that progressive forces can neither ignore nationalism, thus risking total marginalization, nor surrender to it, thus risking losing their voice. Second, in a society shaped by ethno-national conflict, most social and political issues are affected by the conflict but should not be reduced to it. Third, the conflict can be seen as an overall framework, but its many dimensions may be better tackled as political fronts that call for local approaches and contingent alliances. This requires charting a course that would go beyond nationalism without seeking to write it off.

Concretely, a series of campaigns that position Palestinian national demands within a broader framework of rights is one way of establishing a link between particular and universal discourses and opening the way for cooperation between Palestinians and some Israeli Jews on specific issues. Examples may include questions of access to land (affecting Palestinians as well as ethnically and socially marginalized Jewish groups), questions of citizenship and immigration policies (affecting Palestinians as well as many Jews with ambiguous legal status such as recent Russian and Ethiopian immigrants), questions of labour organization, jobs and access to services (affecting Palestinians, working class Jews, and migrant workers from Eastern Europe and Southeast Asia), questions of culture, education and social exclusion (affecting Palestinians, Mizrahi Jews and orthodox Jews), questions of gender and sexuality (affecting everyone), and so on.

Each of these campaigns would involve alliances between different groups working for different causes, but they all share, in their specific domains, a quest for a greater equality and democracy for all regardless of origins. Unlike the traditional approach of the radical Left, this strategy is *not* based on expectations that Jews would renounce Zionist ideology, confront state power directly, and opt for a common socialist future. Rather, it assumes that they may show some willingness to address some of the concerns of Palestinians, working jointly with them, if these were in line with their own concerns.

This approach does not tackle directly all of the core issues of the Israeli–Palestinian conflict, some of which pit Israeli Jews and Palestinian Arabs against each other as mutually exclusive groups fighting over resources and rights. In the short to medium term there is no prospect of weakening the boundaries between these groups or constructing an identity that would transcend ethno-nationalist loyalties. No easy formulas to deal with this situation exist, and debates over one- or two-state solutions miss the crucial point: the Palestinian population was fragmented in 1948 and further in 1967. A holistic political solution would have to address all its components – the 1948 dispersal of refugees, the 1967 occupation, and the fate of Palestinians citizens – but is very unlikely ever to be implemented simultaneously. Hence, forces challenging the status quo must work on each component on its own, instead of seeking to solve all issues in a big bang with some magic formula.

Progress on one front should not be impeded by the lack of progress on another, and the final outcome cannot be predicted in advance. The guiding principle for a solution is common to all components, however: the need for a bi-nationalist approach, which would treat members of each ethno-national group equally, as individuals and as collectives. The combination of a political approach operating on many different but related fronts, with a new mode of activism focused on direct action and creative media, educational, and legal strategies, may be the best way forward. There are not obvious answers here, but posing the right questions is a crucial first step towards a solution.

Notes

CHAPTER 1

1. For the notion of a process of mute peasant resistance see Rashid Khalidi, *Palestinian Identity: The Construction of Modern National Consciousness* (Columbia University Press, 1997), pp. 89–117.
2. See Yakov Rabkin, *A Threat from Within: A Century of Jewish Opposition to Zionism* (Zed Books, 2006).
3. See discussion and translation of this article in Alan Dowty, 'Much Ado about Little: Ahad Ha'am's "Truth from Eretz Yisrael", Zionism, and the Arabs', *Israel Studies*, 5, 2 (Fall 2000), pp. 154–81. It should be noted that these are only three paragraphs in a very long text; the second part of the article says nothing about Jewish–Arab relations, as Ahad Ha'am did not regard the issue as crucial to his overall criticism of the settlement project.
4. Neville Mandel, *The Arabs and Zionism Before World War 1* (University of California Press, 1976), pp. 39–40; other petitions from rural Palestinians are discussed in Yuval Ben-Bassat, *Petitioning the Sultan: Justice and Protest in Late Ottoman Palestine* (London: I.B. Tauris, 2013).
5. See discussion and translation of this article in Alan Dowty, '"A Question That Outweighs All Others": Yitzhak Epstein and Zionist Recognition of the Arab Issue', *Israel Studies*, 6, 1 (Spring 2001), pp. 34–54.
6. Abigail Jacobson, 'Jews Writing in Arabic: Shimon Moyal, Nissim Malul and the Mixed Palestinian/Eretz Israeli Locale' in *Late Ottoman Palestine: The Period of Young Turk Rule*, edited by Yuval Ben-Bassat and Eyal Ginio (I.B. Tauris, 2011), pp. 165–82; Abigail Jacobson, 'Sephardim, Ashkenazim and the "Arab Question" in Pre-First World War Palestine: A Reading of Three Zionist Newspapers', *Middle Eastern Studies*, 39, 2 (April 2003), pp. 105–30; Michelle Campos, *Ottoman Brothers: Muslims, Christians, and Jews in Early Twentieth-Century Palestine* (Stanford, 2011). pp. 158–65, 197–223.
7. Not surprisingly, Epstein's article and another piece by Ahad Ha'am were reproduced immediately after an extract from Theodor Herzl's book Altneuland, in the first publication of the Brit Shalom association from 1927, which effectively launched the bi-national perspective in public.
8. The Hebrew text talks about a Jewish or Hebrew state. The English text refers to Jewish Commonwealth. Document in both languages in Neil Caplan, *Palestine Jewry and the Arab Question, 1917–1925* (Frank Cass, 1978), pp. 205–11.

9. 'Statement of the Zionist Organization regarding Palestine', submitted to the Paris peace conference, February 1919, www.mideastweb.org/zionistborders.htm.

10. King-Crane report, www.ipcri.org/files/kingcrane.html.

11. Variations on these themes are still in use today by the Israeli authorities and their supporters.

12. The Hebrew version of the document can be found in *Al Parashat Darkeinu: A Collection on the Issues of Zionist Policy and Jewish-Arab Cooperation* (March 1939), pp. 25–26, in Hebrew. The English version is in Neil Caplan, *Futile Diplomacy, Vol. 1: Early Arab-Zionist Negotiation Attempts, 1913–1931* (Frank Cass, 1983), pp. 152–53.

13. See a detailed discussion of such diplomatic attempts and original documents in Caplan, *Futile Diplomacy*.

14. Ahad Ha'am, 'The Declaration', 1920, re-published in *She'ifoteinu*, 1, 1927, pp. 5–7, in Hebrew.

15. Quoted in Caplan, *Palestine Jewry and the Arab Question*, p. 137.

16. *Palestine. Disturbances in May, 1921. Reports of the Commission of Inquiry.* London, October 1921, p. 50. The 'Chalukah [Halukkah] Jews' in Jerusalem lived on donations collected in their home countries in Eastern Europe.

17. In *A Land of Two Peoples: Martin Buber on Jews and Arabs*, edited with commentary by Paul R. Mendes-Flohr (Oxford University Press, 1983), p. 61.

18. *Ibid.*, p. 63.

19. Aharon Kedar provides an elaborate and somewhat different picture of trends and personalities within the association: 'On the History of Brit Shalom in the Years 1925–1928', in *Research Chapters in the History of Zionism*, edited by Y. Bauer, M. Davis and I. Kollat (Jerusalem, 1976), pp. 224–85, in Hebrew. Susan Lee Hattis, *The Bi-National Idea in Palestine during Mandatory Times* (Haifa, 1970), pp. 38–58, relies in her analysis on Kedar's unpublished work.

20. Report on meeting Hans Kohn and Hugo Bergmann, 26 May 1928, in Arthur Ruppin, *My Life and Work: The Autobiography and Diaries of Arthur Ruppin, Volume 3* (Am Oved, 1968), p. 149, in Hebrew.

21. Letter to Hans Kohn, 30 May 1928, in Ruppin, *My Life and Work*, p. 149–52.

22. Letter to Dr Jacobson, 3 December 1931, in Ruppin, *My Life and Work*, p. 203. Bold face in the original.

23. Letter to Robert Weltsch, 18 March 1936, in Ruppin, *My Life and Work*, pp. 257–8. Italics in bold face in the original.

24. Diary entry, 16 May 1936, in Ruppin, *My Life and Work*, p. 260.

25. Hans Kohn, 'Report on Brit Shalom Activities', 11 April 1929 in Adi Gordon (ed.), *Brit Shalom and Bi-national Zionism: 'The Arab Question' as a Jewish Question* (Carmel, 2008), pp. 310–11, in Hebrew.

26. Letter by Hans Kohn to Dr Feiwel, 21 November 1929, cited in Buber, *A Land of Two Peoples*, pp. 97–100.

27. Hans Kohn, 'Letter of Resignation', 22 September 1930, in Gordon, *Brit Shalom and Bi-national Zionism*, pp. 313–14.

28. A detailed discussion of possible arrangements can be found in *Brit Shalom's Proposals Regarding Joint Work between Jews and Arabs in Palestine*, August 1930, in Hebrew.

29. Hugo Bergmann, 'The Question of the Regime in Palestine', *She'ifoteinu*, 2, 3, 1931, pp. 94–101, in Hebrew, as are all subsequent quotations from this publication.

30. Ernst Simon, 'The Speech That Was Not Made in the Congress', *She'ifoteinu*, 2, 5, 1931, pp. 164–9.

31. Gershom Scholem, 'What Are We Arguing About?', *She'ifoteinu*, 2, 6, 1931, pp. 193–203.

32. In Bergmann's review of Ben-Gurion's book *We and Our Neighbours*, *She'ifoteinu*, 2, 6, 1931, pp. 204–9.

33. Hugo Bergmann, 'The Thought of Ahad Ha'am and the Proletarian Conception', *She'ifoteinu*, 3, 3, 1932, pp. 84–9.

34. Ernst Simon, 'Against the Sadducees', *She'ifoteinu*, 3, 5–6, 1932, pp. 152–67.

35. Points raised by a number of speakers at the founding meeting of the Haifa branch, Protocol of the Founding Meeting, Haifa, March 1937, in Moshe Gabbai, *Kedma Mizraha, 1936–1939* (Yad Haviva, 1984), pp. 72–84, in Hebrew.

36. Moshe Smilansky, 'Stones for Bread', in Kedma Mizraha, *A Collection of Articles on the Arab Question* (August 1936), p. 69, in Hebrew.

37. Protocol of discussion between Kedma Mizraha and Ben-Gurion, 1936, in Gabbai, *Kedma Mizraha*, pp. 85–106.

38. Ernst Simon, 'Two Years Ago – and Today', in *Al Parashat Darkeinu* (March 1939), p. 1, in Hebrew.

39. *Ibid.*, p. 13.

40. A point made repeatedly over the years by Kalvarisky, 'Plans and Speeches', in *Al Parashat Darkeinu*, pp. 25–40.

41. Moshe Erem, 'The Theory of "National Barriers" and its Consequences', in *Al Parashat Darkeinu*, pp. 47–69; Yaakov Hazan, 'On Zionist Policy', in *Al Parashat Darkeinu*, pp. 87–92.

42. A 1939 statement in Hattis, *The Bi-national Idea in Palestine during Mandatory Times*, p. 222.

43. Quoted in Moshe Smilansky (a member of the group), *Revival and Holocaust* (Masada, 1953), p. 192, in Hebrew.

44. Discussion of the two committees in Hattis, *The Bi-National Idea*, pp. 231–49; Yosef Gorny, *From Binational Society to Jewish State: Federal Concepts in Zionist Political Thought* (Brill, 2006), pp. 109–28; Elkana Margalit, 'The Debate in the

Palestine Labour Movement on the Idea of a Bi-national State', *Ha-Tziyonut*, 4, 1975, pp. 198–215, in Hebrew.

45. In Hattis, *The Bi-National Idea*, pp. 242–3.
46. See details in Aharon Cohen, *Israel and the Arab World* (Beacon Press, 1970), pp. 300–34.
47. Statement from September 1942, in *A Land of Two Peoples: Martin Buber on Jews and Arabs*, p. 149.
48. Judah Magnes, 'Toward Peace in Palestine', *Foreign Affairs*, January 1943, in *Dissenter in Zion: From the Writings of Judah L. Magnes*, edited by Arthur A. Goren (Harvard University Press, 1982), pp. 389–98.
49. Letter to Rabbi Morris Lazaron, 6 October 1942, in Goren, *Dissenter in Zion*, p. 385.
50. Quotes from letter to Alexander Dushkin, 7 January 1943, in Goren, *Dissenter in Zion*, pp. 387–8.
51. Judah Magnes, 'Compromise for Palestine', *New York Times*, 17 February 1945, in Goren, *Dissenter in Zion*, pp. 422–7.
52. In Buber, *A Land of Two Peoples*, 'A Dialogue on the Biltmore Program' (October1944), pp. 161–4.
53. In Buber, *A Land of Two Peoples*, 'A Majority or Many? A Postscript to a Speech' (May 1944), pp. 165–8.
54. Discussion based on *A Binational Solution for Palestine [Eretz Israel]*, memorandum prepared by the Hashomer Hatza'ir Workers Party in Palestine (Tel Aviv, March 1946), in Hebrew.
55. The positions of Ihud are found in *Arab-Jewish Unity: Testimony Before the Anglo-American Inquiry Commission for the Ihud (Union) Association by Judah Magnes and Martin Buber* (London, 1947). The Arab Office's document, *The Arab Case for Palestine*, is reproduced in *Documents on Palestine*, Volume 1, published by PASSIA (Jerusalem, 2007), pp. 381–87. The testimony of Albert Hourani who represented it is in 'The Case Against a Jewish State in Palestine: Albert Hourani's Statement to the Anglo-American Committee of Enquiry of 1946', *Journal of Palestine Studies*, 35, 1 (Autumn 2005), pp. 80–90.
56. In *Arab-Jewish Unity*, pp. 54–5.
57. *Ibid.*, p. 88.
58. Hourani, 'The Case Against a Jewish State', p. 84.
59. In *Arab-Jewish Unity*, pp. 72–3.
60. Judah Magnes, 'A Solution Through Force?', July 1946, in *Towards Union in Palestine: Essays on Zionism and Jewish-Arab Cooperation*, edited by M. Buber, J.L. Magnes and E. Simon (Jerusalem, 1947), p. 20.
61. Martin Buber, 'The Bi-national Approach to Zionism', in Buber et al. (ed.), *Towards Union in Palestine*, p. 9.
62. Report of the Anglo-American Committee of Inquiry: http://avalon.law. yale.edu/20th_century/angch01.asp
63. See responses in Buber et al. (ed.), *Towards Union in Palestine*, pp. 108–14.

64. In *ibid.*, pp. 113–14.
65. 'Oral evidence before the United Nations Special Committee on Palestine, 14th July 1947', in *Palestine – Divided or United? The Case for a Bi-national Palestine Before the United Nations* (Ihud Association, Jerusalem 1947), p. 33.
66. In *ibid.*, p. 34.
67. In *ibid.*, p. 46.
68. In *ibid.*, pp. 50–1.
69. In *ibid.*, p. 56.
70. 'The Case Against Partition', additional memorandum submitted to UNSCOP, in *Palestine – Divided or United*, p. 76.
71. Ernst Simon, 'One Union of Two Nations', statement before UNSCOP, 15 July 1947, in *Palestine – Divided or United*, pp. 85–8.
72. Aharon Cohen, statement before UNSCOP, 15 July 1947, in http://unispal. un.org/UNISPAL.NSF/0/E9D86A501C82C8C68525778500753018.
73. Text of the agreement in Cohen, *Israel and the Arab World*, p. 351.
74. Judah Magnes, 'Report on Palestine', *New York Times*, 28 September 1947, in Goren, *Dissenter in Zion*, p. 451.
75. *Ibid.*, p. 453.
76. Magnes letter to Ernst Simon, 12 November 1947, in Goren, *Dissenter in Zion*, p. 457.
77. Hannah Arendt, 'To Save the Jewish Homeland, There is Still Time', May 1948, in *The Jew as Pariah: Jewish Identity and Politics in the Modern Age*, edited by Ron H. Feldman (Grove Press, 1978). p. 181.
78. *Ibid.*, p. 186.
79. *Ibid.*, p. 187.
80. *Ibid.*, p. 191.
81. Hannah Arendt, 'Peace or Armistice in the Near East?', *The Review of Politics*, 12 ,1 (January 1950), pp. 56–82.
82. *Ibid.*, p. 76–7.

CHAPTER 2

1. Quoted in Jonathan Frankel, *Prophecy and Politics: Socialism, Nationalism & the Russian Jews, 1862–1917* (Cambridge University Press, 1981), p. 129.
2. The term 'Palestinian' here refers to the pre-1948 territory of Palestine and its population, not to a specific ethnic group within it, as it does today. The term 'Israeli' is likewise territorial in nature.
3. On the history of Poalei Zion, culminating in the 1920 split, see Zvia Balshan, *The Jewish Socialist Labour Confederation Poale-Zion, 1907–1920* (The Ben-Gurion Research Institute, 2004), in Hebrew. Internal theoretical debates and their implications for issues of immigration and settlement are discussed in Elkana Margalit, *The Anatomy of the Left: The Left Po'alei-Zion in*

Eretz-Israel 1919–1946 (IL Peretz Publishing House, 1976), pp. 32–64, in Hebrew.

4. 'Conditions of Admission to the Communist International', 6 August 1920, in *The Communist International 1919–1943, Documents*, Vol. 1: 1919–1922, edited by Jane Degras (Oxford University Press, 1956), p. 170.

5. 'Theses on the National and Colonial Question', 28 July 1920, in Degras, *The Communist International*, p. 144.

6. The protocol of the discussion on Zionism is found in www.marxists.org/history/international/comintern/2nd-congress/ch05.htm.

7. On Orientalist assumptions see Avner Ben-Zaken, *Communism as Cultural Imperialism: The Affinities Between Eretz-Israeli Communism and Arab Communism, 1919–1948* (Resling, 2006), in Hebrew.

8. In *Manifesto of the Congress to the Peoples of the East*, 1 September 1920, in www.marxists.org/history/international/comintern/baku/manifesto.htm.

9. 'Protocol of the Meeting of the Executive Committee of the Comintern (ECCI)', 21 September 1920, in Leon Zehavi, *Apart or Together: Jews and Arabs in Palestine According to the Documents of the Comintern, 1919–1943* (Keter, 2005), pp. 25–32, in Hebrew.

10. For the debates over the Jewish socialist and settlement focus, and the gradual abandonment of the Poalei Zion legacy by the MPS in its road to becoming the PKP, see Margalit, *The Anatomy of the Left*, pp. 65–94.

11. In Zehavi, *Apart of Together*, p. 32.

12. Statements of both the right- and left-wings in Y. Peterzeil (ed.), *The Struggle in the International Proletarian Arena: Poalei Zion Collection, Vol. 1, 1907–27* (Ringelblum Institute, 1954), pp. 84–7, in Hebrew.

13. 'Memorandum of the Poalei Zion Bureau to the Communist International', April 1921, in Peterzeil, *The Struggle in the International Proletarian Arena*, p. 113.

14. 'Call by the Executive Committee of the Comintern to members of Poalei Zion', 26 August 1921, in Peterzeil, *The Struggle in the International Proletarian Arena*, p. 134.

15. 'Resolutions of the Council of the World Alliance of Poalei Zion', October 1921, in Peterzeil, *The Struggle in the International Proletarian Arena*, pp. 142–3.

16. 'Resolution of the Executive Committee of the Comintern', March 1922, in *ibid.*, pp. 149–52.

17. 'Extracts from an ECCI Statement on the Decision of Poale Zion', 25 July 1922, in Degras, *The Communist International*, Vol. 1, p. 366.

18. All the preceding quotes are taken from *Palestine, Disturbances in May 1921. Reports of the Commission of Inquiry* (HMSO, Cmd. 1540), known as the Haycraft Commission of Inquiry.

19. Eli Tzur, 'The Silent Pact: Anti-Communist Co-operation between the Jewish Leadership and the British Administration in Palestine', *Middle Eastern Studies*, 35, 2 (April 1999), pp. 103–31.

20. See 'Report on the Situation of the Palestinian Communist Party', 1921, in Zehavi, *Apart or Together*, pp. 36–8.

21. Nahman List, 'Tzadak Hakomintern . . .' Part 4, *Keshet*, 24 (1964), pp. 111–16, in Hebrew. List was a senior Party member, whose critical but well-informed and sympathetic series of articles published in the 1960s – three decades after he had left the Party – is arguably the best source on the early history of communism in Palestine. Its ironic title is 'The Comintern was Right . . .'. On one Arab activist won to the cause in this way see Salim Tamari, 'Najati Sidqi (1905–79): The Enigmatic Jerusalem Bolshevik', *Journal of Palestine Studies*, 32, 2 (Winter 2003), pp. 79–94.

22. That the Party may have continued to some extent to be aligned 'objectively' with the settlement project – even when it explicitly rejected the policies driving it – is an inconceivable notion for mainstream Israeli scholars, who do not bother to disguise their hostile attitude towards it. The seminal work of G.Z Israeli [Walter Laqueur], *MPS-PKP-MAKI: The History of the Communist Party in Israel* (Am Oved, 1953), in Hebrew, stands out in this respect. Large sections of it are reproduced in Walter Z. Laqueur, *Communism and Nationalism in the Middle East* (Praeger, 1956), pp. 73–119. Shmuel Dotan's *Reds: The Communist Party in Palestine* (Kfar Saba, 1991), in Hebrew, is marred by a similar political bias, and at times engages in bizarre speculations, name calling, and fantastic conspiracy theories, but also contains useful historical details alongside malicious gossip. For a discussion of sources and early research on the Party see Alexander Flores, 'The Palestine Communist Party during the Mandatory Period: An Account of Sources and Recent Research', *Peuples Méditerranéens / Mediterranean Peoples*, 11, April–June 1980, pp. 57–84.

23. 'Theses on the Eastern Question adopted by the Fourth Comintern Congress', November 1922, in Degras, *The Communist International*, Vol. 1, p. 393.

24. On Palestinian-Arab identity and ideology see Rashid Khalidi, *Palestinian Identity: The Construction of Modern National Consciousness* (Columbia University Press, 1997), pp. 145–75; Yehoshua Porath, *The Emergence of the Palestinian-Arab National Movement, 1918–29* (Frank Cass, 1974), pp. 31–69.

25. Nahman List reports how Averbuch always immersed himself at home in 'thick tomes' written by English, French, Russian and Hungarian Orientalist scholars, addressing the need to learn about and transform the Middle East as a messianic task. He saw the historical role of the new Jewish proletariat in Palestine as that of raising the consciousness of and mobilizing the Arab masses against imperialism. See 'Tzadak Hakomintern...', Part 4. A brief discussion of the problems with the role played by the PKP in the Arab East is found in Hanna Batatu, *The Old Social Classes and the Revolutionary Movements of Iraq* (Princeton University Press, 1978), pp. 374–86; 1148–55; see also Suliman Bashear, *Communism in the Arab East, 1918–1928* (Ithaca

Press, 1980). A selection of articles on Middle Eastern issues written by PKP leaders (mostly Averbuch and Berger) in the 1920s and early 1930s can be found in 'La Troisième Internationale, la Palestine et le Parti Communiste de Palestine – 1920–1932', on http://321ignition.free.fr/pag/fr/lin/pag_005/pag.htm. The role of PKP members in developing Soviet understanding of the Middle East is discussed in Walter Z. Laqueur, *The Soviet Union and the Middle East* (Praeger, 1959), pp. 76–104.

26. ECCI, 'Resolution on Work in Palestine', 10 May 1923, in Zehavi, *Apart or Together*, pp. 40–1.

27. One attempt to bypass the restrictions imposed by the official unions was the Ihud movement, which focused on Jewish–Arab cooperation outside the Histadrut but with a view to working with its members. Its founder was Leopold Trepper, who became famous later on for running a Soviet spy ring under Nazi occupation in Europe during the Second World War. See his book *The Great Game: Memoirs of the Spy Hitler Couldn't Silence* (McGraw-Hill, 1977), pp. 17–24.

28. Abu-Ziam [Wolf Averbuch], 'Memorandum by PKP Representative to the Comintern', 7 February 1924, in Zehavi, *Apart or Together*, p. 43–7.

29. *Ibid.*, p. 47.

30. Abu-Ziam [Wolf Averbuch], 'Letter to the ECCI', 18 November 1924, in Zehavi, *Apart or Together*, p. 58.

31. Joseph Berger, 'The Communist Party in Palestine and its Work', 2 June 1926, in Zehavi, *Apart or Together*, pp. 77–82.

32. ECCI, 'Resolution Regarding the Report on the PKP', 26 June 1926, in Zehavi, *Apart or Together*, pp. 83–4.

33. Letter from the Comintern, 7 April 1926, in Zehavi, *Apart or Together*, p. 124.

34. In *Hapo'el Hatza'ir*, Vol. 17, No. 28, 8 May 1924, p. 18.

35. For the content of the negotiations see Peterzeil, *The Struggle in the International Proletarian Arena*, pp. 202–15.

36. 'Memorandum to the ECCI from the Delegation of the Palestinian Commune, Gdud Ha'avaoda', 19 May 1926, in Zehavi, *Apart or Together*, pp. 111.

37. Letter to the ECCI by M. Elkind, 'On Gdud Ha'avoda (Left) in Palestine', 13 September 1927, in Zehavi, *Apart or Together*, p. 117. Having become disillusioned with the prospect of building a communist society in Palestine, Elkind and other members of the left wing of the Battalion moved to the Soviet Union shortly thereafter. Most of them perished in the Great Purges of the late 1930s, as did many of the leading members of the PKP from the time.

38. An unsigned internal document, 'Our Disagreements', April 1926, in Zehavi, *Apart or Together*, pp. 133–6. Such disagreements were a constant feature of the Party's life, but those pushing for a more resolutely anti-Zionist direction could not become dominant as long as they included Jewish members only.

Jewish dissidents tended to leave the country and return to Eastern Europe or settle in the Soviet Union, and thus could not sustain a campaign to change the Party's composition and strategy.

39. A. Shami [I. Teper], 'On the Opposition within the PKP', 25 October 1926, in Zehavi, *Apart or Together*, pp.136–7.

40. ECCI, 'The Immediate Tasks of the PKP', 2 February 1927, in Zehavi, *Apart or Together*, p. 128.

41. Letter from ECCI to Central Committee of PKP, 16 June 1928, in Zehavi, *Apart or Together*, p. 144.

42. *Ibid.*, p. 146.

43. A recent comprehensive study of the events from different perspectives is Hillel Cohen, *1929: Year Zero of the Jewish-Arab Conflict* (Keter, Jerusalem, 2013), in Hebrew.

44. The call for 'indigenizing' communist parties based among settler or immigrant populations was not restricted to Palestine, of course. Two cases are discussed in Allison Drew, 'Bolshevizing Communist Parties: The Algerian and South African Experiences', *International Review of Social History*, 48 (2003), pp. 167–202. On Algeria see Emmanuel Sivan, 'Slave Dealer Mentality and Communism', in *Interpretations of Islam* (Darwin Press, 1985), pp, 207–47. Ironically, the call for 'bolshevization' in Palestine came from Jewish members, who worried that Arabization on its own would lead to rapid promotion of unqualified Arab candidates into positions of leadership. The Comintern regarded the slogan of 'Arabization plus bolshevization' as an attempt to avoid the necessary indigenization, and thus rejected it.

45. In 'Extracts from the Theses of the Sixth Comintern Congress on the International Situation', 29 August 1928 in Jane Degras, *The Communist International 1919–1943, Documents: Vol. II, 1923–1928* (Oxford University Press, 1960), p. 456.

46. 'Programme of the Communist International', 1 September 1928, in Degras, *The Communist International Vol. II*, p. 487.

47. *Ibid.*, p. 488.

48. 'Extracts from the Theses on the Revolutionary Movement in Colonial and Semi-colonial Countries', in Degras, *The Communist International Vol. II*, p. 531.

49. *Ibid.*, p. 543.

50. *Ibid.*, p. 546.

51. 'Letter from the ECCI to the CC of the PKP', 25 March 1929, in Zehavi, *Apart or Together*, p. 169.

52. An insider perspective on the Party leadership and the 1929 riots was provided many years later by the sole surviving leader from that period, Yosef Barzilai [also known as Joseph Berger] in his 'Jerusalem, August

1929', *Keshet*, 29 (1965), pp. 122–37, in Hebrew; also in Yosef Berger-Barzilai, *The Tragedy of the Soviet Revolution* (Tel Aviv, 1968), pp. 90–106, in Hebrew.

53. Leaflet issued by the CC of the PKP, 1 September 1929, in Zehavi, *Apart or Together*, p. 174.

54. Brochure issued by the CC of PKP, 'The Bloody War in Palestine and the Working Class', September 1929, in Zehavi, *Apart or Together*, pp. 175–89.

55. ECCI Political Secretariat 'Resolution on the Insurrection Movement in Arabistan', 16 October 1929, in Zehavi, *Apart or Together*, p. 203. Partial English Translation can be found in Jane Degras, *The Communist International 1919–1943, Documents: Vol. III, 1929–1943* (Oxford University Press, 1960), pp. 76–84. I rely here on Zehavi's translation of the full text.

56. An argument that 1929 indeed signified a decisive shift to popular protest politics from below can be found in Rena Barakat, *'Thawrat al-Buraq* in British Mandate Palestine: Jerusalem, Mass Mobilization and Colonial Politics, 1928–1930', unpublished PhD Dissertation, University of Chicago, 2007.

57. ECCI Political Secretariat to PKP, 23 October 1930, in Zehavi, *Apart or Together*, p. 235.

58. *Ibid.*, p. 240.

59. *Ibid.*, p. 241.

60. *Ibid.*, p. 243.

61. Musa Budeiri, *The Palestine Communist Party 1919–48: Arab & Jew in the Struggle for Internationalism* (Ithaca Press, 1979), p. 47. A new edition of this very useful book was published by Haymarket Books in 2011.

62. 'Resolutions of the 7th Congress of the Palestinian Communist Party', in Zehavi, *Apart or Together*, pp. 259–60. Most of the resolutions of what became known as the Arabization Congress can be found in Zehavi's book, pp. 251–76; some of them were included in a 1934 Soviet publication, 'Documents of the Programs of the Communist Parties of the East', reproduced in Ivar Spector, *The Soviet Union and the Muslim World, 1917–1958* (University of Washington Press, 1959), pp. 111–80.

63. In Zehavi, *Apart or Together*, p. 272.

64. 'The Struggle Against Zionism', Theses adopted by the CC of the PKP, 1931, in Tareq Y. Ismael, *The Communist Movement in the Arab World* (Routledge, 2005), Appendix 4.

65. See leaflet from September 1930, calling for solidarity with the dispossessed fellahin of Wadi Hawarith, in Jonathan Frankel (ed.) *The Communist Movement and the Palestine Yishuv 1920–48*, a collection of documents and sources (Hebrew University, 1968), pp. 114–15. On the affair itself, Raya Adler, 'The Tenants of Wadi Hawarith: Another View of the Land Question in Palestine', *International Journal of Middle East Studies*, 20, 2 (May 1988), pp. 197–220.

66. Report by Fred [aka Avigdor, Yehiel Kossoi], Comintern emissary sent to oversee the Arabization of the Party, 1 March 1933, in Zehavi, *Apart or Together*, pp. 290–9.

67. 'Report on the 1929–34 period' by Avigdor [Kossoi], 11 April 1936, in Zehavi, *Apart or Together*, p. 308.

68. 'To the Jewish Working Masses', CC of PKP, November 1935 in *Collection of PKP Publications, 1935–39* (Tel Aviv, 1951), in Hebrew.

69. 'Call to the Masses of Workers and Peasants', CC of PKP, 3 April 1935, in *Collection of PKP Publications, 1935–39*.

70. On the Popular Front policy see the 1935 speech by Georgi Dimitrov, general secretary of the Comintern, in www.marxists.org/reference/archive/dimitrov/works/1935/unity.htm.

71. On the campaign to 'purify' the PKP see Zehavi, *Apart or Together*, pp. 342–52. Most of the 1920s leaders quickly found themselves in a physical – not just political – grave. On the centrality of Arabization to the identity of the new leadership see speech at the 7th Comintern congress by Radwan al-Hilu, the new general secretary of the Party, 31 July 1935, www.marxists.org/history/international/comintern/7th-congress/arab2.htm.

72. Curiously, an alliance with the bi-nationalist movement (referred to as 'the Jewish bourgeois group of Dr. Magnes, which stands on a platform of peaceful realization of Zionist colonization') was cited as evidence, in Zehavi, *Apart or Together*, p. 348. In fact, in 1935 Magnes did not lead any group, nor was he aligned with the PKP in any way.

73. ECCI, 'Resolution on the Palestine Question', 7 May 1935, in Zehavi, *Apart or Together*, p. 350.

74. 'The First Meeting of Communist Parties in the Arab Countries', November 1935, in Zehavi, *Apart or Together*, pp. 322–32.

75. In Zehavi, *Apart or Together*, p. 352. Interestingly, Jabra Nicola's call to establish independent 'red' unions received a critical mention here.

76. Numerous leaflets from the period can be found in *Collection of PKP Publications, 1935–39* and in Zehavi, *Apart or Together*, pp. 366–78. See also Yehoshua Porath, 'Revolution and Terrorism in the Policy of the Palestinian Communist Party (PKP), 1929–1939', *Hamizrah Hahadash*, 18, 3 (1968), pp. 255–67, in Hebrew.

77. On the Jewish Section see Shmuel Dotan, 'The Beginning of Jewish National Communism in Palestine', *Zionism*, 2, 1971, pp. 208–36, in Hebrew. The Tel Aviv committee 1936 leaflet is in *Collection of PKP Publications, 1935–39*.

78. The CC was led by Radwan al-Hilu (known as Musa), the general secretary, and he was supported mainly by Simha Tzabari and Meir Slonim – both indigenous Jews fluent in Arabic.

79. The following discussion relies on the systematic presentation of the positions of the Jewish Section and the Central Committee, based on their own documents, as found in Frankel, *The Communist Movement and the Palestine*

Yishuv, pp. 139–60. The documents include numerous references to internal discussions.

80. 'Memorandum Submitted to the Palestine Partition Commission' by the Jewish Section of the Palestine Communist Party, August 1938, in Frankel, *The Communist Movement and the Palestine Yishuv*, p. 133.

81. 'Memorandum to the International Control Commission of the Comintern', 28 September 1942, in Zehavi, *Apart or Together*, pp. 399–403.

82. 'Report of the Soviet Delegation to Palestine', 15 October 1942, in Zehavi, *Apart or Together*, pp. 403–8.

83. 'Letter to Comrade Dimitrov', 21 December 1942, in Zehavi, *Apart or Together*, pp. 408–11.

84. 'Letter from Emet to the CC', February–March 1942, in *Collection of PKP Documents, June 1941–June 1942*, p. 18.

85. 'Theses on the Party's Policies and its Current Tasks', May 1942, in *Collection of PKP Documents, June 1941–June 1942*, p. 25.

86. *Ibid.*, p. 25a.

87. *Ibid.*, p. 36.

88. Budeiri, *The Palestine Communist Party*, p. 159.

89. On the background to the split see Budeiri, *The Palestine Communist Party*, pp. 153–64. The activist most insistent on the need to create a new party that was not tainted with Zionist tendencies was Bulus Farah, and he discussed his objections to the PKP in great detail in his book, *From the Ottoman Regime to the Hebrew State* (al-Sawt, 1985, Hebrew edition, 2009).

90. Budeiri, *The Palestine Communist Party*, p. 153.

91. The embarrassing neutral position of the Party during the early part of the war, adopted in the wake of the Molotov-Ribbentrop pact of August 1939 and lasting until the German invasion of the Soviet Union in June 1941, was conveniently forgotten.

92. Even before the split, the CC identified this opening but could not act on it: 'The Role of the Party and the Communist Youth in the Arab Street', April 1942, in *Collection of PKP Documents, June 1941–June 1942*, pp. 37–40, in Hebrew.

93. On the NLL's programme see Budeiri, *The Palestine Communist Party*, pp. 212–17; Yehoshua Porath, 'The National Liberation League (*usbat at-taharrur al-watani*): Its Rise, Essence and Dissolution (1943–1948)', *Hamizrah Hahadash*, 14, 4 (1964), pp. 354–66, in Hebrew; Abigail Jacobson, *The National Liberation League, 1943–1948: An Alternative Palestinian Political Discourse*, unpublished MA thesis, Tel Aviv University, 2000, pp. 19–21, 34–38, 40–44, 54–57, in Hebrew. A summary of Jacobson's thesis was published as *Between National Liberation and Anti-Colonial Struggle: The National Liberation League in Palestine*, Working Paper 3, Crown Center for Middle East Studies, Brandeis University, August 2012.

94. Quoted in Jacobson, *The National Liberation League*, p. 38.

95. *Ibid.*, p. 56.

96. From PKP 9th Congress, September 1945, in Ben-Zaken, *Communism as Cultural Imperialism*, p. 138.

97. Vilner's speech, published by *Kol Ha'am*, 5 December 1946, in Frankel, *The Communist Movement and the Palestine Yishuv*, p. 211. An identical position was presented by Vilner already in his evidence for the Anglo-American Committee of Enquiry, earlier in the year, *Kol Ha'am*, 27 March 1946, in Frankel, *The Communist Movement and the Palestine Yishuv*, pp. 234–5.

98. For the NLL's union activities in the context of Arab labour politics see Budeiri, *The Palestine Communist Party*, pp. 116–29; Zachary Lockman, *Comrades and Enemies: Arab and Jewish Workers in Palestine, 1906–1948* (University of California Press, 1996), pp. 303–55.

99. A joint leaflet by the two organizations, 'Solidarity of Jewish and Arab Workers Against the Colonial Government', in *Kol Ha'am*, 26 April 1946, in *Arise, ye Workers from your Slumber: Life and Collected Works of Eliyahu (Alyusha) Gozansky (1914–1948)*, edited by Tamar Gozansky (Haifa: Pardes, 2009). pp. 452–3, in Hebrew. The book includes numerous articles and analyses on the Party and labour conditions in the 1940s.

100. Ben-Zaken, *Communism as Cultural Imperialism*, pp. 137–42.

101. See Soviet position in Andrei Gromyko's May 1947 UN speech http://unispal. un.org/UNISPAL.NSF/0/D41260F1132AD6BE052566190059E5F0.

102. *Kol Ha'am* editorials, 15–23 May 1947, in Frankel, *The Communist Movement and the Palestine Yishuv*, pp. 212–13.

103. All quotes from their 13 July 1947 presentation in Jerusalem, in http:// unispal.un.org/unispal.nsf/0/77d468d8893712ce85256e83005fbc53?Open Document.

104. *Ahdut*, February 1946, in Frankel, *The Communist Movement and the Palestine Yishuv*, p. 240.

105. Testimony of Eliezer Preminger, 17 July 1947, in http://unispal.un.org/ UNISPAL.NSF/0/BFD2A97D81BE51D985256E9B006598DC.

106. 'For Real Independence', *Kol Ha'am*, 17 October 1947, in Frankel, *The Communist Movement and the Palestine Yishuv*, p. 229.

107. *Kol Ha'am*, 19 October 1947, in Frankel, *The Communist Movement and the Palestine Yishuv*, p. 231.

108. *Kol Ha'am*, 3 November 1947 and 10 November 1947, in Frankel, *The Communist Movement and the Palestine Yishuv*, pp. 232–3.

109. On the debates, shifting alliances and eventual reunification between the PKP and NLL see Budeiri, *The Palestine Communist Party*, pp. 231–42. Budeiri concludes that 'The appeal the two hostile communities made on their respective members proved stronger than the promise of an eventual realisation of a community of interests between Arabs and Jews', p. 266. Of the NLL leaders, Tawfiq Tubi, Emile Habibi, and Fuad Nassar were prominent supporters of the resolution. Bulus Farah and Emile Touma

were the main opponents to partition. Touma recanted later and joined Maki while Farah persisted in his position and left active political life. His book *From the Ottoman Regime to the Hebrew State* is full of recriminations over that resolution, and what he regarded as Touma's betrayal.

110. Statement by the CC of the NLL, end of September 1948, published in *Kol Ha'am*, 15 October 1948, in Frankel, *The Communist Movement and the Palestine Yishuv*, pp. 244–5.

111. Statement of the CC of Maki, 5 October 1948, published in *Kol Ha'am*, 15 October 1948, in Frankel, *The Communist Movement and the Palestine Yishuv*, p. 246.

112. The Jordanian Communist Party (JCP) was led by Fuad Nassar of the NLL and – initially – Radwan al-Hilu of the PKP, both of whom became refugees in the West Bank as a result of the war. On the JCP see Amnon Cohen, *Political Parties in the West Bank under the Jordanian Regime, 1949–1967* (Cornell University Press, 1982), pp. 27–93.

113. Tensions in Maki on national grounds are discussed in Joel Beinin, *Was the Red Flag Flying There? Marxist Politics and the Arab-Israeli Conflict in Egypt and Israel, 1948–1965* (University of California Press, 1990), pp. 193–245.

CHAPTER 3

1. This and all subsequent quotations from these exchanges are taken from *Correspondence with the Palestine Arab Delegation and the Zionist Organisation*, presented to the British Parliament June 1922, cmd. 1700 (London, 1922): http://unispal.un.org/UNISPAL.NSF/0/48A7E5584EE1403485256CD8 006C3FBE.

2. Emile Ghory, 'An Arab View of the Situation in Palestine', *International Affairs*, 15, 5 (September–October 1936), pp. 691–2.

3. An argument developed in Rashid Khalidi, *The Iron Cage: The Story of the Palestinian Struggle for Statehood* (Beacon Press, 2006).

4. Albert Hourani, 'The Case against a Jewish State in Palestine: Albert Hourani's Statement to the Anglo-American Committee of Enquiry of 1946', *Journal of Palestine Studies*, 35, 1 (Autumn 2005), pp. 80–90.

5. Amin al-Husayni, 'The Solutions Presented by Britain were a Chain of Deceit', 1954, translated in Zvi Elpeleg, *Through the Eyes of the Mufti* (Vallentine Mitchell, 2009), p. 23.

6. Musa Alami, 'The Lesson of Palestine', *Middle East Journal*, 3, 4 (October 1949), p. 374.

7. Translated into English as *The Meaning of the Disaster* (Khayat College, Beirut, 1956).

8. *Ibid.*, p. 16.

9. *Ibid.*, p. 21.

10. An overview of legal, social and political conditions during that period is found in Shira Robinson, *Citizen Strangers: Palestinians and the Birth of Israel's Liberal Settler State* (Stanford University Press, 2013).

11. Joel Beinin, *Was the Red Flag Flying There? Marxist Politics and the Arab-Israeli Conflict in Egypt and Israel, 1948–1965* (University of California Press, 1990), pp. 193–203.

12. Quotations from *Memorandum on the Arabs in Israel*, al-Ard, 25 June 1964. Thanks to Leena Dallasheh for a copy of the document.

13. In Sabri Jiryis, *The Arabs in Israel* (Monthly Review Press, 1976), p. 190. See also Leena Dallasheh, 'Political Mobilization of Palestinians in Israel: the al-Ard Movement' in *Displaced at Home: Ethnicity and Gender among Palestinians in Israel*, edited by Rhoda Ann Kanaaneh and Isis Nusair (SUNY Press, 2009), pp. 21–38.

14. Court Judgment in www.constitution.org.il/index.php?class=1&id=544&m ytask=view&option=com_consti_comp.

15. Basil al-Kubaisi, *The Arab Nationalists Movement 1951–1971: From Pressure Group to Socialist Party* (unpublished PhD Dissertation, American University, 1971), p. 69.

16. Walid Kazziha, *Revolutionary Transformation in the Arab World: Habash and his Comrades from Nationalism to Marxism* (Charles Knight & Company, 1975), pp. 50–1.

17. *Ibid.*, p. 65.

18. Yezid Sayegh, 'Reconstructing the Paradox: The Arab Nationalist Movement, Armed Struggle, and Palestine, 1951–1966', in *Middle East Journal*, 45, 4 (Autumn 1991), p. 619.

19. All quotations from the Charter are taken from the version in www.un.int/ wcm/content/site/palestine/pid/12363.

20. Fayez Sayegh, *Zionist Colonialism in Palestine* (PLO Research Center, Beirut, 1965), pp. 24–7. Italics in the original.

21. Interview conducted by Lutfi al-Khuli, Editor of *Al-Tali'a*, with Abu Iyad, June 1969, in *International Documents on Palestine, 1969*, edited by Walid Khadduri (The Institute for Palestine Studies, Beirut, 1972), p. 707.

22. On the background to Fatah among Palestinian student movements in Gaza, Cairo and the Gulf see Abu Iyad, *My Home, My Land: A Narrative of the Palestinian Struggle* (Times books, 1981), pp. 19–28.

23. From the Fatah publication *Filastinuna*, 15, March 1961, quoted in Moshe Shemesh, *The Palestinian National Re-Awakening: In the Shadow of Leadership Crisis, from the Mufti to Shuqeiri, 1937–1967* (Ben-Gurion Research Institute, 2012) pp. 247–8, in Hebrew.

24. *Filsatinuna*, 31, May 1963, in Shemesh, *The Palestinian National Re-Awakening*, pp. 248–49.

25. *Filastinuna*, 11, November 1960, in Helga Baumgarten, 'The Three Faces/ Phases of Palestinian Nationalism, 1948–2005', *Journal of Palestine Studies*, 34, 4 (Summer 2005), p. 33.

26. Yezid Sayegh, *Armed Struggle and the Search for State: The Palestinian National Movement 1949–1993* (Oxford, 1997), pp. 100–8. On the Algerian perspective see 'Interview: Mohammed Yazid on Algeria and the Arab-Israeli Conflict', *Journal of Palestine Studies*, 1, 2 (Winter 1972), pp. 3–18.

27. Maxime Rodinson, *Israel: A Colonial-Settler State?* (Monad Press, 1973 [original French in 1967]) p. 90.

28. Nelson Mandela's statement from the dock at the opening of the defense case in the Rivonia Trial, Pretoria Supreme Court, 20 April 1964: www.anc. og.za/show.php?id=3430.

29. In http://thenewliberator.wordpress.com/2011/02/04/footnotes-to-the-book-of-the-setback-by-nizar-qkabbani/.

30. Constantine Zurayq, 'The Meaning of the Nakba Revisited' in *Arab Lessons from Their Defeat*, edited by Y. Harkabi (Am Oved, 1969), pp. 184–210, in Hebrew.

31. Sadik Jalal al-Azm, *Self-Criticism after the Defeat* (Saqi, 2011), p. 85.

32. *Ibid.*, pp. 97–8.

33. 'The Third Round', statement by the Israeli Socialist Organization, 5th July 1967, *Matzpen*, 36 (June-July 1967). English version in www.marxists.org/ history/etol/document/mideast/toi/doc2.html.

34. Article 9 and 10 of the Palestinian National Charter, 1968.

35. In *Documents of the Palestinian Resistance Movement* (Pathfinder Press, 1971), p. 5.

36. *Ibid.*, p. 8.

37. Interview by al-Khuli of Abu-Iyad, *International Documents on Palestine, 1969*, p. 722.

38. For such expectations see Interview by al-Khuli of Abu-Iyad, *International Documents on Palestine, 1969*, pp. 732–33.

39. 'Founding Document of the PFLP', December 1969 in http://pflp.ps/ english/2012/12/founding-document-of-the-popular-front-for-the-libera-tion-of-palestine-december-1967/.

40. All subsequent quotes from 'Strategy for the Liberation of Palestine', February 1969, http://pflp.ps/english/strategy-for-the-liberation-of-pales-tine/.

41. Interview with George Habash, May 1970, in *Documents of the Palestinian Resistance Movement*, p. 21.

42. 'The Political Report of the Popular Front for the Liberation of Palestine', August 1968, in Leila Kadi, *Basic Political Documents of the Armed Palestinian Resistance Movement* (PLO Research Center, Beirut, 1969), p. 156. Although adopted by the PFLP, the report was presented by Nayef Hawatmeh, leader of the left-wing faction that split off to become the PDFLP, and has become associated with that latter group.

43. *Ibid.*, p. 169.

44. Statement by the PDFLP, 1969, in 'The Political Report of the Popular Front for the Liberation of Palestine', p. 11.

45. *The Military Strategy of the PFLP* (Beirut, 1970). Extensive discussion of how the Palestinian struggle was seen by various forces as part of a general anti-imperialist front can be found in Paul Thomas Chamberlin, *The Global Offensive: The United States, The Palestine Liberation Organization, and the Making of the Post Cold War Order* (Oxford University Press, 2012).

46. Interview of Abu-Iyad by al-Khuli, *International Documents on Palestine, 1969*, p. 717.

47. See discussion in Ran Greenstein, 'Socialist Anti-Zionism: A Chapter in the History of the Israeli Radical Left', *Socialist History*, 35 (March 2009), pp. 20–39, and Chapter 4 of this book.

48. Text of UNGA resolution 3379 in http://unispal.un.org/UNISPAL.NSF/0/761C1063530766A7052566A2005B74D1.

49. '10 Point Program of the PLO', June 1974, in www.un.int/wcm/content/site/palestine/pid/12354.

50. In *Palestinian Leaders Discuss the New Challenges for the Resistance*, panel moderated by Mahmoud Darwish (Palestine Research Center, Beirut, April 1974), pp. 9–10.

51. *Ibid.*, pp. 25–26, 30.

52. For Abu Iyad see *Palestinian Leaders Discuss the New Challenges for the Resistance*, pp. 30–34; For Shafiq al-Hout see *ibid.*, pp. 34–39. For Hawatmeh, *ibid.*, pp. 39–54.

53. http://unispal.un.org/UNISPAL.NSF/0/696D540FD7821BCE0525651C00736250.

54. 'Statement by the PLO Central Council', 30 November 1977, in *Journal of Palestine Studies*, 7, 3 (Spring 1978), p. 186.

55. 'Six-point Programme agreed to by all Palestinian Factions', 4 December 1977, in *ibid.*, p. 188.

56. See discussion of oppositional activity in pre-1967 West Bank in Amnon Cohen, *Political Parties in the West Bank under the Jordanian Regime, 1949–1967* (Cornell University Press, 1982), and military organization in the West Bank and Gaza in Shaul Bartal, *The Fedayeen Emerge: The Palestine-Israel Conflict, 1949–1956* (The Author House, 2011).

57. Israeli half-hearted attempts to build up the pro-Jordanian 'notables' as a compliant local leadership are discussed in Avi Raz, *The Bride and the Dowry: Israel, Jordan and the Palestinians in the Aftermath of the June 1967 War* (Oxford University Press, 2012).

58. Weldon Matthews, 'The Rise and Demise of the Left in West Bank Politics: The Case of the Palestine National Front', *Arab Studies Quarterly*, 20, 4 (Fall 1998), pp. 13–31.

59. 'The Palestinian National Front', in *Merip Reports*, 25 (February 1974), p. 22.

60. 'Interview with Palestine National Front', *Merip Reports*, 50 (August 1976), pp. 16–21; Naseer Aruri, 'Resistance and Repression: Political Prisoners in Israeli Occupied Territories', *Journal of Palestine Studies*, 7, 4 (Summer 1978), pp. 48–66.

61. For overview of the early stages see Zachary Lockman and Joel Beinin (eds), *Intifada: The Palestinian Uprising against Israeli Occupation* (South End Press, 1989).

62. Full text of the Declaration of Independence as well as other components of the Palestine National Council resolutions of 15th November 1988 are in http://unispal.un.org/UNISPAL.NSF/0/6EB54A389E2DA6C6852560 DE0070E392.

63. An overview of political conditions within a broad social and economic context can be found in Sabri Jiryis, 'The Arabs in Israel, 1973–79', *Journal of Palestine Studies*, 8, 4 (Summer 1979), pp. 31–56.

64. For surprised and outraged responses to both events by Israeli state officials and commentators see 'Rakah Victory in Nazareth', *Journal of Palestine Studies*, 5, 3 (Spring-Summer 1976), pp. 178–180, and 'Revolt in Galilee', *ibid.*, pp. 192–200.

65. Tawfiq Zayyad, 'The Fate of the Arabs in Israel', *Journal of Palestine Studies*, 6, 1 (Autumn 1976), p. 94.

66. *Ibid.*, p. 103.

67. Emile Touma, 'Palestinian Arabs and Israeli Jews', *Journal of Palestine Studies*, 6, 2 (Winter 1977), p. 5.

68. Interview with Mohammed Kiwan, "Sons of the Village' Assert Palestinian Identity in Israel', *Merip Reports*, 68 (June 1978), pp. 15–18.

69. Azmi Bishara, 'On the Question of the Palestinian Minority in Israel', *Theory and Criticism*, 3 (Winter 1993), pp. 7–20, in Hebrew.

70. Adalah (the Legal Center for Arab Minority Rights), *The Democratic Constitution* (Shafa'amr, 2007), www.adalah.org/eng/democratic_constitution-e. pdf; Mada al-Carmel (Arab Center for Applied Social Research), *The Haifa Declaration* (Haifa, 2007), www.mada-research.org/UserFiles/file/ haifaenglish.pdf; NCHALAI (National Committee for the Heads of the Arab Local Authorities in Israel), *The Future Vision of the Palestinian Arabs in Israel* (Nazareth, 2006), www.adalah.org/newsletter/eng/dec06/tasawor-mostaqbali.pdf.

71. NCHALAI, *The Future Vision*, p. 5.

72. *Ibid.*, p. 9.

73. *Ibid.*, pp. 10–11.

74. Adalah, *The Democratic Constitution*.

75. *Ibid.*, p. 4.

76. This and all the excerpts from the Declaration that follow can be found in Mada al-Carmel, *The Haifa Declaration*, pp. 7–17. Mada al-Carmel, The Arab Center for Applied Social Research, is a Haifa-based policy analysis and

research institute, which aims to become a hub of knowledge and critical thinking about Palestinians in Israel, equal citizenship, and democracy.

77. In 2008, the year after the Haifa Declaration was issued, the Haifa Conference for the Return of the Palestinian Refugees and the Democratic Secular State in Historic Palestine, organized by dissident Palestinians in Israel, the Abnaa al-Balad movement, called for a single state with no ethnic and religious distinctions in the entire country, but without showing any concrete way of linking the disparate struggles of Palestinians in their different locations. A second Haifa conference took place in May 2010. Further information is available at www.ror1state.org/awda.

CHAPTER 4

1. His name was Ygael Gluckstein, and at the time he was an activist in radical socialist circles. He is better known by another pseudonym, Tony Cliff, which he used since he had moved to the UK in the late 1940s to become a prominent leader and theoretician of the British radical Left.

2. L. Rock, 'British Policy in Palestine', *New International*, October 1938, www. marxists.de/middleast/palquest/britpol.htm.

3. L. Rock, 'The Jewish-Arab Conflict', *New International*, November 1938, in www.marxists.de/middleast/palquest/jew-arab.htm.

4. The Spark, 'Zionism and the Arab Struggle', *New International*, February 1939, in www.marxists.de/middleast/palquest/spark.htm.

5. L. Rock, 'Class Politics in Palestine', *New International*, June 1939, in www. marxists.de/middleast/palquest/classpol.htm.

6. The Spark, 'Rebuttal on the Palestine Question', *New International*, October 1939, in www.marxists.de/middleast/palquest/spark2.htm.

7. 'Against Partition!', *Kol Hama'amad*, 31, September 1947: www.marxists.de/ middleast/misc/partition.htm.

8. 'The Trotskyist Position in Palestine: Against the Stream', *Fourth International*, 9, 2, May 1948, pp. 86–9: www.marxists.de/middleast/misc/pal1948.htm.

9. International Secretariat of the Fourth International [written by Ernest Mandel], 'Draft Theses on the Jewish Question Today', January 1947. Published in *Fourth International*, Vol. 9, No. 1, January-February 1948: 18–24, www.marxists.org/archive/mandel/1947/01/jewish.htm See other documents from that period reflecting the Trotskyist positions on the Middle East in www.marxists.org/history/etol/newspape/fi/index2.htm.

10. 'Against Partition!', *Kol Hama'amad*, 31, September 1947.

11. S. Munier [pseudonym of the prominent – future – social historian, Gabriel Baer], 'Zionism and The Middle East – The Aftermath of the Jewish-Arab War (A Report from Israel)', *Fourth International*, 10, 9, October 1949:

277–283, in www.marxists.org/history/etol/newspape/fi/vol10/no09/munier.htm.

12. Michel Pablo, *The Arab Revolution*, 1958 in www.marx.org/archive/pablo/1958/arabrev/main.htm.

13. *Ibid.*

14. His analysis of Egypt, Nasser and the prospects for socialism, appeared in the Fourth International's theoretical magazine under the name of A. Sadi, as "'Arab Socialism" and the Nasserite National Movement', *International Socialist Review*, 24, 2 (Winter 1963): www.marxists.org/history/etol/newspape/isr/vol24/no02/sadi.html.

15. Its marginal position earned it few comprehensive studies. The only substantial one is by Nira Yuval Davis, *Matzpen: The Israeli Socialist Organization* (Hebrew University, 1977), based on MA fieldwork conducted in 1969–70 and covering that period with a focus on issues of organization, structure and membership. In 2003 a documentary film on the organization, *Matzpen: Anti-Zionist Israelis* was made and subsequently screened on Israeli TV: www.matzpen.org/eran/index.html. Michael Warschawski, *On the Border* (South End Press, 2004) is an essential source – a memoir written by one of the main activists in the movement. A more recent book by Nitza Erel, *Matzpen: Conscience and Fantasy* (Resling, 2010), in Hebrew, provides useful information but is weak on political and theoretical analysis.

16. A. Israeli [Moshé Machover and Akiva Orr], *Shalom, Shalom ve'ein Shalom* [Peace, Peace and There is No Peace: Israel and the Arabs, 1948–1961] (Bohan Press, 1961), in Hebrew. A new edition was published in 1999, with additional appendices, www.akiorrbooks.com/files/PEACE.pdf.

17. 'There is an address', *Matzpen*, 1, November 1962.

18. A. Israeli, 'Palestine', *Matzpen*, 4, February–March 1963.

19. A. Israeli, 'Israel-Arab Peace, How?', *Matzpen*, 11, September–October 1963 and *Matzpen* 12, November 1963.

20. S. Meir, 'Al-Ard and Us', *Matzpen*, 21, August–September 1964.

21. S. Meir, 'The Root of the Conflict: Zionism versus Arab Nationalism', *Matzpen*, 23, November–December 1964.

22. ISO Central Committee, 'Statement on the Israeli-Arab conflict, May 1967', in *Matzpen*, 36, June–July 1967.

23. Statement in *Matzpen* 14, January 1964.

24. Moshé Machover, 'Comrade Jabra Nicola, 1912–1974', *Matzpen* 73, March–April 1975.

25. Akiva Orr, 'He Was Not a Teacher But We Learnt a Lot From Him', *Matzpen* 73, March–April 1975.

26. A. Said [Jabra Nicola] and Moshé Machover, 'The Arab Revolution and National Problems in the Arab East', *Matzpen*, 64, May–June 1972 (Hebrew), *The International*, Summer 1973 (English).

27. A. Said [Jabra Nicola] and M. Machover, 'The Struggle in Palestine Must Lead to Arab Revolution', *Black Dwarf*, Vol. 14 (19), 14 June 1969.

28. A. Said [Jabra Nicola], *Theses on the Revolution in the Arab East*: http://98.130.214.177/index.asp?p=english_theses-jabre, 14 September 1972.

29. 'The Third Round', 5 July 1967, Statement by the Israeli Socialist Organization, *Matzpen*, 36, June–July 1967.

30. 'General Declaration by the ISO', 22 March 1968.

31. 'Down with the Occupation', a statement by the ISO, 1 January 1969.

32. A. Orr and M. Machover, 'Against the Zionist Left', leaflet by ISO, 1970.

33. The most complete analysis of the issue was contained in Haim Hanegbi, Moshe Machover and Akiva Orr, 'the Class Nature of Israeli Society', *New Left Review*, 65 (January–February 1971), pp. 3–26. It was written by Machover and Orr, both of whom were residing in the UK, and Hanegbi's name was added to provide an Israel-based co-author. It is reproduced in *The Other Israel*: www.marxists.org/history/etol/document/mideast/toi/chap2–05.html.

34. Almost identical name to that of the pre-1948 Trotskyist organization.

35. 'Towards a New Perspective', *Ma'avak*, 1, October 1970.

36. 'Political Programme of the Revolutionary Communist Alliance', point 12, in *Ma'avak*, 1, October 1970.

37. *Ibid.*, point 16.

38. *Ibid.*, point 19.

39. Oded Pilavski, 'Leftist Phrases and Rightist Meanings', *Matzpen* 56, November 1970.

40. D. Vered, 'On the Split', *Hazit Adumah*, 1, October 1971.

41. 'Abolish Anti-Worker Oppressive Laws', in *Hazit Adumah*, 1, October 1971.

42. In fact, shortly after the split, the new group reproduced the political programme of the RCA as its own, in *Hazit Adumah*, 2, December 1971. However, it added a list of ten membership principles headed by 'it is impossible to realize socialism without a violent revolution supported by the masses'.

43. 'Zionism, Anti-Semitism and Anti-Communism', in *Hazit Adumah*, 2, December 1971.

44. *Ibid.*

45. Whether Arabs in general, in contrast to Palestinians in particular, were indeed 'oppressed' by foreign powers and in need of national liberation is another matter, which has been subject to dispute among the Left.

46. The following quotations are from 'The Red Front Trial: The Depositions of Turki and Adiv', *Journal of Palestine Studies*, 2, 4 (Summer 1973): 144–50. There may be minor problems in the text, since it seems the English text was translated from the Arabic, which in turn was translated from the original Hebrew. We must keep in mind that the text consists of depositions made by people in detention rather than free expression of political views.

47. 'To the Reader', *Hazit Adumah*, 3, April–May 1972.

48. Yehuda Palestinai, 'Matzpen and the Palestinian Resistance Organizations' in *Hazit Adumah*, 3, April–May 1972.

49. Yehuda K, 'Criticism of the ISO (Matzpen)', *Avangard*, 1, November 1970.

50. 'Programme', *Avangard*, 2, January 1971.

51. Matzpen regarded its 'centrism' as an asset: the ability to tackle complex social and historical realities while avoiding a simplistic one-track mode of analysis. See various responses to criticisms by Ma'avak and Avangard in *Matzpen* 56, November 1970 and *Matzpen* 57, January 1971.

52. Organisation Communiste Internationaliste, a French far-left group, led by Pierre Lambert, and referred to by its opponents as the Lambertists.

53. About the conflict see Palestinian Communist Group, *Hanitzotz*, 1, Spring 1977; Yoav Bar, 'The Crisis of the Workers Alliance as Part of the Crisis of the Fourth International', *Avangard*, 29, Summer 1978.

54. 'Programmatic Theses of the Palestinian Communist Faction', *Hanitzotz*, 1, Spring 1977.

55. 'Why do Communists Fight for a Democratic Unified Palestine?', in *Hanitzotz*, 1, Spring 1977.

56. Yoav Bar, 'The Crisis of the Workers Alliance', *Avangard*, 29, Summer 1978.

57. Years later, a member of the original top leadership published an interesting critical analysis of Israeli society, retaining many of the Matzpen insights but devoid of any reference to the class struggle. See Sylvain Cypel, *Walled: Israeli Society at an Impasse* (Other Press, 2006).

58. There were two issues of *Matzpen* number 62, and both sides claimed that the others chose to leave the organization. They continued to number subsequent issues accordingly. To prevent confusion I will refer to the Tel Aviv group and its journal as Matzpen Tel Aviv, and to the Jerusalem group and its journal as Matzpen Marxist.

59. Arie Bober (ed.), *The Other Israel: The Radical Case Against Zionism* (Doubleday, 1972). The book can be found online at: www.marxists.org/history/etol/document/mideast/toi/index.html.

60. 'Basic principles', www.matzpen.org/index.asp?p=51.

61. www.marxists.org/history/etol/document/mideast/toi/chap4-conc.html.

62. 'Statement by the Israeli Socialist Organization (Marxist)', 7 October 1973, in *Matzpen Marxist*, 71, December 1973.

63. The document title is 'The Arab Revolution: Its Character, Present State and Perspectives'. It first appeared in Hebrew in an internal discussion bulletin (no. 6, October 1973), and large sections from it were replicated in 'The Fourth Round', *Matzpen Marxist*, 71, December 1973. In 1975, a French version was published in Paris, listing 'Quatrième Internationale' as author. English version in: www.internationalviewpoint.org/spip.php?article1608.

64. A factional struggle started in 1974 and culminated in the departure of many members. The conflict had many causes, but the concept of the Arab

Revolution was at its core. The document was presented by the faction that eventually re-constituted the organization as the Revolutionary Communist League in 1975. Both adjectives in the original ISO were discarded: 'Israeli' was no longer an appropriate term for those calling for the destruction of the Zionist state, and 'socialist' was too mild for activists who called for a radical social revolution in the region. Matzpen Tel Aviv also changed its name to Socialist Organization in Israel in 1977, to reflect its internationalist character.

65. 'Documents by the Proletarian Faction', March 1975.

66. Yankel, 'Socialism, Nationalism, Israeli Jews and More in *The Arab Revolution*', Internal Discussion Bulletin, Revolutionary Communist League (Matzpen), 14, August 1975.

67. Tamara Nir, '15 Years to Matzpen: Reflections on a Birthday', *Matzpen Marxist*, 100, January 1978.

68. 'Towards Unification', statement by the League's central committee, in *Matzpen Marxist*, 100, January 1978.

69. Michal Schwartz, 'The Unification Conference', *Matzpen Marxist*, 110, May 1979.

70. Its founding members' analysis changed little over the years, though. For a re-statement of the classical positions and their validity for the current conditions see Moshé Machover, 'Israelis and Palestinians: Conflict and Resolution', Barry Amiel and Norman Melburn Trust annual lecture, 30 November 2006, www.amielandmelburn.org.uk/articles/mosheper cent-20machoverper cent20per cent202006lecture_b.pdf.

71. The last issue available electronically, *Matzpen Marxist*, 180, October–November 1990 is dedicated to a critical review of various Left approaches (Zionist, pro-Soviet) from an identical position to that used a decade earlier. A call for a new Left initiative appeared in a subsequent issue *Matzpen Marxist* (new series), 1, February 1992, after more than a year of absence, but this did not seem to have led anywhere, and the magazine ceased publication shortly thereafter. For the Alternative Information Center see www.alternativenews.org/.

72. '30 Years to Matzpen, Have We Been Wrong?', Introduction to a collection titled *30 Years with Matzpen*, www.matzpen.org/index.asp?p=30years.

73. Michael Warschawski, 'The Secret of Matzpen's Magic', *Mitsad Sheni*, 14–15, 2006.

74. All quotes from 'The Olga Document', www.nimn.org/Perspectives/israeli_voices/000233.php?section= , June 2004.

75. But in contrast to the anti-Zionist Left, which always attempted to speak in the name of Jews and Arabs alike and address both groups, the Olga Document was written by Jews addressing other Jews (despite the fact that many of its signatories have been active with Palestinians in other forums and organizations).

76. www.mada-research.org/archive/haifaenglish.pdf.

Index